Social Forces and States

Social Forces and States

Poverty and Distributional Outcomes in South Korea, Chile, and Mexico

Judith A. Teichman

Stanford University Press

Stanford, California

Stanford University Press
Stanford, California

Printed in the United States of America on acid-free, archival-quality paper

Library of Congress Cataloging-in-Publication Data

Teichman, Judith A., author.
  Social forces and states : poverty and distributional outcomes in South Korea, Chile, and Mexico / Judith A. Teichman.
      pages cm
  Includes bibliographical references and index.
  ISBN 978-0-8047-7825-1 (cloth : alk. paper)—
ISBN 978-0-8047-7826-8 (pbk. : alk. paper)
    1. Poverty—Case studies.   2. Equality—Case studies.   3. Korea (South)—
Social conditions.   4. Korea (South)—Economic conditions.   5. Chile—Social conditions.   6. Chile—Economic conditions.   7. Mexico—Social conditions.
8. Mexico—Economic conditions.   I. Title.
  HC79.P6T45 2012
    305.5′69—dc23
                                                                2011036929

Typeset by Thompson Type in 11/13.5 Adobe Garamond

Contents

Figures and Tables

Figures

Tables

Acknowledgments

THE INSPIRATION FOR THIS BOOK arose out of an earlier collaborative work with colleagues Richard Sandbrook, Marc Edelman, and Patrick Heller. This work, which examined four successful cases of social democracy in the global south, led to the publication of *Social Democracy in the Global Periphery: Origins, Challenges, Prospects* (2007). All four cases were ones in which governments had been relatively successful in reducing poverty and addressing human needs. Among the findings was the identification of the important role of democracy, political party pressure, civil society, and trade union activism in these social achievements. The analysis, of course, omitted the experience of the Asian NICs, where rapid poverty reduction and low inequality had been achieved under authoritarian rule. Indeed, the experience of the Asian NICs presents a challenging puzzle because the achievement of rapid poverty reduction with low inequality not only occurred under authoritarian rule but also involved low social spending. This scenario was in marked contrast to many Latin American countries, where social spending had been historically much higher. The social democracy project also inspired me to look comparatively at cases of poor social outcomes. Mexico, a country with enormous promise given its status as one of the Latin American NICs during the 1950s and 1960s, is a case where inequality and poverty have proven to be intractable challenges. For a number of years now, I have added South Korea and Mexico to the comparative mix of cases examined by my senior seminar on poverty, inequality, and social policy. In so doing, I became convinced that a book treating the distinct social outcomes of South

Korea, Chile, and Mexico would find a ready audience among senior undergraduate and graduate students.

Inspiration for this new project was also accompanied by many other important sources of support. I could not have completed this work without the valuable contributions of my research assistants over the years. Two PhD students in the Department of Political Science, University of Toronto, were enormously helpful. Ingrid Carlson contributed in many ways to this project. She was particularly helpful in the collection and analysis of statistical data. Daniella Levy-Pinto provided research assistance on the Mexican case. Jaemin Kim, a Korean national and PhD student in business at the time this research was carried out, provided essential research support for South Korea, tracking down bibliographical sources and translating and summarizing material in Korean.

My colleague in the Department of Political Science, Richard Sandbrook, provided valuable comments on an earlier draft. I would also like to thank Evelyne Huber, Joan Nelson, and the third anonymous reviewer for their careful reading of the manuscript and for their many helpful comments and suggestions. All errors and omissions are, of course, my own.

I am grateful to the Social Sciences and Humanities Research Council, which provided the financial support that make the research possible. A Connaught Research Fellowship provided release time and additional financial support, both of which were essential in affording me the ability to focus on writing the manuscript.

As always, the support and encouragement of my husband, George, contributed in an important way to the success of the project.

Acronyms

AFORES	Retirement Fund Administrators (Mexico)
AFP	Pension Fund Managing Corporation (Chile)
AUGE	Guaranteed Universal Health Access Plan (Chile)
CCE	Coordinating Business Council (Mexico)
CCEJ	Citizen's Coalition for Economic Justice (Korea)
CIEPLAN	Corporation for Economic Research on Latin America (Chile)
CONASUPO	National Company of Popular Goods (Mexico)
CORFO	Chilean Production Development Corporation
CSS	Committee for Social Security (Korea)
CT	Labor Congress (Mexico)
FKTU	Federation of Korean Trade Unions
FOCH	Chilean Labor Federation
FOMEX	Fund for Promoting Manufactured Exports (Mexico)
FONASA	National Health Fund (Chile)
FOSIS	Social Solidarity and Investment Fund (Chile)
IMSS	Mexican Institute of Social Security
INDAP	Agricultural Development Institute (Chile)
INMECAFE	Mexican Coffee Marketing Board
ISSSTE	Institute of Security and Social Services for State Worker (Mexico)

KCIA	Korean State Security Agency
KCTU	Korean Confederation of Trade Unions
KIST	Korean Institute of Science and Technology
KOTRA	Trade Production Agency (Korea)
MAPU	Popular Unity Action Movement (Chile)
NACF	National Agricultural Cooperative Federation (Korea)
NAFINSA	Nacional Financiera (Mexico)
NAFTA	North American Free Trade Agreement
NCTU	National Council of Korean Trade Unions
NHIC	National Health Insurance Company (Korea)
NICs	Newly Industrializing Countries
ORD	Office of Research Development (Korea)
PAN	Popular Action Party (Mexico)
PDC	Christian Democratic Party (Chile)
PIDER	Program of Investment for Rural Development (Mexico)
PNR	National Revolutionary Party (Mexico)
POSCO	Korean State Steel Company
PPD	Popular Party for Democracy (Chile)
PRD	Party of the Democratic Revolution (Mexico)
PRI	Institutional Revolutionary Party (Mexico)
PROCAMPO	Program of Direct Support for Rural Areas (Mexico)
PROCHILE	Program for the Support of Chilean Exports
PROFOS	Projects of Promotion (Chile)
PROGRESA	Program of Education, Health and Food (Mexico)
PRONASOL	National Solidarity Program (Mexico)
PS	Socialist Party (Chile)
PSPD	People's Solidarity for Participatory Democracy (Korea)
SNTE	National Union of Education Workers (Mexico)
SSA	Ministry of Health and Social Assistance (Mexico)
UNT	National Union of Workers (Mexico)

Social Forces and States

1

Social Forces and History
Explaining Divergent Poverty and Distributional Outcomes

IN THE FACE OF REPEATED ECONOMIC CRISES, the failure of market liberalization to produce sustained economic growth in many countries of the global south has eroded the widely held presumption that state intervention was at the root of the economic problems faced by these countries. Numerous authors have recognized the importance of state leadership in the high rates of economic growth achieved by the Asian NICs (newly industrializing countries): South Korea, Taiwan, Hong Kong, and Singapore (Evans 1995; Haggard 1990; Kohli 2004; Wade 1990). At the same time, backed by a rising chorus of criticism from civil society and labor organizations, scholarly and official circles have shown increasing concern about the perpetuation of widespread poverty and evidence of persisting or increasing levels of inequality. By the year 2000, poverty had become a major ethical, political, and economic issue. In that year, the U.N. General Assembly adopted the Millennium Development Goals, which, among other things, included the objective of reducing absolute poverty by one-half by the year 2015. The impact of the recent global financial crisis on the fragile economies of the global south has generated even more interest in such issues.

Mounting unease about the economic and political impact of high levels of intracountry inequality has replaced the early assumption that inequality was inevitable in the early stages of development. Conventional wisdom accepted the Kuznetsian prediction that, while inequality would rise during the early phase of modernization, it would subsequently decline as the labor force in the industrial sector expanded and as industry absorbed labor. At that point, large numbers of people would benefit (Kuznets 1955). Although debate on the issue continues, a number of observers argue that the failure of inequality to diminish in many global south countries is likely an important factor inhibiting the economic growth that is essential for job creation and poverty reduction (Cornia, Addison, and Kiiski 2004, 26, 42–43; de Ferranti et al. 2004, 25; López 2004; Midgley 1987, 38). In addition to raising the risk of civil conflict, high levels of inequality also contribute to rent seeking and predatory and criminal behavior (Fajnzylber, Lederman, and Loayza 1998; Nafziger and Avinen 2002; Wade 2004). Evidence that southern countries have generally higher levels of inequality than the industrialized nations and that inequality increased in many of them over the last quarter of the twentieth century is particularly worrisome (Betcherman 2002, 13; Cornia et al., 2004;).[1] Understanding how inequality becomes established and entrenched is, therefore, of compelling importance.

Poverty, Inequality, and Social Forces

Unacceptable levels of poverty and inequality in many countries of the global south raise the question of why a few countries have been relatively more successful than others have been at reducing poverty and maintaining low levels of inequality. The ability of the Asian NICs to achieve sustained economic growth while eliminating poverty and maintaining relatively low levels of inequality stands in sharp contrast to the general Latin American pattern where stagnant economic growth rates and recurrent economic crises have occurred alongside higher levels of poverty and the failure to reduce preexisting high levels of inequality. Among Latin American countries, however, Chile stands out for its ability to achieve steady levels of economic growth and dramatic poverty reduction since the late 1980s.

This study seeks to explain the distinct poverty and inequality outcomes of three countries: South Korea, Mexico, and Chile. South Korea has had historically low levels of inequality and has been the most successful at reducing poverty. Chile has reduced poverty substantially since 1987 but continues to experience high levels of inequality. Mexico, where poverty has increased since 2006, has struggled with the highest levels of poverty of our three cases and has a high level of inequality (see Tables A-1 and A-2).[2] In addition to these distinct outcomes, I chose these three countries due to their particular historical trajectories, which, on the surface, would seem to suggest outcomes different from those that actually occurred. Prior to 1970, for example, the Mexican economic model was widely regarded as successful. Hailed as the "Mexican miracle," steady annual per capita growth rates between 1950 and the mid-1960s made Mexico one of Latin America's most promising NICs.[3] The country's foray into market liberalization during the late 1980s and early 1990s and the signing of the North American Free Trade Agreement (NAFTA) also earned it widespread international approval. Yet advancement in social well-being has been disappointing. Until the mid-1970s, Chile fared considerably better than Mexico in poverty and inequality indicators, despite having experienced intense political turmoil and one of the slowest economic growth rates in Latin America.[4] Today, Chile has transformed into the "tiger" of the region with steady economic growth from the late 1980s (see Table A-5). South Korea has experienced ongoing success in maintaining both economic growth and comparatively low levels of inequality.[5] This achievement has occurred despite the fact that its more recent political history has begun to reflect the strong popular activism characteristic of much of Latin American history: labor militancy and unrest, political protest demanding social justice, and a much-strengthened propertied class with considerable political clout.[6] In the face of political developments with a potentially polarizing and disruptive impact, Korea has been able to maintain economic growth and comparatively low levels of inequality while expanding social programs.[7]

This work falls within the tradition of comparative historical analysis. As such, it seeks to combine a historically grounded explanation of divergent social outcomes with a causal explanation that emphasizes processes over time and contextualized comparisons (Mahoney and Rueschemeyer 2003, 6). The analysis starts from the premise that particular social structures give rise to social forces whose actions, politics, and ideologies shape institutional development. Institutions, in turn, mold social force strategies, alliances, and attitudes. Hence, whether or not strong, centralized, and efficacious state institutions develop depends on the strength or weakness and configuration of social forces. This is a premise that departs from much of the "new institutionalism" literature, a body of work, which, although admittedly extremely heterogeneous (Hall and Taylor 1996; Steinmo 2008; Thelen 1999), assumes that institutions, however defined, are the most important variable and the starting point in explaining outcome. Generally, those focusing on the role of institutions do not acknowledge institutions as manipulated by powerful social forces to serve their interests. Indeed, proponents of institutionalism view institutions as autonomous forces producing path-dependent sequences that shape action and therefore outcome. In addition, historical institutionalism generally fails to account for the origins of institutions and for institutional change, particularly rapid and momentous change (Pierson 2004, 103). While the analysis presented in this work recognizes the impact of institutions on outcome, it shifts the focuses to social forces, recognizing that powerful social forces may create, destroy, and reconstitute institutions, altering outcome in profound ways.

In many countries of the global south, including the Latin American cases dealt with here, state institutions are weak and fragmented. Strong social forces can and do create and manipulate institutions in their own interests with important implications for distributive outcomes. The actions of social forces may contribute to the fragmentation of state institutions because, in pursuit of their interests, they pull state ministries, departments, and agencies in contrary directions. The result is often policy incoherence (Migdal 1988)—a phenomenon with potentially important implications for economic growth and poverty reduction. At the same time, of course, institutions, once established, can powerfully shape the actions of social forces through a wide variety of measures that may contribute to their mobilization or quiescence. As we shall see, the Korean state proved enormously more resistant to social penetration than the Chilean and Mexican states and, for many years, was able to contain social force pressures, a feat that allowed it to pursue an employment-generating economic growth model. While the specific factors affecting poverty and inequality outcomes vary substantially from country to country, the general approach, which begins with a consideration of the relative strength of social forces and their relation to the state formation, may provide a useful starting point in explaining social outcomes in other contexts.

The term *social forces* refers to both broadly and narrowly constituted social groups that may have either formal or informal organizational features and that have shared interests. Social forces may be social classes in the classic understanding of the term, defined by their relationship to the means of production (peasants, workers, for example), fractions of social classes, groups claiming religious or ethnic identities, or social movements. The state bureaucracy, or factions within it, and the military may come to constitute a social force. All such groups, alone or in coalitions, are capable of acting in ways that can have a powerful impact on social outcomes. As has been recognized elsewhere (Migdal 1994, 19), the term *social class* may not be applicable in global south contexts because southern countries may not only lack sizeable working and business classes but may also display severe schisms within traditionally defined social classes. In two of the cases dealt with in this study (Mexico and South Korea), the working class is divided; in the Korean case, severely so. In Korea, this rift involves distinct social welfare visions. In all three cases, there is a sharp schism between small and medium-sized business on the one hand and big politically and economically powerful conglomerates on the other. In Mexico and Chile, profound divisions within the peasantry entailed very different rural development objectives. Hence, social class fragments can be all-important actors in distributive struggles. In addition, categories such as the military and the bureaucracy, although they *may* draw disproportionately from a particular social class, are not social classes. Social movements cannot be defined in terms of their relationship to the means of production and may draw support from a variety of social classes. In the case of Korea, social movements, acting as social forces, have had a particularly important impact on that country's social welfare regime since the 1990s.

Any statement regarding the relative strength of social forces depends heavily on one's interpretation of the particular historical, social, and political context. Often, a social force exercises power due to its control or ownership of substantial resources, whether land or other capital assets—such is the case for big business interests and big landowners. Business and landed interests, with a conscious understanding of their shared concerns, are likely to act aggressively and in highly organized ways. However, labor groups, peasantries, and social movements, although lacking the same level of resources, may also act in an organized and combative manner. Hence, a social force's effective "strength" (its ability to influence outcome) is very much shaped by the social and political context in which it operates and the condition (size, organizational capacities) of other social forces. The influence of the social force(s) with the most material resources may be mitigated by the militancy of opposing social forces (for example, an alliance of some combination of labor, the middle class, and social movements) or by state action, where the state resists or successfully dominates powerful social force(s). Often the state increases its leverage over powerful propertied interests by mobilizing support. Hence, a social force that is large in number of members, but politically quiescent, may nevertheless affect outcome because a sympathetic political leadership recruits its support (for example, at election time).[8] Explaining why the state is sympathetic to some social forces and not to others is also an important question. The independence of the state may be reflective of the fact that the state itself is the locus of autonomous social forces (the military or the bureaucracy)—groups that have their own policy objectives. These intrastate social forces may have distinct histories and interests and, as a consequence, predispositions to support some social forces over others. Hence, the relationship that social forces have with states is very much a product of particular histories of state formation. States may succeed in subjugating social forces or incorporating them, or powerful social forces may thoroughly penetrate and manipulate the state (Migdal 1994, 25). When social forces penetrate the state, they may do so to different degrees and through different mechanisms. They may gain access to the state by means of a clientelistic relationship with a bureaucrat or politician, or they may secure direct representation within the state through membership in a government body. Differing degrees and modes of incorporation will have important implications for policy and distributional outcomes.

Social forces and the state are key actors in the creation and perpetuation of inequality, and inequality is, as noted, closely related to the prospects for economic growth and poverty reduction. If social forces become distinct social categories that are tightly interconnected, have shared awareness and consciousness, and interact with those outside of the group differently than with those from within, then the stage may be set for the emergence and perpetuation of a high degree of inequality. According to Tilly, whether inequality occurs and is perpetuated depends on whether repeated transactions across social categories regularly yield a disadvantage to a certain group or groups (2005, 21). Categorical inequality is based on one group's control of an important resource or resources; the most effective and enduring form of inequality occurs when one social category is able to dominate the state. The control of this all-important resource allows a social force, or a coalition of social forces, to institutionalize and therefore perpetuate inequality through building the unequal treatment of the "out" social categories into the operation of state structures. In this work, I refer to the creation of marked distinctions among social forces and the absence of deep knowledge within a group about those in other social groups as *social compartmentalization*. This phenomenon is particularly salient to this study because of the sharp categorical and social distinctions brought about by the colonial experience in Latin America.[9] However, modernization also gives rise to new social forces and to new possibilities for social integration. In this context, the sequencing of events and pace of transformations are key ingredients in explaining divergent outcomes. The timing and pace of industrialization are particularly important in shaping the attitudes, the relative strength, and configuration of social forces and the prospects for societal integration and cohesion. The rapid pace of industrialization in the case of South Korea contributed to working- and middle-class concern for the maintenance of low levels of inequality, while its prolonged nature in the other two cases contributed to social compartmentalization.

The approach outlined here is rare in comparisons of the Latin American and East Asian experiences. Hence, the following section reflects selectively on some of the main points of comparison in the comparative literature on the two regions, pointing out the ways in which this study diverges from, and adds to, what we already know about the differences between the two regions.

Grappling with Divergent Outcomes in East Asia and Latin America

Much of the literature comparing Latin America and East Asia has not focused specifically on poverty and equality outcomes nor considered broader contextual historical processes, including the role of social forces, as primary causal factors.[10] Instead, there has been much greater interest in economic growth and a predisposition to identify the different nature and role of the state as the crucial ingredients explaining East Asia's more robust and sustained economic performance. The "weaker" Latin American state, so the argument goes, has produced ineffective economic policy and low or stagnant growth, while the "strong" East Asian state has produced coherent and effective economic policy, responsible for high economic growth rates. Relatively few works have explored the historical origins of the East Asian strong state. Some have examined Japanese colonial rule and argue that it contributed to the later economic success of colonized countries through the construction of a strong colonial state that promoted technological change in rice agriculture, the expansion of the education system, and policies that stimulated industrialization (Amsden 1989, 79–80; Cumings 1987; Myers and Ching 1964). Kohli argues that Japanese colonial rule swept away the old predatory state and carried out reforms in the civilian bureaucracy and policy that established the basis for the postcolonial state (1994, 128).[11] European colonial rule, on the other hand, left a legacy of weak states and contributed to social fragmentation and to the intensity of intrastate political conflict in the postcolonial period (Blanton, Mason, and Athow 2001). In the case of Latin America, colonial rule left behind a particularly rigid social structure that placed a wealthy European oligarchy in control of the economy and politics, a mixed-blood population in the middle ranks of economic and political power, and a poor and powerless indigenous population at the bottom. This situation made nation building and state formation very difficult and often protracted tasks.[12] Hence, colonial rule shaped the configuration of social forces with profound implications for state formation and state strength.

However, colonial rule was but the first step and was one of a number of influences, shaping social forces and political institutional outcomes. In fact, in the immediate aftermath of independence from Japan, the Korean state between 1945 and 1961 shared a variety of features with its Latin American counterparts, including the fact that it was heavily penetrated by private interests and apparently incapable of producing a coherent and effective economic program. Yet, as we shall see, South Korea successfully produced a strong state by the mid-1960s. Furthermore, while Mexico and Chile shared a history of Spanish conquest and colonialism, their twentieth-century achievements in poverty reduction, as noted, are substantially different. This study demonstrates that, while colonial experience marks an important starting point, the postcolonial evolution of social forces and their impact on state formation and capacity have weighed heavily on outcomes.

Land redistribution—extensive in East Asia and insufficient or non-existent in Latin America—is frequently cited as one of the main variables explaining their distinct experiences in industrial growth and equitable social outcomes (Haggard 1990, 236–238; Kay 2006; Morley 2001, 64; Sen 2000, 45). There is clearly a strong relationship among land redistribution, economic growth, and poverty reduction over the long term. This link is due to the greater incentive to farmer productivity that occurs when producers work their own land rather than work for a landowner on large holdings. Land redistribution is also important because it eliminates unproductive landowners and allows more dynamic producers to improve agricultural productivity through modernization (Birdsall and Londoño 1997; Cornia et al. 2004, 50; Deininger and Squire 1998). Furthermore, government support of rural dwellers, in the form of credit and technical support, is crucial to the achievement of good social outcomes because such support makes possible the healthy levels of agricultural production required to feed the growing labor force as economic growth and industrialization continue. I use the term *land reform* in this work to refer to those transformations involving both land redistribution and state support (credit, technical support) to land redistribution beneficiaries. In Latin America, the absence of land reform, combined with insufficient educational opportunities, particularly for the rural poor, has further aggravated poverty and inequality. While Latin American governments focused educational spending on urban centers and squeezed rural incomes to support industrialization, the Asian cases involved more equitable educational opportunities for rural dwellers.

While the general observation that land reform was important in securing equitable development and poverty reduction in East Asia is an important one, substantial land redistribution did occur in some Latin American countries, including in Mexico and Chile. Kay makes the important observation that land redistribution in East Asia had the equality-enhancing impact it did because it occurred early in the history of industrialization (2006). However, we need to explain why land reform was earlier, more complete, and more sustaining in Korea than in Chile and Mexico. For the most part, the answer lies in an examination of social forces—in particular in a consideration of levels of peasant mobilization and sources of resistance from powerful social forces and their allies.[13]

The East Asian state has demonstrated greater bureaucratic capacity and the ability to engender cooperation with state policy on the part of its private sector. Korea's trained bureaucrats, for example, were able to devise and implement effective economic policies that stimulated the growth of new industrial activities, expand exports and export earnings, and keep the fiscal deficit in check, while collecting taxes sufficient to cover state expenditures. In a by now classic formulation, Peter Evans speaks of the autonomy of the "developmental" state as embedded in a concrete set of social ties that provide institutionalized channels for the continual negotiation and renegotiation of goals and policies with the private sector—an arrangement that secured the sector's cooperation (Evans 1995, 12). While this "embedded autonomy" is a feature of the East Asian states, Latin American countries either lack the feature, or it is only partially present; hence Latin American states are less capable of policy coordination and are prone to personalistic solutions. However, Silva (2006, 106, 108) has challenged this argument in the case of Chile. He argues that, since 1983, Chile has had many of the features of East Asian states, such as state strength and an effective state bureaucracy with embedded autonomy in state–private sector relations. Others have dealt with the differences in the quality of state intervention with attention to the corrosive impact of rent-seeking behavior on bureaucratic capability, development policy, and social outcomes in Latin America (Boyd 2006; Cho 1997). Once again, however, a full understanding of state capacity or weakness requires an exploration of what historical circumstances molded the relations between states and social forces. This study finds that a historical moment of weak social forces allowed the emergence of a strong state in Korea, capable of leading industrial growth and employment expansion with low inequality, while strong social forces represented an obstacle to state efficacy in Mexico and Chile. Furthermore, embeddedness fails to capture the coercive capability of the Korean state. Nor does it convey the limitations of the Chilean state, which, although much strengthened in the past two decades, is able to encourage but not *ensure* private sector cooperation. While all countries are restricted in their policy options by the surge of international regulations governing trade and investment stemming from various World Trade Organization (WTO) Agreements, the Korean state stands out for its ability to continue stimulating export-led growth that is employment generating.[14]

Closely linked to bureaucratic capacity is the issue of policy choice—particularly the choice of an export-oriented industrial strategy. The often-made observation is that the East Asian choice of an export-oriented industrial strategy that was labor intensive and produced a sustained upward swing in employment was instrumental in reducing poverty. Further, in the Korean case, when demand for light industrial products began to decline, the state was able to shift its industrial strategy to ensure the maintenance of economic growth and employment growth. Observers typically contrast this experience with Latin America's less effective import substitution industrialization, which focused on producing primarily for the domestic market, a strategy that ran into serious difficulties when foreign exchange earnings from volatile primary product exports fell (Haggard 1990, 3; Ludovic 2003, 478).[15] Industrial growth subsequently ground to a halt because of its dependence on imported machinery and inputs, and companies laid off workers. Moreover, heavy protection in Latin

America produced an inefficient industrial sector that could not expand into export markets once domestic production fully supplied the domestic market. However, Mexico has become a successful manufacturing export economy with 67 percent of its exports accounted for by manufactures by 2008 (see Table A-11), although, as noted, this success has coincided with a high level of inequality and a persistent and relatively high level of poverty. Chile's export-led strategy, initiated in the mid-1980s and focusing largely on nontraditional agricultural exports, has been much more effective at employment generation and poverty reduction. Clearly, South Korea's industrial strategy was by far the most effective in generating employment. Essential to understanding these differences in policy outcome is a grasp of the historical evolution of social forces, their social and political attitudes and interests, and the ways in which different social force configurations affected the state and the specific aspects of industrial policy.

Cultural explanations—the difference between Confucian values and Iberian Catholic ones—have also been considered as important by a variety of observers. One difficulty is that there is no consensus among Korean experts on the developmental impact of Confucianism. There are those who argue that Confucianism, insofar as it posits mutual support among family members, discourages the state from assuming public responsibility for the well-being of the population and therefore is counterproductive to good social outcomes once modernization is underway (Woo 2004, 5). However, others point to Confucian values as supporting the ongoing concern for equity and human welfare on the part of the state. This perspective views the "Confucian state," as grounded in benevolence because it is an extension of the family (Lee 1997, 119). The role of the state, therefore, is to build a community of plenty and care for the everyday needs of all people because the ethical life is possible only for people who have achieved freedom from socioeconomic misery (B. Kim 2000, 65).

A large body of literature on Latin America deals with the impact of Iberian Catholic values. Some of this literature sees such values, because of their hierarchical nature, as counterproductive to economic growth, social improvements, and greater equality (Harrison 1998; Lipset 1967). Observers see Iberian Catholic values as deeply embedded in unequal social and power structures. Elite adherence to the nineteenth-century philosophy of positivism, a philosophy that identified the key to development as the application of Western science through the economic leadership of a Europeanized modern business class of bankers and industrialists, was inclined (as in the Mexican case) to denigrate the indigenous population and exclude it from development. At the same time, however, values are mutable. The rise of liberation theology within Roman Catholicism is a testament to the capacity of Catholic "values" to change and to the possibility that a hitherto wholly conservative Church could produce a theology that questioned hierarchy and social injustice. Similarly, traditional Iberian Catholic business attitudes, such as aversion to risk taking and a propensity to appoint close family members rather than the highly trained individuals, diminish once the opportunity structure changes (Cardoso 1972).

I take the position that, while cultural values may be relevant explanatory variables, they are powerfully shaped by historical structural realities and evolve with socioeconomic changes. Hence, I do not treat them as causal factors independent of the historical evolution of social forces and state formation. Larger structural conditions create the context shaping which ideas will survive, strengthen, or diminish. In fact, this is largely an interactive process in which it is difficult to separate cultural norms from societal practices and social forces.

The Context: Geopolitics and the International Political Economy

External factors—geopolitics, U.S. foreign policy, and the operation of international political economy—have often been cited as key factors shaping the different outcomes in Latin America and East Asia (Chase-Dunn 1987, 290; Deyo 1987, 232; Haggard 1990; Kong 2000, 151). Until 1985, U.S. policy toward East Asia was governed by its concern with issues of national security and the containment of communism. The East Asian countries not only benefited from high levels of U.S. aid but also had considerable maneuverability in mitigating U.S. pressure and in diverging from U.S. wishes (Ick-jin 2006, 57; Woo 1991, 4–8; 45–48). Hence, because the United States saw Korea not as a potential market and investment opportunity but as the front line for containing communism, U.S. policy advice and pressures tended toward a pragmatism that tolerated an activist economic role for the state and excused otherwise unacceptable policy choices as long as the overall result satisfied security concerns. Meanwhile, Latin American countries have been subject to greater U.S. interference and more direct forms of investment pressure. Furthermore, in the Asian cases, the United States did not ally itself with traditional landed elites, and it supported thorough land redistribution, perceived as necessary to secure popular support against communism. In Latin America, on the other hand, where the U.S. economic interests were supreme, alliance with traditional landed elites was common, as was U.S. intervention, including military intervention, carried out to secure the overthrow of political leaderships seeking land redistribution and other measures threatening private property.[16] U.S. involvement in the overthrow of the Chilean socialist government of Salvador Allende in 1973 (Petras and Morley 1975, 79–118, 134), a regime in the process of carrying out land reform at the time along with other redistributive measures, is an example of intervention that bolstered conservative and propertied forces, thereby reinforcing poor social outcomes. Finally, the ongoing threat from communist North Korea was instrumental in cementing a strong South Korean commitment to make capitalism work in a way that would reduce poverty and keep inequality low. Doing so would mitigate social unrest and reduce the appeal of Communism (Kong 2000, 117). In short, the differing impact of geopolitics in the two regions has had very different consequences. In South Korea, the threat from communist North Korea and U.S. geopolitical concerns was conducive to an equitable outcome and successful export-oriented economic growth.

The international economy is also instrumental in shaping the success or failure of chosen economic and development strategies. As East Asia turned to the production of light consumer goods for export in the 1960s, it faced an expanding world market (Deyo 1987, 227). The Vietnam War gave an important impulse to South Korea's efforts to support the development of its heavy and chemical industrial sector (Woo 1991, 85), and improvements in the country's terms of trade contributed to the country's rapid recovery from the 1981 economic crisis. On the other hand, in the early 1970s, an inhospitable world economy contributed to Mexico's inability to pursue redistributive measures, while the dramatic drop in petroleum prices through the first half of the 1980s was an important ingredient in the depth of the country's economic downturn and to the rise of poverty.

However, we need to account for the redistributive features of the economic strategies chosen and for the ability and willingness of some states to exercise whatever leverage they have in the international realm in ways conducive to equitable and poverty-reducing outcomes. Social force configuration, state formation, and politics are instrumental in the formulation of economic policy and the extent to which policymakers contemplate social outcome. Furthermore, states may win or lose international market opportunities or may grasp them in different ways with distinct redistributive outcomes. A particular social force configuration may be conducive to adaptability in the face of international opportunities, while a different configuration may foster constraints in grasping opportunity.

Social Forces, Regime Type, and Social Outcome

There are two key ingredients shaping poverty and equality outcomes: economic growth and state-orchestrated redistributive measures. Economic growth, in providing employment opportunities, lifts people out of poverty and will be especially equality enhancing if, over the long term, employment opportunities are well remunerated. State redistributive measures, involving progressive taxation and social spending, are important for both poverty and inequality reduction. Income transfers, of course, are by themselves poverty and inequality reducing. Progressive spending on health care and education is particularly important because it provides opportunity for upward mobility to the more disadvantaged members of the population. Hence, poverty and inequality are not simply matters of income level; they are also inextricably linked to equitable access to health care and education. Disease due to lack of access to health care may thrust a household into poverty. Furthermore, inequality in wealth has a tendency to magnify all other disparities because, as Sen points out, it creates sharp differences in opportunities owing to a variety of non–income-related handicaps (2000, 119). Hence, employment-generating economic growth and equitable access to health care and education appear to be essential ingredients in reducing poverty and inequality. Economic growth and redistributive measures are closely linked because economic growth generates the revenue that makes redistribution possible.[17] However, the mix between these two elements is highly variable, particularly in the global south.

There is a long-standing debate about regime type (whether democratic or authoritarian) and its relevancy for the achievement of good human development indicators. The distinct features of the three cases amply illustrate the variable impact of regime type on social inequality and poverty. South Korea achieved rapid egalitarian economic growth under a military regime, which vacillated from soft to hard (repressive) authoritarianism between 1961 and 1979. Following its transition to electoral democracy in the late 1980s, the country has continued to maintain steady economic growth, low poverty, and relatively low levels of inequality, but more recently with expanded social welfare provisioning. Chile achieved social improvement through social welfare expansion, with slow economic growth, under a highly competitive electoral democracy between 1938 and 1973, but the country witnessed a sharp increase in poverty and inequality under military rule (1973–1989). However, improvement in poverty levels, with steady economic growth, began in 1987. This achievement has accelerated under electoral democracy from 1990 on, a period that combines healthy economic growth rates with an increase in social protection. Mexico experienced healthy growth rates, only a slow reduction of poverty, and a rise of inequality under an authoritarian one-party regime that lasted until 2000. Since then, its electoral democracy has witnessed slow economic growth and comparatively high levels of poverty and inequality.

Most of the literature dealing with socioeconomic equality and democracy makes a strong case for a close link between the two. For the most part, this literature assumes the efficacy of electoral processes and party competition and the ability of social forces to work through these institutions to achieve redistributive gains.[18] Capitalist growth, according to this argument, produces a social structure amenable to democracy and, eventually, to improved social outcomes because of pluralist political activity and elections. Capitalist growth gives rise to new social forces (whether workers or middle class) who push for redistributive measures (Huber and Stephens 2001, 9–10; Lipset and Lakin 2004, 100). Those examining the welfare regimes in the global south have made the case that democracy is more likely to produce greater responsiveness to the poor (Haggard and Kaufman 2008, 362) and is associated with a decline in infant mortality because it is conducive to state-provided basic social services (McGuire 2010, 63). Sen (2000) draws our attention to the fact that no democracy has ever experienced a famine, arguing that democracy and political rights can help prevent humanitarian disasters because democratic governments have to face elections and public criticism. The Korean case, however, might seem to suggest the efficacy of authoritarianism (even military rule) in achieving economic growth and good social outcomes. Indeed, authoritarianism might be conducive to economic growth and improved social conditions over the long run because the authoritarian state can resist public pressure and is therefore better able to direct resources into investment rather than to consumption (Haggard 1990, 262).

A careful examination of the social forces behind particular regimes, rather than drawing conclusions based on whether a regime is democratic or authoritarian, may go some distance in helping to resolve such debates. Authoritarian regimes may in fact be backed by popular social forces on which the leadership heavily depends, while formal democratic regimes may be characterized by narrow social bases. Elected politicians concerned about improving social welfare may be constrained by powerful informal groups. Such observations may be particularly salient to transitional or recently transitioned democracies, a category into which our three cases fell from the mid- to late 1980s. As Przeworski observes (1991, 95), the prospect of a new or transitional democracy achieving improved social outcomes depends on the "concessions" made by prodemocratic forces to obtain agreement for the transition. If income distribution and property relations are highly unequal at the time of transition, and the agreement is to leave these untouched, then the consequence will be conservative, economically and politically. Such pacts become particularly challenging problems because many late industrializing democracies have faced serious social deficits and high levels of inequality.[19] Hence, in the case of transitional democracies, the presence of democratic institutional frameworks may encourage, but by no means guarantees, progress in poverty or inequality reduction. When pacts involve not just the continued influence of powerful social forces from the authoritarian period but also institutional legacies that impede changes in policy direction, change in distributional outcomes can be particularly slow and difficult. Many years may pass before the removal of institutional obstacles and popular pressure produces sufficient policy change to have an impact on distributional outcome. On the other hand, if the transition to democracy involves both a political opening and pressure from below for greater social justice, then there will be a greater likelihood of improvements in social protection.

The three cases of this study represent different forms of political transition with distinct social consequences. As a political transition pushed from below (1987–1992), the South Korean case is one in which strong popular social forces pushed the posttransition governments to address social concerns with expanded programs. Chile's political transition, which culminated in the election of a center–left alliance in 1990, was a pacted elite-driven one with a strong and restrictive institutional legacy that stymied a more vigorous pursuit of redistributive objectives until after 2000. The narrow electoral focus of the Mexican transition, in combination with a potent informal and institutional legacy that left powerful business groups and organized labor with inordinate power, has been among the factors blocking more effective redistributive and poverty reduction measures despite the achievement of electoral democracy in 2000 and a subsequent competitive and free election in 2006. In addition, Mexico's legacy of authoritarian political control, which has involved a highly effective form of co-optation and control of popular organizations, has contributed to that country's weak civil society and commensurately weaker pressure from below for social improvements.[20]

Social Forces and Redistributive Pacts: North and South

A consideration of social forces has been a central preoccupation of a great deal of the general literature dealing with distributive outcomes. The body of work explaining the nature of welfare states in the industrialized nations (the key redistributive mechanisms in these countries) places considerable weight on the configuration and relative strength of social classes and on the nature of the political settlement reached between contending groups. This settlement involved a process in which a strong state mediated the interests of strong social forces (business and labor). Where social forces and states were the strongest, in northern Europe, the most equitable redistributive settlements ensued; where the social compromise was the weakest (the United States), inequality has been higher.[21] In northern Europe, where state-orchestrated redistributive compromises produced policies conducive to full employment, a generous welfare state, and a progressive tax system, basic material security was a citizenship right (Berger 2002, 16–18; Huber and Stephens 1998). The state also engaged in an active industrial policy geared to the creation of a competitive manufacturing sector that provided expanded employment opportunities. In short, in the societies with arguably the best social outcomes, social forces were powerful but states even more so. A crucial ingredient of the class compromise of the industrialized nations is the fact that private property ownership was not questioned (Berger 2002, 14), an issue that was especially problematic in Mexico (pre-1980) and Chile (pre-1973) and an important ingredient inhibiting redistributive settlements.

Although the extent of social welfare protection in the global south varies quite markedly, the social welfare arrangements of individual countries are often minimal. Indeed, even in those cases, particularly in Latin

America, in which there are relatively high overall levels of public expenditure on social security, social welfare protection is usually very unequal in nature and covers only a proportion of the population, often less than one-half (Haggard and Kaufman 2008, 31–33; Pierson 2005, 398–399; Segura-Ubiergo 2007, 30). Meanwhile, social assistance, the support measures provided that part of the population lacking social security protection, is minimal or nonexistent. Hence, highly limited and unequal state-supported social security arrangements combined with regressive tax regimes may render the "welfare" system regressive for the population as a whole (Atkinson and Mills 1991, 104; Huber 2005, 78). Welfare regimes in the south have often developed in situations of state weakness and permeability. Indeed, when the state is weak and permeated by social forces, social policy is not independent and therefore serves to reinforce privilege and private short-term gain (Barrientos 2004; Gough 2004, 32). Hence, in some circumstances, particularly in Latin America, the welfare regime may actually contribute to inequality.

The lower level of state-funded social protection in the East Asian NICs has resulted in these welfare regimes being characterized as "productivist welfare regimes" (Holliday 2000). Because social spending is low in productivist regimes, welfare provision is considerably less generous than that found in Western industrialized nations; productivist regimes also compare unfavorably with Latin American welfare regimes where social spending has also been much higher. Yet, achievements in poverty reduction and the maintenance of low inequality have been superior to Latin America. One important explanatory factor is that productivist regimes provide relatively higher levels of spending on education but provide much less on potentially inequality-enhancing social security protection than is the case for Latin America (Haggard and Kaufman 2008, 28). In addition, the productivist welfare regime's provision of basic social services to the poor, which, in addition to education, includes family planning and basic maternal and infant care, has probably been important in improving human development indicators such as infant mortality (McGuire 2010, 21) with positive implications for poverty and equality levels. However, much of the discussion characterizing the East Asian welfare regime as underdeveloped may well arise from a narrow definition of what policies and programs ought to be included in the definition of redistributive or welfare programs. Consideration of surrogate policies, such as government-mandated private enterprise welfare, subsidies, and regulations favoring small farmers, including guaranteed purchase prices and regulations against foreclosure, gives a much more generous picture of the extent of East Asian state intervention in support of social welfare (Kim 2010).

All of the three cases depart in important ways from the experiences of industrialized nations in which redistributive settlements involved the combination of strong states *and* strong social forces. In the case of Korea, weak social forces early in the historical process facilitated the emergence of a strong state. The condition of weak social forces and a strong state made possible the construction of institutions and state decisions having a positive distributive impact. In Mexico and Chile, on the other hand, strong social forces made state building difficult and created distributive conflicts that weak states, permeated by the most economically powerful, did not mediate. The consequence was damaging for distributive outcomes. Hence, the distributive and poverty outcomes for all three cases involved long historical trajectories during which initial starting points were iterated over time. The following section outlines the conceptual framework used for the analysis of these historical paths.

The Analytical Framework and the Argument of the Book

The concept of critical *con*juncture used in this work is inspired by the term *coyuntura,* employed in Latin American historical sociology, *and* by the notion of "critical juncture," found in mainstream comparative historical analysis. While the latter tends to focus on the events in temporal sequences and on formal institutional outcomes, the former pays closer attention to economic structure, including international structures, the way economic structure shapes social structure, and the emergence, relative strengths, and projects of social forces.[22] This work pays attention to social structures and the relative strengths of social forces, including how these are shaped by a country's insertion into international markets *and* the ways in which social forces shape institutions and are shaped by them. For both critical junctures *and* critical conjunctures, key developments early in history produce causal chains that explain later unexpected or unpredicted outcomes. However, critical conjunctures, unlike critical junctures, involve the intersection of two separately determined sequences that connect only through a coincidence of timing (Mahoney 2000, 528; Pierson 2000, 87). The intersection of these sequences produces an outcome distinct from what would have resulted from either one of the sequences alone. Critical conjunctures also differ from critical junctures insofar as they mold more than political or institutional outcomes. Critical conjunctures produce change that is more fundamental; in particular, they result in not only institutional change but also an alteration in the configuration and relative strength of social forces. The social force or coalition of social forces that emerges as dominant and in control of the state now constructs a new set of institutional arrangements that shape future outcomes. Finally, the term *critical juncture* by itself is insufficient because of its strong association with path dependency: Normally, the term connotes a rupture that produces a self-reinforcing sequence. As we shall see in the following discussion, the notion of path-dependent–producing critical junctures does not provide a sufficient explanatory framework for the two Latin American cases.

The choice of a particular period in history as marking a critical conjuncture arises from its apparent determinant importance in the causal chain producing distinct outcomes—in this case its importance in molding particular equality or inequality and poverty outcomes. In all three cases, the impact of events on that all-important equalizing event—land reform—heavily influenced the choice of initial critical conjunctures. Critical conjunctures span a period of years because it takes time for them to materialize and for their impact to be full felt. Figure A-1 indicates the critical conjunctures and their impacts in the three cases. For Korea, the key equality-enhancing critical conjuncture is located between the years 1930 and 1953. Korea's critical conjuncture, which involved the intersection of domestic sequences and an international sequence, was by far the most transformative of the three cases. The domestic sequences involved the increase in peasant mobilization from 1930 on and the rebellion of 1946. The international sequence included the end of World War II in 1945, with its profound domestic impacts (the expulsion of the Japanese as Korea's colonizing power), the division of Korea into North and South and the U.S. military occupation of Korea until 1948, and the Korean War between 1950 and 1953. An election in 1948 brought a civilian Korean government to power, a government supported by the United States and initially dominated by landlords and domestic capitalists (Kwon and O'Donnell 2001, 17). The intersection of the two sequences propelled forward that country's extensive land redistribution program, eliminating an already weakened landowning class. The impact of these events was profound: South Korea emerged as a homogeneous society of small farmer-producers and a country bereft of mineral resources and industry, which had been largely located in the north.

Chile's initial critical conjuncture with long-term equality and poverty implications begins with the Great Depression, includes the election of the Popular Front government in 1938, and ends with the disintegration of the Popular Front government in 1941. The intersection of the Great Depression, with its devastating impact on the Chilean economy, and the rise to power of an alliance of parties representing the middle and working class had profound political and economic implications. The severity of the economic downturn propelled forward a new industrial economic model. The alliance of the middle-class-supported Radical Party, the Communists, and the Socialists represented a new social force coalition and opened the possibility of more radical redistributive measures. However, the legislative deal to secure the new industrial development program was instrumental in consolidating the power of the rural landholders by guaranteeing them control over the countryside for decades to come, thereby making land reform impossible. Mexico's initial critical conjuncture spanned the period from 1890 to the mid-1920s. The domestic sequence of events involved the struggles of peasants, who fought in the Mexican Revolution (1910–1917) for land, and of workers who joined the struggle for better wages, benefits, and state ownership of natural resources. While the Revolution and its aftermath raised the possibility of radical land redistribution, the dynamism of the U.S. economy, both before and after the Revolution, facilitated the emergence of a new class of big agricultural exporters from the postrevolutionary leadership. This group, in alliance with the propertied interests that had survived the Revolution, allowed land redistribution to go forward only very slowly.

Critical conjunctures are not defined by the fact that they necessarily generate a path-dependent process. In fact, the sequences that follow critical conjunctures may be reactive (therefore producing substantial change or elimination of existing institutional arrangements) or self-reinforcing (Mahoney 2000, 509). The premise of the path-dependency literature, on the other hand, argues that initial institutional arrangements arising from critical junctures are self-reinforcing because there are "increasing returns" over time. The key mechanism involves some form of positive feedback loop, such as when the groups benefiting from the new arrangements act to prevent their dismantling or dilution. In addition, critical junctures generate social understandings and basic outlooks on politics, which also contribute to path dependence (Pierson 2000, 79). In this way, the new direction initiated by the critical juncture becomes locked in. On the other hand, critical conjunctures may also give rise to reactive sequences, which represent strong oppositional backlashes. In this process, the initial events are crucial not because they generate a powerful feedback loop but because they produce a powerful oppositional response. Mobilization and countermobilization create their own distinctive dynamic over time.

Reactive sequences occurred in Mexico and Chile; see Figure A-1. In these cases, elites and middle-class groups[23] (or their representatives) reacted against popular mobilization and/or the accession to power of representatives of the popular classes. These reactive sequences blocked redistributive measures in contexts that offered redistributive possibilities, including land redistribution. Faced with the prospect of losing wealth and political power, propertied and middle-class groups reasserted political control and blocked change. This, in turn, engendered mobilization from popular classes and redistributive episodes that, once again, engendered a hostile reaction on the part of propertied groups. In Mexico, brief redistributive episodes (including land redistribution) occurred between 1934 and 1938 and again in the early 1970s, but intense reactions on the part of the propertied groups ended these attempts. In Chile, middle-class and elite groups purged the left from the Popular Front government, contributing to the radicalization of the left. Increasing popular demands for radical redistributive measures provoked a harsh reaction from the propertied class, producing the 1973 military coup, the reversal of social gains, and a sharp increase in poverty and inequality. In Mexico and Chile, the profound oppositional reactions of those threatened by mobilization from below led to new critical conjunctures with profound distributional consequences (see Figure A-1).

In sharp contrast, Korea's critical conjuncture produced a largely self-reinforcing sequence in which the configuration of social forces allowed for the creation of institutions and policies that mitigated inequality and reduced poverty well into the twentieth and even the twenty-first centuries. The weakness of Korea's propertied classes substantially reduced the likelihood of reactive sequences. The early establishment of low levels of inequality through land redistribution and rapid progress in the eradication of poverty made losses or threatened losses in these achievements unacceptable. Hence, the large class of small farmers created by land reform and, later, the urban working and middle classes all resisted increases in inequality. In Mexico and Chile, on the other hand, long histories involving the subjugation of the peasantry and workers became entrenched in institutional policy and practice and in social attitudes.

Preexisting historical legacies, international pressures and opportunities, and resource endowment shaped critical conjunctures. As noted above, Korea's geopolitical importance to the United States produced policy preferences, such as land redistribution, that weakened big landowners and contributed to a good distributive outcome. In addition, different experiences of colonial rule also contributed in powerful ways to the nature, relative strength, and attitudes of social forces. The expansion of commercial agriculture patterned rural class structure and the prospects for land reform.

Resource endowment determines a country's trade profile and the extent and nature of foreign investment; for example, a country rich in mineral resources is likely to have extensive foreign investment in its mining sector and to become highly dependent on minerals for its foreign exchange earnings. In Chile and Mexico, the development of mining exports molded the ways social forces emerged and shaped how conjunctural circumstances developed. The establishment of foreign-dominated mineral enclaves in the early twentieth century, along with the much earlier onset of industrialization and its prolonged nature, contributed to the strength of the propertied interests that blocked redistributive measures. Mineral enclave economies also produced working classes with a high level of political consciousness whose rejection of the institution of private property made redistributive compromises especially difficult. The fact of much greater U.S. capital penetration in Latin America than in East Asia (Evans 1987, 203) complicated and polarized redistributive struggles because nationalization and anti-imperialism became closely linked with redistributive demands. Conjunctures under these circumstances could quickly become zero-sum conflicts. Taken all together, the combination of external influences served to strengthen path-dependent sequences in Korea and to invigorate reactive ones in Chile and Mexico.

According to Couch and Farrell (2004), one of the problems in the path-dependency perspective is its difficulty in accounting for change or for deviations from the expected path-dependent pattern. They point out that, while path dependency is powerful, past values, thinking, and alternatives are never entirely extinguished but continue to exist somewhere within agents' repertoires. There remains the possibility that agency could resurrect one of these hidden alternatives (20). In understanding divergent poverty and inequality outcomes, it is useful to consider this possibility in connection with the resiliency of popular notions of social justice at times when movements espousing such values are defeated politically. The persistence of old ideas and alternatives, over time, means that agency can resurrect one of these hidden alternatives if the opportunity presents itself. In fact, for a "new" direction in policy to be successful, the political leadership is likely to incorporate aspects of defeated alternatives into the rhetoric and policy even if only for the purpose of neutralizing opposition and asserting political control (Laclau 1977, 162, 178). Hence, old ideas may, in fact, come to influence policy choices. The persistence of a past repertoire was evident in South Korea after 1961, where social justice remained an important issue despite the defeat of the left, and in Chile after 1990, where social justice reemerged after years of repression under military rule. The survival of past repertoires is also evident in the survival and reemergence of state-led export growth in Chile after 1985.

This work makes the following argument with regard to the distinct social outcomes of the three cases. In Korea, a critical conjuncture giving rise to a unified Korean peasantry and a weakened landed class made land redistribution possible and ushered in the establishment of a strong state, unencumbered by strong social pressures. A reinforcing sequence followed, involving a population increasingly accustomed to equality, even in the face of rapid economic and political change, and a leadership motivated to lead employment-generating economic growth and secure social improvements because of its basis of support in the rural poor. In Mexico and Chile, on the other hand, strong propertied classes and weak and divided peasantries precluded thorough land reforms. Critical conjunctures gave rise to reactive sequences that stalled or overturned redistributive gains. The prolonged nature of the Chilean and Mexican industrialization and modernization process allowed rigid social compartmentalization, with origins in the colonial period, to strengthen. Korea's compressed history of modernization, on the other hand, facilitated social homogeneity and empathy across social classes. In both Chile and Mexico, from the 1950s to the early 1970s, weak states permeated by propertied, working-class, and middle-class interests produced suboptimal economic strategies, unequal welfare regimes, and neglect of rural welfare.

In Korea in the 1980s and 1990s, the past success of employment-generating export-led growth with its equitable features reinforced continued state efforts at employment-generating export expansion and shaped civil society and labor pressure for the expansion of social protection. In Chile and Mexico, on the other hand, the crises faced by their respective industrialization models contributed to support for their dismantling and to the onset of radical market liberalization with negative social outcomes. With a pacted political transition characterized by a still-powerful propertied class and a prostrate labor movement, Chile's success in poverty reduction from the mid-1980s stemmed largely from state-led export expansion. It has only been since 2000 that civil society activism has begun to propel a more invigorated effort to achieve inequality reduction. Mexico, with the poorest social outcomes of our three cases, displays sharp social compartmentalization in which the indigenous peasants of the south have been the most disadvantaged. The legacy of institutional arrangements established by the postrevolutionary elite to contain recalcitrant social forces remains key in explaining continuing poor social provisioning. Those institutions left a legacy of weak popular forces, a powerful business sector, and privileged middle- and working-class groups. Unlike Korea and Chile, Mexico's export model has not been employment generating—a feature stemming from state weakness and the ability of powerful industrial interests to resist a basic change in direction.

The following three chapters are devoted to an examination of the historical roots of poverty and equality in each of the three cases, examining the contextual conditions and the causal chains that produced different outcomes. Chapter 5 combines the insights of the three country chapters with an analysis of the timing and pace of events. It argues that the compressed nature of Korea's historical experience contributed in an important way to social homogeneity (an absence of social compartmentalization) and to better social outcomes. Chapter 6 examines the experiences of each country in the 1980s and 1990s and shows how past legacies continued to shape different experiences with, and reactions to, the debt crisis of the early 1980s. It was in the 1980s that Korea surpassed the two other cases in terms of per capita income while it continued to maintain low levels of inequality. Chapter 8 examines poverty and inequality in the three cases since 2000. In this chapter, I argue that, while the pressures of economic globalization are having a homogenizing impact on labor regimes, there are still important differences in social outcomes, and social welfare regimes remain distinct. The relative political strengths of social forces provide the explanation for these differences.

2

South Korea
The Historical Origins of Equitable Growth

COMPARED WITH CHILE AND MEXICO, South Korea has been remarkably successful in improving the welfare of its population. With an economic growth rate averaging over 7 percent per year between 1965 and 1980 (see Table A-5), poverty declined from 41.4 percent of the population to 14.6 percent of households between 1965 and 1975, and inequality has remained comparatively low (see Tables A-1 and A-2).[1] One of the striking features of the South Korean case is that generally equitable growth occurred within the context of a rightist/conservative regime, backed by the military closely aligned with powerful business conglomerates known as *chaebols*. Two policies, early land reform and labor-intensive export-oriented industrialization, were the most important factors accounting for both equitable growth and poverty reduction. Land reform mitigated rural poverty and inequality, while state-led export-oriented industrialization produced high growth rates, generating jobs and increased wages. In this way, Korea avoided the high levels of underemployment and its associated poverty, so common in Latin America. There is a consensus that the country's employment-generating industrial strategy is attributable to the presence of a strong state and a meritorious bureaucracy with a high degree of policy capacity (Amsden 1989, 204; Deyo 1987, 229; Haggard and Kaufman 2008, 77; Koo 1993b, 236).

Korea's incorporation into the world economy as a grain producer and the nature of its landholding system produced a homogenization of misery among an ethnically homogeneous Korean peasant population. The country's equality-enhancing program of land reform was possible due to the combination of high levels of peasant mobilization and a weakened landed class. The ensuing context of weak social classes (following land reform), combined with the elimination of the political left, allowed for the emergence of a strong and efficacious state with a strong social base in the peasantry. The defeat of the political left did not signify the abandonment of concern for improved living standards for the peasantry and for equity in general, however. These themes persisted both in rhetoric and in policy. Concern for equity, bereft of notions of class conflict and calls for the eradication of private property, remained an important driving force behind policy decisions. The rapid pace of industrialization produced a large new urban middle class with recent memories of rural poverty and concerns about the importance of equality.

Setting the Stage for Equitable Growth: Social Forces, Land Reform, and the Korean State

The weakening of the traditional landowning class under Japanese colonial rule (1910–1945) and intense mobilization on the part of the popular classes, particularly the peasantry demanding land redistribution, set the stage for land reform. Hence, between 1930 and 1953 South Korea experienced a transformative critical conjuncture that would shape an equality-producing outcome within the context of rapid industrial capitalist growth. Domestically, the surge of peasant mobilization, culminating in the peasant rebellion of 1946, weakened big landowners. However, the push toward a thorough land reform would likely not have been possible without another series of transformative events: the end of World War II, the expulsion of the Japanese landowners, the American occupation, and the Korean War. While the government effectively repressed the small working class, neither the American occupation government nor the Korean government of Syngman Rhee (1948–1960) that followed it could ignore the claims of the much more numerous peasantry for land.[2] Particularly in the Cold War context, communist aggression from the north was instrumental in driving land reform.

From 1876, with the signing of Kanghwa Treaty with Japan, Korea was incorporated into the world economy as a grain producer (rice and beans) for the Japanese economy (Shin 1996, 27). Under Japanese colonial rule, rural class polarization rose as large landowners benefited the most from the commercial opportunities presented by the Japanese market, while the fortunes of small landowners, semitenants, and tenants diminished, particularly when grain prices weakened. With the Great Depression, many highly indebted small owners lost their land and were pushed into tenancy, owner-tenants became tenants, and tenants often found themselves without any land to work as landlords had canceled tenancy contracts. Hence, there was a significant decline in small owners and in owner-tenants and a rise in tenancy (Yong-ha 2003, 147). Increasingly impoverished, peasants took part in rebellions. Tenant protests, particularly in the south, occurred through the 1920s and accelerated after 1933. As a consequence, the Japanese colonial government began to withdraw its support from landlordism and attempted to address rural discontent with reforms restricting the ability of landlords to displace tenants or raise tenant rents (Shin 1998, 1327). Landlord power began to decline as rented land became less and less profitable. In 1941 through 1945, the freezing of agricultural rents and the colonial government's appropriation of agricultural surplus for the war effort further eroded landlord power (1329). Finally, the peasantry's perception that the traditional Korean landowning class was collaborating with the hated Japanese colonial rule reduced the legitimacy of its authority (Cole and Lyman 1971). This weakening of the traditional Korean landholding class helped clear the way for land redistribution after independence from Japan.

The nature of landholding, particularly in the south, created a set of conditions that would drive the mobilization for land redistribution. Big landowners parceled out their land to numerous peasant producers who worked the land in exchange for a portion of the crop, usually 50 percent. The increase in tenancy under colonial rule meant that at the time of independence, big landowners, 3 percent of the rural population, owned 60 percent of the land, while 80 percent of the population consisted of landless tenants or tenant-owners with little land (Shin 1996, 5). Extreme poverty was widespread: According to one estimate, 38 percent of the population was starving while 68 percent of the population was near starvation (Yong-ha 2003, 170). Commercialization of agriculture had done nothing to alter the mode of production, which continued to be based on cheap exploited labor, not on improved methods. New laws under Japanese colonial rule encouraged tenant demands for redress of grievances, and landlords had few mechanisms with which to contain tenant demands.

The distant nature of landlord–tenant relations made mobilization against landlords likely. The ties between landowners and tenants were weak. The biggest landlords, and many smaller ones, were absentee landlords, employing agents to administrate their estates. Furthermore, while landholdings were sometimes in a single estate, landowners' hold-ings were more frequently scattered widely throughout various districts with the result that peasants did not develop any sort of attachment to the landed estate (Yong-ha 2003, 47). While the power of the indigenous landed class was being eroded and peasants increasingly mobilized, Ko-rean nonagricultural business and organized labor were small and weak. Under colonial rule, the Japanese had dominated commercial/business activity as Japanese colonial rule restricted the development of an indig-enous capitalist class (Kwon 1999, 32; Minns 2001, 1029). Hence, few Koreans owned businesses, and none owned businesses of any substan-tial size. Only a few former members of the Korean landed class, despite the relatively small compensation given for their lands, were able to take advantage of the opportunities presented by the expansion of industry beginning in the 1950s (Kay 2006, 28).[3] Moreover, the division of Korea into North and South meant that South Korea lacked heavy industry, major iron ore, and coal deposits and was left with only 10 percent of the former colony's developed power capacity (Kim and Roemer 1979, 24). The absence of a mineral resource base and industrial development linked to it meant the absence of sufficiently strong social forces (such as indigenous industrialists) that could thwart an industrial export strategy.

While peasant revolts were numerous, the most important mobi-lization was the nationwide peasant uprising that occurred in October–November 1946, involving some 2.3 million peasants demanding land (Minns 2001, 1030; Shin 1998, 1318). Although the government severely repressed the rebellion, the extent of the unrest strongly influenced U.S. policy in the direction of decisive support for land redistribution. U.S. authorities and later the Korean government were convinced that the vast majority of South Koreans would not accept anticommunism and capital-ism if these meant preserving the structure of concentrated land owner-ship (Choi 1993, 19).[4] Hence, in the spring of 1948, the U.S. occupying force distributed the land it had confiscated from the Japanese. This initial land redistribution, accounting for about 30 percent of tenanted landhold-ings at the time, went forward rapidly in large part because the Korean landed class had already been considerably weakened. Intense pressure from a mobilized peasantry and fear of the popular appeal of the commu-nist land reform would ensure the completion of redistribution after the

Americans left. Given that the concept of private property ownership was firmly entrenched, no group in Korean society contested the nature of the land redistribution and the creation of a small landowning class.[5]

The introduction of elections and universal franchise[6] not surprisingly saw key politicians promising land titles to tillers with the consequence that land redistribution accelerated (Ban, Moon, and Perkins 1980, 288). The Korean War (1950–1953) was instrumental in further entrenching land redistribution and weakening the old landowning class because North Korean occupying troops forced land redistribution without compensation in areas that they occupied (Shin 1998, 1339).[7] Distribution of remaining landholdings occurred between 1948 and 1952. The impact was profound: While in 1945 only 13.8 percent of cultivators were full owners of the land they tilled, in 1964, 71 percent were full owner-cultivators while the proportion of tenants fell to around 5 to 7 percent from 48.9 percent in 1945 (Ban et al. 1980, 285, 286; Mason et al. 1980, 238).[8] Even though tenancy increased in subsequent years, by 1970 land ownership was far more equitable than in Mexico. The Gini coefficient[9] for land inequality in 1970 was 0.37 for South Korea and 0.77 for Mexico (Shin 1998, 1313).

Land redistribution produced redistribution of both land and income and, in virtually eliminating tenancy, created a large class of small farmers. Incomes of farmers increased because farmers no longer had to give half of their crop to the landlord, which meant a per capita rise in income of 33 percent (Ban et al. 1980, 290). Although the reform may have been somewhat detrimental to production, given the very small size of many plots, redistribution was instrumental in removing the threat of future peasant unrest. It created what has been described as a "structurally atomized and homogeneous society" (B. Kim 2000, 76). However, land redistribution would not have continued to be effective in assuaging peasant demands had not public policy in subsequent years sought to improve the lives of the peasantry and support agricultural production. This development was important in explaining both social peace and social welfare in the countryside. The high degree of equality arising from land redistribution meant that subsequent policy initiatives, such as credit and input opportunities, would benefit the rural population equally. In addition, because peasants marketed approximately the same percentage of produce, agricultural prices and variations in the terms of trade had a similar impact. Hence, the distribution of income in the rural sector remained unchanged between

1963 and 1974. There was also little change in the distribution of size of farms during this period (Ban et al. 1980, 306).

Greater land equality in the countryside also produced an equitable response to the expanded educational opportunities in rural areas.[10] With an overall illiteracy rate of 78 percent in 1945, rural illiteracy declined to 10 percent by 1970, an illiteracy rate even slightly better than the urban rate (see Table A-6). By 1967, 68 percent of the rural population had primary education or more. This situation is in sharp contrast to Mexico and Chile, where higher rates of rural illiteracy were evident in 1970. While family expenditure on education, especially in rural areas, was just as important as government expenditure (Mason et al. 1980, 349), increases in rural incomes, a consequence of both land reform and a variety of government policies discussed further in the following pages, made that extra personal expenditure possible. Moreover, state expenditure on education as a percentage of GNP (gross national product) increased steadily through the 1960s and early 1970s (Mason et al. 1980, 356).

While, in the immediate postindependence period, land reform was crucial in assuaging the discontent of the peasantry, repression (not just against peasants but also against worker organizations and against the political left) also played a role in removing oppositional pressure and paving the way for the emergence of a strong state. Guided by the Cold War objective of containing the Soviet Union and North Korea, the U.S. occupation government fiercely repressed the political left, eradicating mobilization politics from the political scene. The U.S. administration oversaw the destruction of leftist trade unions and other political organizations and secured the establishment of an anticommunist right-wing labor federation, the Federation of Korean Trade Unions (FKTU), an organization that would control labor under the tutelage of subsequent regimes. The absence of ideologically distinct leftist political parties meant the unlikelihood that either workers or peasants would become the object of high levels of political party mobilization (B. Kim 2000, 68).[11]

A combination of factors—a weak traditional landlord class and a small business class, elimination of popular class activism through repression, and a satisfied (and therefore quiescent) class of small farmers—created a power vacuum into which the state could move and develop strength. South Korea, on the threshold of industrialization, was a homogeneous society united by a shared ethnic identity, with weak social forces. The relative weakness of social forces, through the 1960s until the mid- to late 1970s, allowed state managers the time to establish institutions that could direct capitalist growth during its initial years. Due to this historical legacy, the South Korean state had the luxury, at least for a time, of the absence of effective challenges from domestic social forces. It was not necessary to construct elaborate methods of political containment that would thwart coherent economic policy (as occurred in Mexico). Nor was the state hampered in its economic policy choices by intense political pressures (Chile). For at least a decade, the Korean state could force the cooperation of a weak business class, as discussed further in the following pages.[12]

The fact that the Korean state, liberated from political pressures from the political left, nevertheless pursued an economic model with positive poverty and redistributive outcomes requires an explanation.[13] Although repression had eliminated the political left, concerns on the part of both society and state managers about poverty, inequality, and general human welfare had not been. The results of a 1960 survey carried out by the government demonstrated the predominance of socioeconomic demands among the Korean public. These demands included, in order of importance, the following: relief from unemployment, price stability, the elimination of usurious loans, and equitable taxation (Oh 1999, 2, 47). Although subordinate to the larger goal of economic growth, social concerns, particularly concerns about equality, would survive through the 1960s and 1970s, providing the impetus for policies that would mitigate poverty and keep inequality in check.

However, formal *levels* of social spending were not an indicator of the regime's redistributive concerns. Indeed, on issues of social welfare spending, Korea compares quite unfavorably with Chile, although less so with Mexico. Social spending in Korea reached only 4.6 percent of GDP by 1980 (see Figure A-3). While there was some improvement in state social spending between 1970 and 1980, the impact of formal social policy and taxation on equality was not great, although it is important to emphasize that it was not regressive.[14] However, it is the *composition* of social spending that played an important equalizing role. Korea spent considerably less, as a proportion of total social spending, on social security (a contributor to inequality, especially in Mexico, as we shall see) and relatively more on education—an important equalizing social expenditure, particularly if offered equitably as it was in Korea (see Figure 2-1). In 1974, 77.6 percent of total social expenditure went to educational spending. It is not until the 1990s that social security and social welfare expenditures begin to rise.

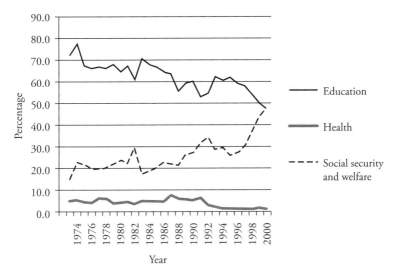

FIGURE 2-1. Korea: Education, health and social security/welfare, percentage of total social expenditures, 1973–2000. Sources: Data from International Monetary Fund, *Government Finance Statistics Yearbook,* 1985, 1991, 1999, 2001, 2003, 2005.

As Gough observes (2004, 79), in the South Korean case equality and improved living standards were secured "by other means"—full employment, job security, price subsidies, price controls, corporate (as opposed to public) welfare provision, and kinship obligation. Private transfers, particularly from family members, appear to have been especially important, accounting for 15 percent of the market income of the poorest quintile (Kwon 1999, 109). This is an important ingredient in the maintenance of relatively low levels of inequality and poverty reduction not present in either Mexico or Chile.

Furthermore, there is considerable evidence that public concerns about inequality, particularly regional differences that began to emerge with industrialization, became important once the problems associated with absolute poverty had been solved (Kwon 1993, 98; Song 2003, 195).[15] There is, moreover, evidence that, despite its overwhelming preoccupation for economic growth, the Korean administration was also very much concerned about social welfare and equality issues. The elimination of poverty is a recurrent theme in rhetoric and in policy throughout the administration of General Park Chung-hee (1961–1979) and reemerges more strongly by the mid-1980s, as we shall see. General Park himself framed his economic goals in terms of the elimination of poverty and publically called attention to welfare spending during his time in office (K. Kim 1990, 95). Preoccupations with social issues and the goal of meeting the basic needs of all citizens were clearly enunciated in the Constitution of the First Republic (1948), which called for the "development of a balanced national economy that can satisfy the needs of citizens" (Chapter 6, Article 84) (Kim 2001, 15–16; Oh 1999, 28). As we will see in the following section, the social origins of the political leadership (in the class of small farmers) would shape its concern for rural welfare, while a new urban middle class would increasingly articulate social concerns.

The Rule of Park Chung-hee: Economic Growth and Improved Human Welfare in the Countryside

The rule of Park Chung-hee, from his coup in 1961 until his assassination in 1979, is widely associated with the period of rapid and successful industrialization. The Park regime was a paternalistic/bureaucratic/nationalist variant of populism. His regime was an alliance involving the military and the bureaucracy (with power heavily concentrated in Park's leadership), with rural dwellers (the majority of the population at the time) incorporated in a subordinate manner.[16] Once in power, the political leadership brought a select group of business interests, the powerful *chaebols*, into the coalition. The alliance excluded organized urban labor and the urban middle-class groups, particularly students, dissident intellectuals, and opposition politicians who wanted liberal democracy. Initially, in fact, the regime pitted the military bureaucracy and the smallholders against the national business and urban popular sector (Han 2004, 92).[17]

General Park's populism was an authoritarian "populism from above," one he himself admitted had little sympathy for liberal democracy because democracy, in the absence of economic equality, was, in his view, a "useless concept" (Oh 1999, 51). On assuming office, Park made a "revolutionary pledge" to eradicate poverty and famine (Moon and Lin 2001, 207) and to provide jobs. The Park regime articulated a rural populist aversion to a corrupt capitalist oligarchy, with special antagonism directed toward the banking sector, hostility toward traditional politicians, and a nationalism that rejected the country's heavy dependence on foreign aid. One of the new government's first actions was the arrest of some 17,000 civil servants and military officers. Initially, the regime banned 4000 citizens from political activities (Mason et al. 1980, 461). Park's arrest of many of the country's leading businessmen, who also had their assets confiscated, amply demonstrated the regime's hostility to the capitalist oligarchy.

The fact that the regime's social base was in the peasantry was the driving force behind its concern for rural welfare. Despite a seeming lack of concern for procedural democracy, for the first ten years of Park's rule, the fact of periodic elections (a consequence of U.S. pressure) was important in government measures supportive of the rural sector.[18] The fact that the opposition made constant gains in the 1967 and 1971 elections contributed to the government's interest in propeasantry policy initiatives (Lee 2001, 149).[19] Farmers were also Park's natural constituency. Park and members of the military, as the sons of small landowners, were acutely aware of rural needs.[20] Indeed, Park was no stranger to peasant radicalism against oppression, poverty, and inequality. His father had joined the Tonghak peasant rebels, who had risen up in 1884 demanding equality and the elimination of class distinctions (Lee 1997, 119; Oh 1999, 49). Other factors no doubt amplified this concern for rural welfare. The threat from North Korea, where per capita income and industrial productive capacity were considerably higher at the time, was an additional incentive driving the regime's goal of eliminating poverty (Kong 2000, 117). Given the country's history of rural mobilization, Park was no doubt anxious to pursue measures that would ensure rural quiescence.

Hence, under Park, a variety of state measures improved the lives and prospects of peasants. Almost immediately on assuming power, Park increased agricultural credit and provided debt relief to farmers. The National Agricultural Cooperatives Federation (NACF), established in 1961, assumed rural debt (Jacobs 1985, 102). In addition, the NACF supplied fertilizer, pesticide (at subsidized prices), credit, and assistance in marketing. A new law made loans available on the basis of trust rather than on good collateral. By the 1970s, funds available to farmers were rising faster than agricultural output (Mason et al. 1980, 223). The NACF also handled storage, transportation, and marketing of rice. In addition, the government divided up reclaimed land among those with less than one *chongbo*. The Office of Research Development (ORD), an agency of the Ministry of Agriculture and Fisheries, provided extension services and distributed improved seed and information on cultivation techniques. Between 1960 and 1966, the number of extension workers supplied by ORD increased six times (Cole and Lyman 1971, 152). Some of this support for agriculturalists clearly served a social assistance function for poor farmers. At the local level, the NACF was under considerable pressure from village elders for an equitable distribution of loans to poor farmers who needed the money to feed their families and overcome crisis. Hence, these loans were used to support private consumption (Ban et al. 1980, 274; Choi 2000, 352). Furthermore, the NACF co-ops also operated retail stores that sold consumer goods cheaply (Ban et al. 1980, 274).

The tripling of fertilizer use between 1956 and 1966 was the most important factor in the increase in farm output (Cole and Lyman 1971, 146; Mason et al. 1980, 221). From the early 1970s, new rice varieties were developed. These improvements, in producing double or triple yields, were instrumental in ending the spring famine (Boyer and Ahn 1991, 72; Choi 2000, 352). As a consequence, by 1965, there were no longer food shortages during the off-harvest season, there was a noticeable increase in the availability of consumer goods, and investment in education had made a noticeable impact (Song 2003, 197). As shown in Table A-1, by the mid-1970s, rural poverty was below urban poverty, in sharp contrast with Mexico and Chile.

While living standards improved in many respects in rural areas, cultivators were hurt by the fact that grain prices (rice and barley) were held down between 1963 and 1968 to alleviate the impact of inflation on city dwellers. It was during this period that economic surplus was extracted from cultivators because fixed agricultural prices allowed only a meager profit, with the consequence that rural incomes declined relative to urban.[21] However, the government quickly stepped in, raising grain prices from 1969 on (Han 2004, 63). In addition, the Third Five Year Plan called for investment in agriculture that was four times that of the Second Five Year Plan (Mason et al. 1980). Because of these policies, the gap between urban and rural incomes began to narrow (Mason et al. 1980, 423), and rural living standards improved.[22]

Another factor contributing to rural living standards, particularly when the terms of trade were against agriculture, was the fact that out-migration to the cities and opportunities for employment there (a consequence of the success of the export-oriented labor-intensive industrial strategy discussed further in the following pages) provided an outlet for surplus rural population. Rural out-migration was substantial. Agricultural labor as a percentage of total employment declined from 65.9 percent of total employment in 1960 to 34.0 percent by 1980 (see Table A-7). Rural youth, who became educated, were able to find economic opportunities in the cities, inhibiting otherwise lower living standards in the country-side. Without this out-migration, farms would have become smaller over time (and less efficient) as they were divided among an ever-expanding rural population. If, on the other hand, land ownership had become more concentrated, increased landlessness would have been the consequence. Under both scenarios, the rural sector would have had to absorb increased population with consequent lower living standards.

Park received only 51.2 percent of the popular vote in the 1971 election (Buzo 2002, 117). This decline in Park's support base arose from the decline in the country's peasant population and the increasing transformation of Korea into an industrial urbanized society (see Tables A-7, A-8, and A-9). Faced with rising urban unrest, the Park regime now took a marked turn from "soft" to "hard" authoritarianism. The new Yushin constitution, rejecting the notion of procedural democracy that had taken root in urban centers where Park faced growing opposition from intellectuals and students, enhanced the power of the president, giving him the right to dissolve the National Assembly and to nominate one-third of the national assemblymen (B. Kim 2000, 74). It also provided a six-year presidential term with no limitation on the number of terms and denied the opposition the possibility of winning the presidency through requiring the indirect election of the president by a rubber-stamp electoral college (Kwon 1999, 37). Opposition parties were effectively blocked, and the regime severely curtailed labor organizing and deprived workers of the right to participate in collective action (Koo 1993a, 139).

This turn to "hard" authoritarianism did not signify an abandonment of the peasantry, however. Perhaps the most important government initiative aimed at improving rural living standards was the New Community Movement (*Saemaul Ungong*). With this program, the government provided technical and financial assistance for improving health, education, housing (elimination of thatched roofs, for example), roads, electrification, and communication in rural communities (Mason et al. 1980, 480). Improvements in water supply and in sewage contributed to improvements in health. By 1975, electricity reached 64.9 percent of all villages, up from just 15.9 percent in 1966 (Ban et al. 1980, 314). Expanded investment in the rural areas meant that, by the mid-1970s, the government was allocating as much as 10 percent of total national investment to rural areas. The new program also sought to raise agricultural production through higher-yielding varieties of rice and barley and better extension services and infrastructure (Boyer and Ahn 1991, 46). Other aspects of the New Community Movement reflected its strong egalitarian ethos insofar as the movement sought to reduce the power of the traditional village leaders and empower the young. The movement also emphasized the lowest rungs of society and promoted the egalitarian aspects of the Korean village tradition (Han 2004, 92). In this respect, the program attempted to incorporate something of the populist opposition *minjung* ideology that, among other things, "emphasized the lowest rungs of society" (Han 2004, 88).[23]

The consequence of all of these policies was that the rural sector did not become mired in severe inequality or in high poverty levels. In fact, the lives of the rural poor generally improved during the period. According to one estimate, in 1975 farm income was roughly 80 percent higher than in the 1930s. Half of this increase was due to increases in agricultural productivity per family, and half was due to land reform (Mason et al. 1980, 239). Poverty rates showed a steady decline in the rural sector: from 35.8 percent of rural households in 1965, to 27.7 percent in 1970, to 11.7 percent in 1976 (see Table A-1). Inequality, very low among farmers in 1965, increased up to 1976 but declined thereafter and was consistently below the national figure for all of these years (Joung-woo 2006, 204). While General Park's regime demonstrated an ongoing concern for rural welfare, his policies also stimulated high rates of industrial growth—the other key ingredient in poverty reduction. Indeed, the state's role in industrial growth was a central one.

The Strong State, Industrial Policy, and the *Chaebols* under Park Chung-hee

The ability to carry forward an industrial policy that would both provide high rates of economic growth and reduce poverty was closely linked to the presence of a strong and efficacious state—and that state arose and consolidated at a time in Korean history when social forces were weak. As indicated in Chapter 1, it was by no means a foregone conclusion that the strong state of the period of Japanese colonial rule would continue into the postcolonial period. The administration of Syngman Rhee (1948–1961) was characterized by the extensive use of patronage within the bureaucracy, a feature that had politicized it and reduced its autonomy (Koo 1993a, 134). There was also considerable corruption in the distribution of bank loans and in the approval of import licenses to the private sector (Cole and Lyman 1971, 25). The government financed the budget deficit by borrowing from the Central Bank, while an overvalued exchange rate discouraged exports. In addition, there was heavy dependence on U.S. aid, decried by much of the public as economically harmful and as proof that the Rhee administration had failed to use foreign aid productively and responsibly. Rhee also confronted growing economic difficulties, particularly inflation, and he resisted policies to help the rural poor (Cole and Lyman 1971, 43). When an election win for Rhee's Liberal Party candidate in 1960 prompted charges of fraud and massive student demonstrations, Rhee resigned, and new elections were held. However, the new government, deeply divided and riddled with corruption, did not last long: It fell victim to constant demonstrations, growing labor strife, and the 1961 military coup, which brought General Park to power.

A well-trained techno-bureaucracy, recruited beginning in the Park years, took over economic policy, formulating development plans and designating which economic sectors the government would support (Ban et al. 1980, 261). Indeed, despite the fact that Park had risen to power through a military coup, the military did not take power as an institution; rather, officers who assumed government positions or who ran for elected office were required to resign their commissions (Jun 2001, 128). The most important institutions in the country's industrialization drive arose during the 1960s and would prove enormously resilient through the coming decades. These institutions included the state-owned banking sector; the Economic Planning Board, which played a key role in directing domestic and foreign credit toward sectors favored to achieve export markets (Cumings 1987, 72); the Korean Development Institute, which formulated the overall economic plans; and the Trade Promotion Agency (KOTRA), which surveyed the world for needed markets, capital, and technology (Cumings 1987, 72). Other institutions were the Korean Institute of Science and Technology (KIST), established 1966, which developed advanced technologies for industry (Mai 2006, 55), and the Export Promotion Fund, established in 1969. At the same time, the military establishment, which had expanded dramatically due to the Korean War, gained in prestige as it acquired improved training and discipline. It increasingly attracted the best students and eventually came to be comprised of upwardly mobile members of the middle class (Kim 2001, 175). It played a crucial role in modernization in its contribution to physical infrastructure (roads, highways, and bridges) (Jun 2001, 139).

Korea's public enterprises, numbering only 100 in 1972 and producing 9 percent of GNP (Mason et al. 1980, 372), were able to focus solely on tasks of economic development. Given the absence of strong social force pressures, they were able to avoid the sort of political role characteristic of the Mexican case—a role that proved harmful to economic growth and export competitiveness. The involvement of Korea's public enterprises in research and development and in training programs (rapid learning and absorption of imported technology) through research centers played an important role in increasing productivity. The state steel company (POSCO), for example, was able to increase its productivity and thereby provide cheap steel to the private sector without decapitalizing the company (Park 1998, 163). Hence, while state investment as a percent of GDP was relatively low, it played a crucial role in economic growth.

While the government invested in key economic sectors, it, at the same time, kept its budget balanced. It did this through establishing an efficient tax system and through the mobilization of resources, both domestic and foreign, through the state-controlled banking system. A highly efficient Office of National Tax Administration, established in 1966, eliminated corruption and tax evasion, resulting in tax collection as a percentage of GDP increasing from 6 percent of GNP to 17 percent by 1975 (Kim and Roermer 1979, 54).[24] Furthermore, taxes on farm income remained low (Mason et al. 1980, 210) while the government, concerned about "highly visible consumption disparities" (Song 2003, 139), taxed heavily items used by the upper class, particularly luxury items such as vehicles with more than four cyclinders and colored televisions.

The relative weakness of Korea's business class made it possible to direct the country's industrialization drive in a way that was impossible in Chile and Mexico. The principal instrument by which the state directed private investment into its industry was through its control of the banking system, nationalized by the Park regime soon after taking power. The government handpicked bank managers and required that the finance minister approve bank budgets. To gather together investment capital, the government set annual and quarterly targets for the increase in deposits for each bank, which bank managers dutifully complied with to court the approval of the government (P. Kim 1990, 196). With this virtual

monopoly over bank credit, the government was able to direct the investment decisions of the country's conglomerates. In 1962, President Park ar-
rested the country's top businessmen and then proceeded to strike a deal
by which he agreed to exempt them from criminal prosecution and, with
the exemption of banking assets, provide compensation for confiscated
assets, if they would agree to establish new industrial firms (Mason et al.
1980, 263; Woo 1991, 83).

Lacking their own banks, *chaebols* became heavily dependent on the
state for credit. Indeed, state policymakers encouraged *chaebols* to borrow heavily, thereby keeping them in an almost constant state of technical
bankruptcy (Cumings 1987, 72; Song 2003, 122). Companies requiring foreign loans also had to go through the government banking system because
the acquisition of such loans was dependent on loan guarantees provided
by the Bank of Korea and the Korean Development Bank. The government selected "winner" industrial enterprises and provided them with low-
interest loans and loan guarantees in exchange for their agreement to meet
export targets and invest in new factories in sectors that the state wished to
stimulate. It also gave large firms export targets, which the affected firms
regarded as "orders" (Minns 2001, 1028). Failure to fulfill targets without a
plausible explanation risked the recall of loans (and certain bankruptcy) or
tax investigation (Song 2003, 118). In exchange for loans, the government
demanded "voluntary" financial contributions to the tune of 20 percent of
corporate profits to be handed over to the ruling political party (Woo 1991,
9). Hence, at least during these early years, the relationship between the
state and its private sector was coercive, rather than "embedded," with the
private sector having little influence over industrial strategy.

The first five-year plan (1961) reflected the government's desire to
develop heavy industrial sectors (fertilizer was especially important),
contrary to the U.S. recommendation that emphasis be placed on light
consumer-export-oriented industry (Young-chol 2006, 112). However,
this original priority was altered due to the unanticipated success of labor-
intensive exports, and priority was diverted to light industries such as raw
silk, cotton fabrics, leather, radio, electrical appliances, and wood products
(Mai 2006, 155; Sang-cheol 2006, 86).[25] By the late 1960s, probably the
period of most extensive government intervention, the government had
once again altered its priorities to heavy and chemical industries (HCI),
targeting industries such as iron, steel, nonferrous metals, shipbuilding,
electronics, and chemicals.[26]

State support for light industry and light industrial exports resulted in the share of output of this economic sector reaching 60.3 percent by 1972 and its share of exports hitting 86.3 percent in that same year (Woo 1991, 130). Because of the new HCI program, the share of heavy industry in manufacturing exports rose from 39.7 percent in 1972 to 54.9 percent in 1979 and the proportion of exports of heavy manufactures from 13.7 percent in 1971 to 37.7 percent. Meanwhile, light industry's share of exports dropped to 62.3 percent by 1979 (130). By 1968, total exports were fourteen times greater than they had been in 1960, while the share of manufactured exports of total exports had risen from 10 to 20 percent of total exports to nearly 75 percent in the same period (Cole and Lyman 1971, 159). Employment in manufacturing, at only 6.8 percent in 1960, rose to 21.7 percent by 1980, higher than Mexico and Chile at the time (see Table A-8). Manufacturing as a percentage of GDP, at 27 percent in 1980, had risen above the figures for Mexico or Chile (see Table A-9).

A distinguishing feature of South Korean industrial development, important in overall economic growth, was the fact that its manufacturing sector became increasingly integrated, with the fastest degree of integration occurring between the new heavy industry, which purchased its inputs from domestic producers, and other industrial sectors (Albala-Bertrand 1999, 162). As we will see in the following two chapters, the permeation of the Chilean and Mexican states by those countries' comparatively more powerful industrialists was instrumental in precluding such integration. Industrial integration was important for employment generation and poverty reduction because it meant significant expansion and growth beyond simply the sectors or firms targeted by government support. Indeed, Korean government policy explicitly promoted backward and forward linkages among industrial sectors. For example, the state fostered the development of the synthetic fiber industry to provide that vital input to the textile industry. Another important linkage occurred between the public steel company and steel-consuming industries such as construction and metals. The state steel company provided Korea's shipbuilding industry, a sector that became a leading exporter, with steel plates.[27] This input had been 100 percent imported before 1966. By 1976, dependence on imported steel plates had declined to 27 percent (Woo 1991, 135).

The Korean bureaucracy with its panoply of institutions and policy instruments was the main factor in the formulation of most of these industrial development decisions. At the same time, it was mindful of the social implications of its policy choices and, as explained in the following discussion, a fraction of it became increasingly concerned with social policy. The choice of which light industries to promote for export in 1965, for example, was based not just on the anticipated impact on the balance of payments and on linkages with other industries but also on employment considerations (Mai 2006, 155). The subsequent program to promote heavy and chemical industry was prompted by fear of the loss of international markets for labor-intensive exports due not only to increased international competition but also to the fact that the United States had threatened quota restrictions on textiles (Woo 1991, 125). Korea was also hit by the quadrupling of oil prices and the increased borrowing that this had prompted. This new economic direction in heavy and chemical industry, given its capital-intensive nature, had the potential to increase inequality. It did, for a time, but as explained in the following pages, the government quickly took measures to mitigate this impact.

The Antilabor State and Social Welfare

The Korean industrialization process was carried out under the auspices of a military-backed populist regime with strong roots in the countryside. While that regime mounted a vague populist appeal to rural dwellers and would cultivate a close alliance with the powerful economic conglomerates, wage labor remained excluded as a basis of regime support. The regime was harshly antilabor and became increasingly so after 1970. Labor unrest met with harsh repression. With the Yushin Constitution, labor's right to defend its interests was heavily restricted.

For at least the first decade, the Park regime was successful in keeping the cost of labor down. Although labor unrest did increase from the 1970s onward and would burst onto the political scene by the 1980s, pressure from the labor movement was far less of a problem than in Mexico and Chile. This is perhaps not surprising because living standards improved for Korean workers throughout the period. Despite harsh working conditions and labor repression, urban poverty continued to decline (see Table A-1). The context of rapid industrialization drawing on a peasantry for its labor force also made an important contribution to worker quiescence. The first-generation factory workers were from the poor farming regions, without a history of collective trade union action, and were perhaps more likely to endure poor urban working conditions silently

(Koo 2007, 111). In addition, the fact that the compulsory draft forced all young men into the military perhaps also contributed to the rapid formation of a disciplined and quiescent workforce. Finally, recent migrants from the countryside may have been too absorbed in adapting themselves to factory work to act collectively (Deyo 1987, 285; Koo 1993a, 137).

At the same time, however, the fact that a strong state was in place on the threshold of industrialization enabled the state to establish a variety of measures inhibiting collective action even as social forces became stronger. The FKTU, created in 1946 but reconstituted by Park in 1962, controlled its member trade unions on behalf of the state. Park resurrected it as South Korea's only official labor movement with the leadership hand-picked by the state security agency (KCIA) (Hamilton and Kim 2004, 73; Koo 1993a, 135). Revisions to the labor law prohibited unions from participating in political activities. Workers could not establish unions without joining one of the nationwide unions affiliated with the FKTU, and bargaining occurred at the enterprise level only (Sam-soo 2006, 172). The state intervened directly in the determination of wages through its establishment of wages in the public sector. It would then direct private sector managers to follow its lead (Ick-jin 2006, 77).

Despite this control, between 1961 and 1971 organized labor faired relatively well economically in comparison with labor in Mexico and Chile. While repression increased after 1972, before that date labor was able to bargain collectively (at the enterprise level) and engage in collective action (Davis 2004, 68–69, 204). In the two decades prior to 1980, real wages were running ahead of productivity. Between 1973 and 1979, the average annual rate of increase in real wages reached 12.7 percent, 2.4 percent higher than the increase in GDP. The trend in 1964 through 1970 was roughly similar. Particularly in 1977 through 1979, labor's share of income increased from 40.6 percent in 1971 to 51.2 percent in 1978 and to 54.2 percent by 1987, with the consequence of increased spending power in the late 1970s (C. Kim 1990, 310; Woo 1991, 179). Wages of blue-collar workers increased more than white-collar workers, while workers in larger enterprises in capital-intensive industries and male workers gained the most from wage increases (Sam-soo 2006, 180). Despite harsh working conditions, this increase in wages likely dampened collective action. In addition, by the late 1970s, larger firms tended to provide a variety of social welfare measures, such as housing benefits and assistance with private education fees (Gough 2004, 176). Probably most important for maintaining living standards was the fact that the ethic of communitarianism (the idea of the firm as a "second family") inhibited employers from laying off workers, a practice that no doubt helped keep unemployment—a main cause of poverty—low. Indeed, Korean workers enjoyed virtual lifetime employment during the period of high growth (Hamilton and Kim 2004, 82).

While this ethic may have been a factor in allowing the authorities to forgo consideration of more extensive welfare protection, there was nevertheless pressure from society and, later, from within the state for expanded social welfare measures. For the most part, however, the Park regime resisted this pressure and sought to establish the legitimacy of its rule through economic performance. In general, the Park administration had little interest in cultivating organized labor. Nevertheless, the minimal social programs initiated between 1961 and 1980, mostly benefiting workers in large enterprises, arose in the face of various bouts of political turmoil and were probably devised, at least in part, to enhance regime legitimacy (Kwon 1999, 19).

Social welfare measures were not simply a reaction to political unrest, however. They were also a consequence of growing pressure from middle-class interests both inside and outside the state. The government agency most involved in the drafting of most social programs at the time was the Committee for Social Security (CSS). This body first arose from outside the state: It started as a private group of doctors, intellectuals, and civil servants concerned about social welfare programs. It gained official status in 1962, acting as an advisor to the minister of health and social affairs, and it drafted social policies until 1972, when the Korean Development Institute took over its responsibilities (Kwon 1999, 31). During the period of its existence, it endeavored to persuade the president and other policymakers of the importance of social development and to counter the then-prevalent viewpoint that social welfare programs would hamper economic development (31). It considered all the major social programs: industrial accident insurance, unemployment insurance, and health care. Even at this early date, it pushed for a universal compulsory health care program, arguing that this would provide the greatest benefit to the lowest income groups.

From the early 1960s, various programs such as unemployment insurance, accident insurance, and universal health care were under consideration. However, because President Park was not convinced of the importance of generalized social welfare protection, the social programs introduced during the 1960s and 1970s were limited. The government introduced accident insurance in 1963 to cover workers in enterprises with more than 500 employees and gradually expanded this program. By the mid-1960s, the government had enacted pension schemes and industrial accident insurance for the military and public officials. In the early 1970s, it seriously considered a national pension program but ultimately rejected it at the time due to problems with inflation. Instead, the government introduced legislation that temporarily waived income tax for low-income households. In 1977 a National Health Insurance Program, restricted to employees in work places with more than 500, was introduced (Kwon 1999, 80, 41, 53).[28]

While the turn to "hard" authoritarianism of the 1970s involved an ever-closer alliance with the *chaebol,* it did not signify an abandonment of poverty and inequality issues. Indeed, the fact that the new economic strategy, involving a turn toward industrialization in heavy and chemical industries, triggered a rise in inequality increased the pressure on the state to take measures to address it. The Third Five Year Plan (1972–1976) and the Fourth Five Year Plan (1977–1981) both called for measures to promote a greater degree of equality (Song 2003, 160). Hence, there was, during this period, an ongoing concern for issues of equality and social welfare—a concern belied by the seemingly restricted nature of the welfare programs that actually emerged. This concern was reflected in the substantial support programs for rural dwellers, in the nature of the industrial strategy pursued (it was employment generating), and by measures taken to mitigate rising urban rural disparities and inequality once they began to emerge. Furthermore, although, overall, minimal standard social programs appear to have had relatively little positive impact on income redistribution, social policy did not contribute to inequality because the state did not make substantial contributions to social security protection for the few. The state's social base in the peasantry, and its autonomy and strength relative to its business class, explains much of this. However, the rapid rise of the urban middle class would become important in pushing forward social justice issues and keeping inequality in check through the 1980s and 1990s.

The Emergence of Class Politics and Redistributive Struggles

From the early 1960s, the political conditions (relatively weak and malleable social classes) had facilitated the state-led growth of the 1960s and 1970s. By the late 1970s, however, it is clear that this situation was changing rapidly; by 1980, South Korea had become a class society. With rapid industrialization, the social structure of the country changed dramatically between 1960 and 1980. The working class, which constituted 8.9 percent of the population in 1960, had risen to 31.3 percent by 1980. During that same period, the middle class increased from 19.6 percent to 38.5 percent of the population, while farmers by 1980 constituted only 31.3 percent of the population (Arita 2003, 204).[29] Further, over three-quarters of those in the middle class had fathers who were not middle class, with a high percentage coming from the agricultural class—48.6 percent of the new middle class and 62.1 percent of the old middle class (207).

The middle class and a faction of the working class would soon join forces in demanding both democracy and social justice. Beginning in the early 1970s, the authoritarian Yushin Constitution had sparked the emergence of a loose oppositional alliance among certain middle-class groups (religious groups, students, and human rights groups), demanding change in the constitution toward greater democracy (Oh 1999, 90). Given the restrictions on leftist ideology, the alternative *minjung* ideology, arising from a multiclass movement comprised of middle-class members, workers, and peasants, arose to address issues of political exclusion and social injustice. It opposed the authoritarian state, had a strong nationalist desire for economic and political independence, and was opposed to the distributive injustice that had arisen because of the recent period of HCI-led economic growth (Koo 1993a, 145). Thousands of its middle-class adherents, particularly students, became factory workers to help organize trade unions (Lee 2007). Growing labor unrest was a key component of the prodemocracy struggle as well. By the early 1970s, more active labor resistance began to emerge, triggered by a Korean worker's self-immolation carried out to call attention to the need for labor rights and better working conditions. In 1979, a slowdown in economic growth triggered riots among the textile workers while repression engendered more resistance (Moon and Lin 2001, 207). The state now faced increasingly powerful social forces, but the country's development trajectory had, by now, been firmly established, and the emergent social forces, particularly the new middle class, were driven by social justice as well as by political concerns.

Conclusions

The origins of South Korea's equitable development have roots deep in history. Japanese colonial rule (1910–1945) was short lived and far less intrusive than in the Latin American cases and did not produce new racial categories.[30] As peasant mobilization mounted, the state withdrew support for landlords, thereby further stimulating peasant mobilization. The impact was homogenizing. Extensive land redistribution was the essential starting point for the establishment of social equality in modern South Korea. It arose within the context of a profound conjuncture involving high levels of peasant mobilization, the end of World War II, the expulsion of the Japanese, and the American occupation. Once land reform had occurred, a historical moment of weak social forces allowed the emergence of a strong and efficacious state. Powerful business interests did not permeate or manipulate the state. Indeed, relative to the state, businesses were weak and were initially coerced into following its direction.

However, a grasp of South Korea's equitable development requires recognition that this was a strong state with an agenda of employment-generating growth and an ongoing concern with poverty reduction and low levels of inequality. Moreover, this was a state with an abiding concern for the small landowners—they comprised the majority of the population and the regime's electoral base for years and constituted the Park regime's social base. A host of measures implemented by the Park regime ensured that the rural poor did not suffer inordinately from industrialization and that rural urban inequalities remained minimal.

Furthermore, even though the state did not put in place important formal social welfare measures during the period, it is clear that there were aspirations to do so within a growing segment of the middle class and within the state. Despite the fact that the political left had been silenced early in South Korean history, concerns about social equality, poverty, and social welfare (a past repertoire) survived in rhetoric, in policy, and in the new Munjung movement. These issues would be forcefully resurrected when the moment was right. By the late 1970s, social forces had gained appreciably in strength and would begin to influence policy and social outcomes in important ways. South Korea would eventually begin to face challenges similar to those faced by Mexico and Chile— but it already had a much stronger starting point, and the country's long history of equitable development would make it considerably more difficult to resist equity aspirations.

3

Chile
The Historical Origins of Inequality

DESPITE SLUGGISH ECONOMIC GROWTH through the 1950s and 1960s, Chile was fairly successful at reducing poverty until the military coup of 1973. In addition, its level of inequality was considerably lower than Mexico's during these years. However, both inequality and poverty shot up during the 1970s and 1980s (Tables A-1 and A-2). The causal chain producing these outcomes has its origins in early historical conditions and political developments.

Chile's early dynamic mineral export economy provided it with employment expansion and resources that produced improvements in urban living standards in the early twentieth century. Yet its mineral-led growth was also conducive to the emergence of a unified propertied class that maintained tight control of the rural masses and blocked land reform and an increasingly militant working class that challenged the institution of private property. By the late 1930s, the critical conjuncture of the Great Depression and the prospect of a new industrialization drive, combined with growing working-class militancy and the rise of leftist political parties, brought about the possibility of social reform, including the possibility of land redistribution. While land reform was blocked, the country's pluralist democratic institutions, combined with pressure from its organized middle and working classes, facilitated improvements in social welfare until the last quarter of the twentieth century. However, effective resistance from the landed/business class and its middle-class allies to more extensive redistributive measures, including land reform, resulted in a reactive sequence—beginning with the disintegration the Popular Front

Government in 1941. This reactive sequence reached its pinnacle with the military coup of 1973 and the initiation of a second critical conjuncture that ushered in a transformation of politics and a new direction in economic policy, reversing the social achievements of earlier years. For most of the twentieth century, the Chilean state was weak, heavily permeated by social forces.

The Early Historical Origins of Inequality: Land, the Oligarchy, and Mineral Exports

Several aspects of nineteenth-century Chilean history augured well for future social outcomes. Although rural social class relations would prove enormously resistant to change, the country did not begin with sharp ethnic compartmentalization involving a large indigenous population and a white elite, features that characterized Mexico and many other countries of the region. The indigenous population in Chile was sparse. The Araucanian Indians, who had been struggling against encroachment on their lands, were defeated in 1883 and confined to reserves in the south. Through the colonial period, miscegenation between Europeans and the indigenous people produced a mestizo (mixed-blood) population that quickly came to outnumber the Spanish. With the indigenous population pushed to the frontier, the Chilean population became remarkably homogeneous by Latin America standards, composed largely of a mass of mestizo peasants and a criollo (Spanish, American-born) elite of landowners.

Chile also stood out from other Latin American countries in its early establishment of political stability: From 1830, the leadership of Diego Portales, backed by the landowners, produced sixty years of stable autocratic rule. While Portales was uninterested in agricultural modernization, the administrations he backed[1] placed public finances on a solid footing, introduced income and property taxes, and embarked on a program of modernization involving impressive infrastructural development (particularly railways). The 1833 constitution, with its heavy property and literacy restrictions on voting, ensured that power rested in the hands of the traditional landed oligarchy.

Beginning in 1850, Chile was incorporated into the international market as a grain producer. As in the Korean experience, this process produced the increasing impoverishment of the peasantry, but, unlike the Korean case, it consolidated, rather than loosened, the control of big landowners over peasants, thereby heavily discouraging the peasant mobilization that might have contributed to earlier and more extensive redistributive measures. In response to increased international demand for wheat between 1850 and 1880, big landowners expanded their production by expanding their landholdings (known as *fundos*) and by extracting more work from peasants.[2] Hence, *fundo* owners imposed ever-heavier workloads on workers (*inquilinos*), requiring them to work more days or demanding work from family members, in exchange for ever-smaller land allotments. Despite the harsh conditions, rural rebellions were relatively rare and large-scale mobilizations practically nonexistent.

The large landholdings were isolated, workers seldom left, and the landlord was all powerful. Peasants did not reside in independent villages. Rather, the *inquilino*'s entire world was the *fundo*—and the landlord could eject him and his family from that world on a whim. In exchange for labor, the peasant received payment in kind, usually a house, a subsistence plot of land, and perhaps a ration of supplies from the *fundo* store. Entirely dependent on the landlord for survival, the *inquilino* lived in mortal fear of being cast off the land. This arrangement conferred tight patriarchal control over rural workers, ensuring a quiescent labor force and guaranteeing the landowner control of the rural vote. The *inquilino* system persisted well into the first half of the twentieth century: In 1935, an estimated 75 percent of *fundo* workers were still *inquilinos* (Bauer 1975, 135). The attitudes of the landowners, whose racist outlook shaped a view of the rural poor as mentally backward and of poverty as part of the natural order of things, were further obstacles to the eradication of rural poverty.[3] Small landholders were mostly located in the south of Chile, where, during the 1840s, the influx of Chilean and German colonists increased their ranks. The heterogeneity of rural dwellers was another factor contributing to the absence of widespread mobilization demanding land.

Meanwhile, early mining development shaped both economic development and, with it, social structure. The expansion of railways carried out by British interests and financially supported by the Chilean state, along with mineral discoveries, stimulated nitrate and copper mining in the north, developments that would soon transform Chile into a foreign-controlled mining enclave. While between 1845 and 1850 agriculture accounted for 45 percent of the value of exports, by the 1880s nitrate accounted for 60 percent of the value of exports (Subercaseaux 1988, 132). Although initially Chilean entrepreneurs played an important role in mining, the industry soon fell into foreign (British and American) hands (Blackmore 1974, 22). From then on, the state's ability to guide economic development became heavily contingent on the international volatility of a single export commodity due to the state's heavy dependence on mining for tax revenue and for foreign exchange. Customs duties were the main source of government revenue, and, with nitrate as the country's major export, it was that industry that filled government coffers, financing, between 1900 and 1930, more than one-half of government expenditures (Mamalakis 1976, 38).

Among the landed elite, there was little interest in improving the conditions of the rural poor and strong opposition to land redistribution. However, by the 1850s, a more reformist attitude emerged among a newer mining/commercial business class, artisans, small landowners, and intellectuals in the northern and southern parts of the country. The most radical among these reformers, who demanded a splitting up of the large *latifundia* and an end to *inquilinaje,* were defeated in the insurrection of 1851.[4] The overthrow of President José Manuel Balmaceda (1886–1891) marked the consolidation of a conservative propertied coalition. Social reform, particularly in the countryside, would now depend on the growing strength of reformist political parties drawing support from the growing middle- and working-class groups.

Mining exports gave an especially strong impetus to the service sector. Employment in services, expanding in response to the need for transportation and banking services, reached 44.5 percent of the economically active population by 1910 (Mamalakis 1976, 176). At the same time, an upsurge in government expenditures, funded by the booming nitrate market, contributed to the rapid expansion in government employment.[5] Mining development also stimulated the growth of industry. Rural migrants from the central agricultural region to the northern mines and the Santiago area provided the workforce for the new urban-consumer-oriented industry. Between 1908 and 1918, the number of factories in the country increased 60 percent, and by 1920 there were more Chileans employed in manufacturing than in mining (Morris 1966, 82).

Mining development did not, however, produce a decline in the political power of the country's landed class nor a diminishment of its dominance and control over the masses of rural poor. However, there were important social improvements during the period, at least in urban areas. The nitrate boom enabled the Chilean governments of the late nineteenth and early twentieth centuries to make huge investments in infrastructure and education (Cortés Conde 2006, 219). Educational expansion, perceived as a way to raise the masses to avoid the anarchy evident elsewhere in the region, was a priority.[6] While illiteracy declined substantially from the middle of the nineteenth century to 56 percent by 1900 (see Table A-6), the expansion of public education occurred largely in the urban areas with the consequence that the vast majority of people in the Chilean countryside could not obtain even a minimum of education (Loveman 1988, 139). Due to the changes stimulated by mining development, by 1910 employment in agriculture stood at only 37.7 percent of the economically active population (see Table A-7).

A new middle class of white-collar workers, government officials, and professionals emerged in this early period (Grant 1983, 153). Two political parties came to represent this new social class: the Radical Party and the Democratic Party. The Democratic Party, in particular, supported a reformist program involving social protection for workers and obligatory primary education (Petras 1970, 116). The entry of Arturo Alessandri (president, 1920–1925, and again from 1932–1938) onto the Chilean political stage signified the entry of the country's middle class, from whom he had received most of his votes, into politics. Indeed, most of the social gains of the Alessandri years, especially the country's first social security legislation, benefited the middle class and privileged strata of the working class. Unfortunately, the Democrats had no interest in land redistribution or in the plight of the urban or rural poor. Parties addressing the plight of these groups would not emerge until the middle of the twentieth century.

Chile's mining enclave status shaped the development of worker organization and ideology, giving the latter a Marxist and anti-imperialist tone that would powerfully mold future possibilities. While mine workers tended to be better paid than factory workers, their working conditions were deplorable. The conditions of northern mining communities—their isolation and the common experiences of exploitation and oppression faced by workers—rendered them open to leftist radical political ideas. By the early 1890s, labor strife was beginning to emerge in the country's northern nitrate mines and in the coal mines of the south, where harsh working conditions, the erosion of salaries due to inflation, and periodic layoffs fueled unrest. Drops in nitrate prices produced numerous recessions between 1896 and 1927, triggering surges in strike activity and worker militancy. Workers migrating from mining communities in search of employment spread their ideology of worker militancy among factory workers in urban areas (Loveman 1988, 203). The harsh repression meted out in the face of mounting strikes and other forms of worker unrest promoted even greater worker militancy.[7] A militantly anticapitalist labor federation based in the coal, copper, nitrate, and railway workers (the Chilean Labor Federation or FOCH) was established in 1909. Its founder, Luis Emilio Recabarren, established the Workers Socialist Party in 1912, a revolutionary Marxist party.[8] While between 1919 and 1925 the FOCH had begun to penetrate the countryside in an attempt to organize rural dwellers and lead strikes, landlords, with the full support of the state, successfully quelled rural unrest. With court orders and the support of local police, landlords punished union supporters by evicting *inquilinos* from their homes (Loveman 1976, 140).

State-Dominant Industrialization and Limited Redistribution (1931–1964)

With the Great Depression and the rise of a new ruling coalition, Chile's critical conjuncture momentarily opened the door to the possibility of more substantial redistributive measures, including the possibility of change in the countryside. The Depression hit Chile harder than any other Latin American country, shattering the country's elite cohesion and shaking its stable institutional framework.[9] Chile's exports of copper and nitrate plummeted by 88 percent, the steepest decline in the world, and over 50,000 workers lost their jobs. Between 1929 and 1931, the country's GDP dropped by almost 40 percent in real terms (Loveman 1988, 230, 231). This sharp economic decline rendered the need for a new economic strategy, particularly further industrialization, an unavoidable necessity.

The regime that initiated Chile's import substitution industrialization drive was the Popular Front government of 1938–1941. The presence of the worker-backed Socialist and Communist Parties in the new ruling coalition, headed by the Radical Party, signaled the possibility of social reform. However, while working-class interests received more attention, the regime failed to address the plight of rural dwellers despite the desire of its Socialist and Communist coalition partners that it do so. Indeed, activists within both the Communist and Socialist parties continued their attempts to organize the countryside during this period (Loveman 1976, 143–165). These efforts produced growing resentment on the part of big landowners, who pressured for restrictions on rural labor rights. The Radical Party drew support from the country's middle class but also counted some of the big landowners among its most important leadership figures.[10] To win support from the congressional political right and its big landowner supporters for the new industrialization drive, the Front effectively agreed to the abandonment of any possibility of social improvements in the countryside.[11] This deal between the Popular Front and the country's landed interests cemented the poor social conditions faced by rural labor and entrenched inequality for decades to come. In addition, these developments produced an ongoing reactionary sequence of ever-increasing political intensity. The failure of the Popular Front regime to produce more substantial reform resulted in the exit of the Socialist Party from the Front in 1941 and prompted its move toward revolutionary Marxism and the abandonment of its personalistic and clientelistic features (Drake 1978, 39).

As the state promoted import substitution, the manufacture of previously imported light consumer goods, it neglected agriculture. Manufacturing's share of GDP rose from 16.7 percent in 1950 to 23.9 percent by 1965, and employment increased in construction and manufacturing from 20.9 percent of total employment in 1940 to 26.3 percent by 1965 (see Tables A-8 and A-9). Stagnation in agricultural production meant that net agricultural imports increased from $7.6 million (U.S.) in 1942 to $83 million in 1962 (Mamalakis 1976, 311). Meanwhile, between 1950 and 1960, less than 3.7 percent of public investment went to the agriculture and only 2.7 percent in 1962–1966 (Mamalakis 1976, 268), compared with 10 percent in South Korea in the 1970s. The benefits that the state provided to agriculture went overwhelmingly to big agriculturalists, who received credit and large subsidies to improve irrigation and transportation for agriculture (Drake 1978, 222–223; Zeitlin and Ratcliff 1988, 213).

One of the most important implications of the industrialization drive was the rapid expansion of the country's middle class. By 1970, the middle class accounted for 41 percent of the economically active population (Guardia B. 1979, 537).[12] However, those entering the middle class were not proletarian in origin but arose from segments of the business class and their descendants (Grant 1983, 165). The Radical Party became increasingly conservative and antilabor, reflective of the growing conservativeness of its middle-class support base: In 1946, it expelled the Communist Party from the Popular Front coalition and repressed trade unions. Frightened by the growing ferment among the working class, in 1952 the middle class supported the antilabor regime of President Carlos Ibañez (1952–1958), whose policies produced a calamitous decline in workers' income and in economic growth (Mamalakis 1976, 197), a consequence that solidified labor solidarity and leftist unity. Indeed, a 1958 survey found that a majority of the middle class exhibited strong authoritarian tendencies, were aware that the country lacked equality of opportunity, supported the current system of land tenure, and aspired to become large landowners themselves, amply demonstrating the middle class's lack of enthusiasm for social reform, particularly in the rural sector (Petras 1970, 146–149). The middle-class movement away from social concerns has been explained by the fact that it had benefited the most from the period of Radical Party dominance, obtaining the best wage increases and by far the most generous social security protection. This development produced a growing distance between it and the working class (Grant 1983, 156; Petras 1970, 131).[13]

With industrialization, wealth remained heavily concentrated. In the 1950s, 9.7 percent of landowners owned 86 percent of the arable land (Drake 1978, 36). As industrialization progressed through the 1940s and 1950s, the old economic elite fused with the new industrial and commercial families. A few families controlled companies spanning banking, industry, and commerce and were closely tied to the landowning class, constituting the powerful "inner core" of families who controlled the country's economy (Zeitlin and Ratcliff 1988, 169). By the late 1940s, repression had pushed left-wing rural labor organizers underground, and by 1952 agricultural wages were 300 percent below industrial wages (Loveman 1976, 173; Mamalakis 1976, 102.). Meanwhile, the rural workforce remained very heterogeneous. In the late 1950s, 40 percent of the agricultural labor force were landless (equally divided between *inquilinos* and pure wage laborers), 6 percent were sharecroppers, and 53 percent were small and medium-sized landowners. About half of this 53 percent were small landowners who together owned only 1 percent of the land (Petras and Zeitlin 1968, 255). In 1962, the Alessandri government introduced a timid land reform, redistributing idle land to some 1,066 families (Sigmund 1977, 26).

While state activities expanded quite dramatically, pressures exerted by industrialists inhibited the emergence of a growth-producing industrial policy that might have reduced social tensions and mitigated political polarization. The instruments of industrial stimulation included the usual panoply of import substitution policies: tariff and nontariff barriers; an overvalued exchange rate; state investment; the allocation of credit to the private sector through the state-owned development bank, the CORFO; and the establishment of state companies providing basic industrial inputs. By 1958, business was effectively directing industrial policy through its representation on state boards and commissions. Through their voting power on the commission granting import licenses, for example, business groups secured a protection policy that provided overly generous protection to already existing and powerful business interests. Within industry, sectors that received privileged treatment (food processing, clothing, shoes, textiles, beverages, and leather) were all granted net effective protection in excess of 100 percent, while the least protected were machinery and equipment and a few intermediate products (Mamalakis 1976, 172). Hence, Chilean industry, in marked contrast with Korean industry, remained not only uncompetitive, because its light consumer goods industry was so highly protected, but also unintegrated and heavily dependent on imported inputs. Unlike the South Korean case, the Chilean state lacked the power and the policy instruments to shape private sector investment. In fact, while the private sector invested a decreasing share of its profits (Mamalakis and Reynolds 1965, 75), state investment increased in an apparent effort to compensate for the private sector decline (Universidad de Chile 1963, 129; Vergara 1983, 74). CORFO, the state's industrial development agency, played an important role, establishing companies in steel, oil, cement, and electricity, but it exacerbated the problem of import dependency because the activities it promoted remained heavily dependent on imported inputs.

The ambitious investment activities of the state and the increasing expansion in social programs, particularly social security (discussed further in the following pages), required a solid and growing source of state revenue that was not forthcoming. While tax revenue as a percentage of GDP was fairly high compared to the other two cases (see Table A-10), it was never enough to meet the ever-growing pressures for increased state expenditure and investment. Meanwhile, both economic circumstances and powerful business interests inhibited an increase in tax revenue. The government abandoned the idea of paying for CORFO by taxing wealthy Chileans due to strong resistance from business and decided instead to fund its activities by a 15 percent tax on the profits of the foreign-owned mining companies (Mamalakis and Reynolds 1965, 55). However, squeezing the mining industry produced a decline in mining investment, a reduction in export earning, and a fall in mining's share of employment

(Fáundez 1988, 50; Mamalakis and Reynolds 1965, 54). Chile's share of the world copper market declined from 20 percent in 1940 to 13 percent by 1953 (Fáundez 1988, 106). One "solution" to the shortage of revenue flowing to the state became increasing transfers from the lower classes through higher indirect taxes. The state also resorted to the printing press with inflationary consequences—inflation hit a high of 80 percent by 1955 (Aguilara Reyes 1994, 13; Velasco 1994, 390). As inflation accelerated, it became the cornerstone of political conflict as competing groups sought to recoup their lost share of income—contributing to increasing political polarization and political difficulties. This development also led to a series of cycles between 1955 and 1964 during which governments attempted to stem inflation through recessionary stabilization programs but then reversed course in the face of public opposition, engaging in expansionary policies.[14] Uncontrolled state spending, chronic budget deficits, and spiraling inflation became the order of the day.

With a weak state, a competitive political system, a powerful landed/business oligarchy, and a militant labor movement linked to ideologically driven political parties, the Chilean bureaucracy could not provide independent development leadership. There had been numerous attempts to build up bureaucratic/technocratic capacity within the state, including within CORFO, by incorporating highly trained people (Montecinos 1998, 5). However, civil servants found it impossible to remain independent. As political polarization between right and left accelerated through the 1960s, civil servants fell in line with the current ideological trend. In addition, Chilean ministries and public agencies were accustomed to bolstering their demands for scarce state resources by recruiting societal support (Cleaves 1974, 23, 29). Various presidents attempted to provide more centralized oversight of policy, but these attempts failed.[15]

Despite the neglect of rural social welfare, the lack of a coherent industrial policy, profligate state spending, and the absence of trained bureaucrats in charge of policy (all difficulties arising from strong and contentious social forces), living standards for most Chileans probably improved during the period. By 1970, the level of poverty was below that of South Korea although, notably, there was twice as much poverty in rural areas as in urban (see Table A-1). However, as early as 1950, agricultural employment was only 32.2 percent of total employment. Improvements that focused on the urban sector, therefore, benefited the majority of the population. Furthermore, by 1960, inequality was substantially lower than Mexico's (see Table A-2). Social improvements were due, in large part, to the incorporative capacity of the country's pluralist electoral system, to the expansion of state employment, and to the state's development of new economic activities. Left-wing political parties, with close ties to the trade unions, as explained further in the following discussion, pressed the interests of the organized working class.

The comparatively low level of poverty probably would not have been possible without the country's low population growth (Drake 1978, 217). In addition, as we saw, early dynamic export-led growth in agriculture and minerals had important employment-generating spin-off effects. Those migrating to cities tended to find employment in the continuing expanding industrial and service sectors. The higher levels of industrial protection afforded light consumer industries (compared with Mexico) may have been important in employment maintenance insofar as a large number of small industrial firms provided about one-half of industrial employment (Mamalakis 1976, 144). Between 1940 and 1965, the fastest rate of labor absorption, however, was in the service sector and, within this, the state sector, due to the expansion of state employment. Under pressure from urban middle-class and working-class groups to expand employment, the state responded with a more than threefold increase in employment between 1925 and 1965 (Loveman 1988, 323, 234).

As formal employment became widespread, social security protection came to cover a substantial portion of the population: 68 percent of the economically active population by 1964 (Borzutsky 2002, 52). Political parties in Congress, anxious to provide benefits to their electoral clienteles, acceded to a myriad of requests for new social security funds and to the expansion of special benefits and privileges within existing ones. Hence, by 1964 there were 160 different funds (Borzutsky 2002, 46). The most generous benefits went to white-collar workers and organized blue-collar workers in such sectors as transportation and mining. On the other hand, social security provisions for less powerful unions involved meager services whose funds often had had large deficits (Borzutsky 2002 16; Drake 1978, 225; Mamalakis 1976, 199). Meanwhile, unorganized workers, the self-employed, and the rural sector—tenant farmers, rural wage earners, and *minifundistas* (very small landowners)—all lacked access to social security. The regressive nature of the system was reinforced further by the fact that, during the decade between 1960 and 1970, the unsecured population, through their taxes, financed 49 percent of the cost of social

FIGURE 3-1.   Chile: Education, health, and social security/welfare, percentage of total social expenditures, 1973–2000. Sources: Data from International Monetary Fund, *Government Finance Statistics Yearbook,* 1985, 1991, 1999, 2001, 2003, 2005.

security protection being provided for the secured population (Mamalakis 1976, 200). The system was very costly: Government spending on social security accounted for the greatest portion of social spending during the 1970s, as shown in Figure 3-1. Social security spending in Chile accounted for the highest portion of GDP of the three cases (see Figure A-3). Indeed, in relation to GDP, the cost of Chile's social security regime became one of the highest in the world (Borzutsky 2002, 61).

There were, however, important social improvements that benefited the entire population. The establishment of preventive health care in 1938 helped reduce infant mortality rates and contributed to higher life expectancy while bringing under control and eliminating a number of infectious diseases (Borzutsky 2002, 51, 62). However, the neglect of agriculture and the rural population had an impact on welfare. Infant mortality rates, although greatly reduced, at 102.8 per 1,000 live births in the mid-1960s remained high (World Bank 1983, 20). Neglect of agriculture and the consequent low level of agricultural production may have been responsible for the low level of animal protein intake, contributing to nutritional deficiency and difficulty in making better progress in lowering infant mortality (Mamalakis 1976, 197). Given the neglect of spending on social services in the rural areas, rural illiteracy was considerably above national levels (see Table A-6).

By the late 1950s, land reform was making it onto the political agenda of political parties. The clientelist grip of landed elites over the peasantry began to erode in the face of increased rural urban migration, a consequence of improved transportation routes into the countryside. In addition, the expansion of the monetary economy into remote rural areas was resulting in the growing corporate ownership of agricultural enterprises and an increase in the landless workers. These developments contributed to the weakening and breakdown of patron–client ties and opened the way for the radicalization of the peasantry as political parties began to compete for their vote. The electoral law of 1958, which increased penalties for electoral bribery, making it increasingly difficult for land-lords to control the votes of peasants, stimulated the entry of the left-wing and center parties (the Socialist, Communist, and Christian Democratic Parties) into the countryside. By early 1961, the parties of the old elite (the liberals and conservatives) began to see a drop in their seats in congress (Loveman 1988, 265). As the 1960s wore on, the country's political center began to crumble as the center parties, the Christian Democratic Party (an offshoot of the Conservative Party) and the Radical Party, moved left-ward and the country's powerful propertied interests became increasingly fearful of threats to private property.

The Popular Mobilizational State and Radical Redistribution (1964–1973)

From 1964, the state increasingly distanced itself from the country's powerful propertied class. However, this autonomy was heavily contingent on the mobilization and pressure exerted by the popular groups, a mobilization that increasingly pushed radical redistributive measures forward. Hence, the social basis of the state shifted during the period, beginning with the withdrawal of business support from the Christian Democratic regime and that party's increasing recruitment of working-class and peasant support. In the 1964 election, presidential candidate Eduardo Frei received support from the political right, fearful of the growing strength of the opposition left. However, he had also promised progressive reforms, including agrarian reform, the right to rural unionization, and the enforcement of labor laws. As Frei attempted to meet these election promises, he alienated his rightist supporters. While powerful propertied interests felt the most threatened, middle-class Chileans, generally, were also not supporters of radical social reform. The coalition Popular Unity regime of Salvador Allende (1970–1973) drew support largely from the organized working-class and rural workers (especially those engaged in wage labor) with the private sector and much of the middle and upper class in strong opposition.

The competition for rural support during these years contributed to a sharp rise in political mobilization and political polarization. The process deepened the political divisions among rural dwellers. By 1964, the left coalition, with Salvador Allende as its presidential candidate, was winning support among rural wage earners and others in rural areas close to mining communities from where workers spread their militant ideology. Meanwhile, the Christian Democrats recruited support from isolated tenant and medium-sized farmers and, once in control of the presidency (1964–1970), used state agencies, particularly INDAP (Agricultural Development Institute) to compete for support from rural wage earners. Big landowners, calling for the defense of property rights, engaged in a massive drive for the support of small landowners (Hernández 1973, 137), a move that proved to be highly effective because Chilean small landowners were geographically atomized and tended to see themselves as part of the propertied class (Petras and Zeitlin 1968, 264). By 1971, there were five nationwide agrarian organizations: one linked to the left-wing parties; two to the Christian Democratic Party; one to MAPU (Popular Unitary Action Movement), a radical break-away from the Christian Democratic Party; and one linked to the rightist National Party. Not until the MAPU's defection from the Christian Democratic peasant organization in 1971 (that is, after the election of the left-wing Popular Unity Coalition in 1970) did the political left command a majority of organized peasant support (Castells 1974, 344). The Popular Unity's peasant support and the major beneficiaries of its land reform program were largely wage earners on the big landholdings.

Growing ideological polarization was occurring, rendering any sort of compromise settlement impossible. As mobilization mounted, the middle and upper class grew increasingly apprehensive. For the most part, Popular Unity identified landed and business elites as the class enemy, taking the position that there was no place for the capitalist class in an economic order that was truly just and redistributive.[16] Popular Unity rejected the notion of private property and carried out the most extensive land reform ever once it was in power. The regime also took over a large number of firms in a wide range of financial and industrial areas (Foxley, Aninat, and Arellano 1979, 204–205). These measures angered the country's business/landed class and frightened the middle classes, most of whom saw their way of life overturned.[17] The gulf between the Popular Unity government and the political right became insurmountable.

Land redistribution began in earnest in 1965 under President Frei, who initiated the process by expropriating holdings over 80 hectares (198 acres). President Allende oversaw the expropriation of 76 percent of the total landholdings expropriated between 1964 and 1973 (Martner 1988, 155). By 1973, about 60 percent of Chile's irrigated land and 50 percent of total agricultural land was under the control of the public sector (Hudson 1994). Support for the establishment of individual smallholdings—a defining feature of the Korean land reform—was effectively defeated during the Christian Democrats' tenure in office (1964–1970). With Christian Democrats divided between supporters of smallholder agriculture and "communitarian" (communal) holdings, rural workers obtaining land under the 1965 Christian Democratic land reform were to decide the ultimate form of land holding. In practice, however, the support of key Christian Democratic policymakers for communitarian arrangements meant that this option invariably won out (Loveman 1976, 272). The idea of establishing a small landowning peasant class, a land redistribution vision compatible with capitalism and the capitalist class, found no support within Popular Unity. The Allende administration favored the establishment of farm cooperative ownership and state-run farms over the assignment of individual peasant ownership. The regime was apparently reluctant to create a new capitalist peasant class and argued that cooperative ownership would extend the benefit of land reform to the mass of landless peasants (Sigmund 1977, 182).

Political pressures from strong popular social forces drove economic and social policy during both the Frei and Allende administrations, defeating some policy preferences that might have produced better results in terms of both economic growth and social welfare. The Frei government, for example, sought to achieve greater social equality through more progressive taxation and the expansion of credit to small and medium-sized enterprises (Montecinos 1998, 23). This administration also supported the expansion of export markets and called for the elimination of the excessive protection provided to industry. Frei even attempted to coordinate and centralize economic policy through the establishment of the Economic

Committee of Ministers to oversee economic management—but to no avail (Cleaves 1974, 70). The second half of the Frei administration witnessed an upsurge in inflation that diverted government attention to the more immediate problems of economic stabilization and mounting worker unrest. As the political situation deteriorated in 1968–1969, plans for further trade liberalization and measures to enhance industrial efficiency were shelved (Velasco 1994, 392). Meanwhile, direct pleas to the president by the heads of government ministries and agencies for budget increases routinely stymied efforts by the finance ministry to control fiscal expansion (Cleaves 1974, 64).

Under President Allende, the political pressures exerted by popular social forces drove public policy, producing policies that alienated the middle and upper classes and were problematic in their redistributive outcome. The executive branch became increasingly captive to powerful political pressures that it had mobilized but could no longer command.[18] While it is certainly true that many new programs targeted the urban and rural poor who had hitherto been excluded from social improvement, benefits went disproportionately to the organized groups, including the middle class. Having won the presidency with only 36 percent of the vote, Allende needed to expand his electoral support base due to upcoming municipal and congressional elections. Employment expansion, a key measure necessary to keep party supporters on side, occurred in the new land reform sector, in the state bureaucracy, and in newly acquired state companies (Foxley et al. 1979, 205, 211, 218).[19] At the same time, Allende abandoned his attempt to reform the social security system to benefit the poorer members of society (small farmers, temporary rural labor, and the urban poor) due to the resistance from the middle and organized working classes. Hence, the expansion of social security coverage to 76 percent of the population went to further coverage for middle-class groups in the hope this change would bolster his support base at election time (Borzutsky 2002, 140). Nor did land redistribution have a widespread redistributive outcome. Only permanent workers on the largest landed estates benefited from land reform, leaving out *minifundistas* and temporary rural workers. In addition, resistance from landowners made minimum wage legislation for rural workers difficult to enforce.

While at the height of political mobilization (1964–1970) the Chilean state was at the behest of powerful social forces, a layer of technocracy had emerged within CORFO that had been able to insulate itself from much of the political fray (Drake, 1978, 219; Fáundez 1988, 46). CORFO became involved in the development of a variety of new programs, particularly in the 1960s, that would become essential ingredients in later economic growth and employment creation (Montecinos 1998, 21). During the Frei years, CORFO advanced the idea of developing an internationally competitive agricultural processing industry and began to research the best foreign and local business practices. It promoted the creation of "leader processing firms" that would assist in the adoption and diffusion of modern processing industries. In 1967, CORFO established a Plan for Fruit Development, which provided a variety of measures essential for export success: market analysis, technology, credit, and tariff drawback (Kurtz 2001, 5). In this same period, it also laid the basis for a new export infrastructure in such sectors as fishing, chemicals, and pulp.

There were additional state-directed measures that would also contribute to later export success. The expansion of the university system from 1964, especially in technical/engineering programs focusing on the training of agricultural economists and agronomists, was important (Agosín 1999, 94). The 1965 National Forestry Plan established goals for government plantings, and in 1970 the state directly planted 46 percent of total forestry plantings; by 1973, this figure was 96 percent (Wisecarver 1992, 485). All of these initiatives would eventually contribute, in important ways, to economic growth and employment creation after 1985. However, in the early 1970s, the intensifying political polarization and growing political and economic crises preoccupied both government and opposition forces.

Despite the extensiveness of the redistributive measures during the Allende years, the power of the propertied class had not been broken; As the economic situation deteriorated, these interests plotted both the return of their assets and their return to power. Capital flight and a precipitous decline in investment contributed to the difficult economic situation. As land reform progressed, agricultural production declined, forcing the country to use precious foreign exchange to import food (Loveman 1988, 298). Widespread shortages of basic goods ensued. The expanded social programs in combination with the difficulties in economic growth and copper exports placed heavy pressure on government expenditures: by 1972–1973, government expenditure as percentage of GDP stood at over 40 percent, with social expenditures hitting a record high of 25.6 percent of GDP by 1972 (see Figure A-3). The government deficit reached nearly 13 percent of GDP (see Figure A-8). In the absence of sufficient resources, the government resorted to the printing press (Hira 1998, 53). By 1973, the country was experiencing the highest rate of inflation in the world at over 500 percent (Larraín 1991, 89).

External factors played no small role in the growing economic and political difficulties faced by the Allende administration, particularly in the balance-of-payments difficulties and public deficit. The fall of copper prices on the international market exacerbated an already difficult foreign exchange situation. With the nationalization of the American-owned copper companies, Anaconda and Kennecott, the legal actions taken by the companies made it difficult for Chile to market its copper. At the same time, the U.S.-sponsored credit blockade prevented the administration from obtaining much needed credit (Petras and Morley 1975). The United States aided Chile's political right by supporting the truckers' strike and the right-wing media. These actions contributed to the growing political destabilization and economic difficulties.

The Propertied and Middle Classes React: Military Rule and Radical Neoliberalism

The country's most powerful industrial, financial, and landed interests enthusiastically supported the 1973 military coup, thereby ushering in Chile's second critical conjuncture. Indeed, a number of the country's top businessmen had been key actors behind the coup—in particular the two most powerful conglomerate executives who opposed Allende and who had had their firms intervened by his government when they refused to sell them to CORFO (O'Brien and Roddick 1983, 71). Owners of small and medium-sized businesses, who faced particularly acute conflicts over wages and working conditions (Martínez and Díaz 1996, 77), and members of the middle class, concerned with the recent economic deterioration, also supported the coup.

The Pinochet era featured the dismantling of many aspects of state intervention in the economy, a draconian trade liberalization program, and, by the mid-1980s, the successful introduction of sustained export-led economic growth. It is also associated with rising unemployment and increased levels of poverty and inequality. An important aspect of Chilean society that made the disregard for the social implications of the new economic program possible was that it had become not only politically polarized but also heavily compartmentalized, with its middle and upper classes and military establishment having had little contact with, or knowledge of, the lived experiences of the lower classes. Indeed, Constable and Valenzuela describe Chile as a "country of parallel subcultures that never touched" (1991, 140). As noted earlier, the distance between the Chilean middle class and the working class had increased, and the middle class had lost its earlier reformist concerns.

The Chilean military, drawn from the lower middle class, was also insulated from the broader society. Like the Korean military, the Chilean military had developed contempt for politicians and politics in general. The Chilean military blamed politicians for the political and economic crises of 1970–1973, strongly supported the national security doctrine, and adhered to a strong ideology of anticommunism. A number of important characteristics account for the military's disregard of the social consequences of its policies, however. While most of its officers were recruited from the lower middle class, by the early 1970s the Chilean military had undergone decades of cultural isolation from the rest of society as sons followed their fathers' career paths into the military (Angell 1988, 94). The law banned military officers from voting, and the military lived in segregated housing and generally socialized only with each other (Constable and Valenzuela 1991, 45, 49). While the Korean military had recent links with the rural poor, the Chilean military lacked both knowledge of and sympathy for the rural and working poor—an attitude that was reinforced by its exposure to the national security doctrine. Its insulation from society made the Chilean military a natural ally of another group that had also been isolated from mainstream society—the technocratic group of economists known as the Chicago boys (Teichman 2001).[20] Moreover, the Chilean military was confronted with a very different set of problems than those of its Korean counterpart: It faced an angry and extremely powerful private sector that pressed for intervention on its behalf and that firmly rejected asset redistribution. The Chilean military also faced highly mobilized workers and peasants and a militant leftist movement that rejected the institution of private property.

Initially there was a plurality of right-center views within the military regime as each member of the four-man military junta headed up a council with specific policy responsibilities—security, social welfare, economy, and agriculture. Each council maintained ongoing contact with civilian advisors who played an important role in shaping policy (O'Brien and Roddick 1983, 47). However, as Pinochet consolidated his power, those able to influence policy became an ever more restricted group that included military leaders, the Chicago boys,[21] and a very small number of conglomerate executives who had close personal ties with those technocrats. The renewed economic downturn in 1974 convinced Pinochet that the state must take drastic action. He therefore agreed to the Chicago boys' draconian adjustment program known as the "shock treatment," which involved drastic cuts in government expenditures, deregulation of financial markets, steep trade liberalization, and privatization. Trade liberalization immediately pushed up unemployment as small and medium-sized light consumer goods industries went bankrupt. Manufacturing, as a percentage of GDP, dropped from 25.5 percent in 1970 to 21.5 percent by 1980 (see Table A-9). Unlike South Korea, imported inputs did not complement domestic production but replaced it. Manufacturers who survived increased their imports of inputs with the consequence that the amount of integration within the country's manufacturing sector weakened even further (Albala-Bertrand 1999). Privatization benefited conglomerate executives as they used state-provided low-interest loans to purchase privatized companies, which were auctioned off at bargain-basement prices to single bidders (Oppenheim 1993, 152). The low prices of public companies constituted an important subsidy to the private sector (Edwards and Cox Edwards 1987, 97).

As the regime dismantled labor protection, workers became unable to defend themselves. The military suspended the right to strike and to bargain collectively, withdrew legal recognition from the umbrella labor confederation, closed unions, and confiscated their goods. Repression and the disappearances of union activists and leaders were frequent. There was a dramatic drop in union membership from 41 percent of the workforce in 1973 to 9 percent by 1981 (Oppenheim 1993, 185). The 1979 labor code, while allowing bargaining at the plant level, severely restricted union activities, leaving labor almost no recourse against arbitrary and numerous layoffs and unsafe and unhealthy working conditions. Rural workers were especially disadvantaged because one of the aims of the new military regime was to weaken and depoliticize the rural lower classes. In privatizing the agricultural land taken over by the Popular Unity government, the military regime excluded all those peasants who had participated in land invasions from the opportunity of purchasing land and assigned land only to "apolitical" peasants (Kurtz 2004, 84). In 1979, the regime repealed the law allowing rural unions. In addition, after 1975, small landowners were excluded from the formal private sector credit market (Kurtz 2004, 66).

Smallholders were forced to buy seeds from landlords using very expensive in-kind loans and had to sell their produce at low prices at harvest time. The regime focused on the creation of large and medium agricultural capitalists. As the nontraditional agricultural export sector gained ground, small farms declined, as did full-time permanent jobs. Everywhere, wages declined sharply, and unemployment rose to record levels, skyrocketing, with the economic crisis of the early 1980s, to 22 percent by 1982.

Moreover, privatization in health care and in the educational and social security systems in 1979 contributed to the generation of sharp inequalities in the coming years. The establishment of a two-tier system in health care involving a private system for the well-off and a public system for the remaining 85 percent of the population would quickly produce a sharp deterioration of health services as both government and upper-class financial contributions to public health care dropped. New inequalities emerged as the health care companies discriminated against women and the elderly. The privatization of the pension system involved the creation of private pension administrators (AFPs, Pension Fund Managing Corporations). While the new law gave the currently employed a choice of remaining in the old system or transferring to the new one, it required all those hired after 1982 to join an AFP.[22] Under the privatized system, employers did not make contributions. AFPs invested workers' contributions in individualized capitalized accounts. Finally, not only was the newly privatized social security scheme extremely costly, but it would fail to generate adequate pensions.[23] There was still no social support for the self-employed—those in the informal sector and small farmers.

At the same time, reforms carried out in the educational system would soon produce a sharp distinction in quality between publicly funded schools, attended by the poorest, which did not charge tuition, and the private tuition-charging schools used by the middle and upper classes. A system of vouchers assigned per student attending classes was the principal mechanism of assigning resources to education while the educational law expressly prohibited the government from giving additional resources to public schools. The military regime created three types of schools: schools run by municipalities, privately run schools that received state subsidies, and privately run schools receiving no subsidies. The latter two types charged tuition and were of higher quality and available to the middle and upper classes. As the state reduced its subsidies, the publically funded part of the educational system experienced a sharp deterioration in quality. After 1981, education spending declined sharply (see Figure A-4). The government replaced university administrators and fired professors. Student enrollment, particularly in postsecondary institutions, dropped.[24]

Poverty and inequality increased. While the percentage of households living in poverty stood at 17 percent in 1970, that figure had risen to 39 percent by 1987 (see Table A-1). Income distribution also became more unequal, with the Gini coefficient increasing from 0.46 in the late 1960s to 0.56 by 1984 (see Table A-2). By the late 1980s, the top 10 percent of households had increased their share of national income to 45 percent from 35 percent in the late 1960s. This figure contrasts sharply with the Korean case where, in the late 1980s, the wealthiest 10 percent accounted for 25 percent of national income. Meanwhile, the bottom 40 percent of Chilean households saw their proportion of national income decline (see Tables A-3 and A-4). In the late 1980s, the share of the bottom 40 percent of Chilean households of national income was one-half the figure for South Korea. Social spending as a percentage of GDP dropped in the immediate aftermath of the military coup before rising to almost the level of the Allende years, but it declined sharply thereafter (see Figure A-3). The upsurge in the early 1980s occurred largely due to the sharp increase in social security payments made necessary by the steep rise in unemployment in the early 1980s.[25] See Figure 3-1 earlier in this chapter.

The military period left a legacy of power concentration and authoritarian institutional arrangements that kept the new economic model firmly in place and made it difficult for civilian governments in the post-military period to effectively address social issues, particularly inequality. The most important among these institutional provisions included the provision for nine appointed senators who ensured right-wing strength in congress because they were appointed by Pinochet; military control of the National Security Council, whose advice the Cabinet was obliged to listen to; and an electoral system that gave disproportionate weight to the right-wing coalition.

Conclusions

While developments during the 1950s and 1960s produced important social improvements, aspects of the country's early economic modernization were conducive to later sharp social compartmentalization. The expansion of commercial agriculture resulted in increased exploitation of the peasantry, while the emergence of Chile as a mining enclave produced an ideologically militant working class and facilitated a unified propertied class. Chile's first phase of industrialization also produced a middle class that emerged at the end of the nineteenth century and expanded dramatically with import substitution after 1938. While the middle class initially showed a tendency to mobilize workers around social reform demands, it became increasingly conservative over time and, unlike the case of Korea, did not become an important force for social reform.

The initial most important historical feature contributing to socioeconomic inequality in Chile was the fierce resistance to land redistribution, agrarian reform, and social improvements in the rural areas on the part of the country's powerful oligarchy of landed and business interests—a resistance that was successful well into the last part of the twentieth century. However, the Great Depression and the rise of the Popular Front to power offered the possibility of change. The period ushered in a new economic model and provided access to political power for the political left for the first time in Chilean history. The pact arising from the Front, however, entrenched rural exclusion and set in motion a reactionary sequence that, with the 1973 military coup, ultimately deepened inequality and increased poverty by the early 1980s.

Meanwhile, the country's import substitution model lacked the dynamism to improve living standards over the long term. The Chilean state became increasingly weaker over time. Business interests penetrated the state and sought to protect their interests, while bureaucrats rallied their societal clienteles in pursuit of particular policy objectives. Preoccupied with political pressures, public policy ignored agriculture, squeezed mining, expanded social spending, particularly social security, and failed to engage in industrial development planning. The consequence was stagnant growth by the mid-1950s, chronic balance of payments difficulties, huge budget deficits, and inflation.

Working-class militancy, fed by the intransience of the political and economic elite and by the growing conservativeness of the middle class, increased through the 1950s and 1960s. The pluralist nature of the political system made possible selective improvements benefiting the middle class and the organized sectors of the working class. By the late 1960s, high levels of political mobilization of workers and peasants were propelling radical redistributive measures forward. The ensuing political polarization, however, set the stage for the 1973 military coup orchestrated by the fearful powerful conglomerates and supported by the middle class, the final event in an increasingly intense reactive sequence. It marked a critical conjuncture that set in motion far-reaching economic and political changes with profound implications for poverty and inequality. The increasing ideological polarization involving the left's rejection of capitalism and the concept of private property made compromise over land redistribution and other redistributive issues impossible. However, a number of new economic initiatives during the Frei and Allende years would make an important contribution to employment-generating economic growth much later, although not until an important adjustment was made in the radical market reform model.

4

Mexico
The Historical Origins of Poverty and Inequality

ALTHOUGH MEXICO'S ECONOMIC GROWTH RATE from 1950 to the late 1960s was better than Chile's, by 1970 its poverty was twice as high (see Tables A-1 and A-5). Mexico's poverty level was also considerably higher than South Korea's in 1970. Inequality in Mexico was the highest of the three countries: In the mid- to late 1960s, the wealthiest 10 percent of households accounted for 51.7 percent of national income compared with 34.8 percent and 25.8 percent in Chile and Korea, respectively (see Table A-3). Although the Mexican Revolution raised the possibility of redistribution, faced with strong social forces, the propertied interests that came to control the state in its aftermath constructed political arrangements that made it possible to resist redistributive reforms. In addition, Mexico's mining and agricultural enclave status shaped an early industrialization drive that was not employment generating, and this tendency continued through the twentieth century. The failure to effectively address social well-being, however, generated bouts of political mobilization and two reactive sequences that put an end to attempts to grapple with the social inadequacies of the country's development model. As in Chile, social forces penetrated the state, inhibiting the emergence of an independent state bureaucracy with a coherent development vision.

Setting the Stage for Exclusionary Capitalist Development

Mexico, unlike Chile, began its modern history with a substantial indigenous population, a feature that gave a marked racial facet to socioeconomic inequality and poverty and provided the basis for entrenched social compartmentalization.[1] Although the indigenous population declined sharply with the conquest, by 1810, a decade before independence, it had recovered to more than 60 percent of the population (Brown 2000, 274), although it declined thereafter.[2] Concentrated in south central rural Mexico, these were the country's poorest citizens. With a high level of miscegenation, by mid-twentieth century, mestizos (the descendents of European and indigenous peoples) came to constitute about 60 percent of the population. Mestizos generally occupied an intermediate level in the social, economic, and political hierarchy, although many were poor urban and rural dwellers. A small white population of around 10 percent occupied the highest levels of economic and political power and resided in the urban centers.

During much of the nineteenth century, civil wars raged in Mexico, defying attempts to establish centralized authority. In fact, between 1821 and 1860, Mexico had fifty separate governments, each lasting on average less than one year (Smith 1979, 31). While intraelite struggles were an ongoing source of civil strife, many conflicts also sprang from the racial and cultural heterogeneity that characterized the countryside. Conflicts between mestizo and Indian villages and between those villages and haciendas (large landholdings) were common (Hart 1997, 33). Indian rebellions raged as commercial agriculture impinged on village communal property.[3] It was not until the rule of Porfirio Díaz (1876–1911) that political stability and centralized authority were established.

The Porfiriato[4] made mineral development and exportation and commercial export agriculture the driving forces of economic growth—a strategy that produced Mexico's first industrialization phase. Díaz's technocratic advisors, known as *científicos,* adhered to an extreme form of the philosophy of Positivism that involved the conviction that the country must achieve modernization through the application of modern science, a feat that could only be achieved by the leadership of the country's white *criollo* (American-born) oligarchy (Cumberland 1968, 191). Mexico's indigenous and mixed-blood population, on the other hand, was an obstacle to modernization. The regime was an especially strong opponent of Indian communal landholdings because it regarded such arrangements as an impediment to capitalist development (Miller 1985, 263). The Porfiriato's social base, therefore, was in the foreign and domestic business interests that became the major beneficiaries of its modernization strategy. The rural masses and the emerging working class, on the other hand, were the big losers. State repression kept them in line.

The state-led nature of this early modernization phase arose because, in large part, Mexico's big landowners had no interest in agricultural modernization or in investment in mining or industry.[5] The lack of state access to investment capital, given the decades of political instability, encouraged Díaz to pursue foreign investment in mineral development and commercial agriculture. Although Díaz's policies gave rise to a domestic capitalist class, foreign capital from the United States and Europe was the most important driving force behind economic modernization, accounting for 67 to 73 percent of total investment (Haber 1989, 12).

To encourage foreign investment, the Porfiriato granted economic privileges, monopolies, and guaranteed markets to foreign and domestic entrepreneurs. Foreign investment in railways was the most important measure, stimulating both mining and agriculture for export. In fact, 87.5 percent of the railways that existed in Mexico in 1875 were built during the years of Porfirio Díaz, and most were foreign owned until 1908, when the government acquired ownership of over half of them and merged them with the National Railways of Mexico (Solís 1981, 54). Railway expansion was also the main factor in peasants losing land as the fiscally strapped government encouraged railway investment by offering builders land grants.[6] Peasants also lost land when the state gave land survey companies one-half of the land they surveyed as payment for their services and allowed companies to purchase the remaining land at bargain prices (King 1970, 5). In the nine years following the institution of this practice in 1883, an estimated 30 million acres went to surveyors and 40 million to private individuals and companies (Cumberland 1968, 198).

As railway lines reached the northern border, the movement of minerals and agricultural foodstuffs northward accelerated, and the United States became Mexico's most important export market and most important source of investment (Solís 1981, 65). Americans came to own three-quarters of the mines and one-half the oil fields and were heavy investors in sugar and cotton plantations and cattle ranches. By 1910, half of Mexico's exports were accounted for by minerals and the other half by commercial agricultural products (King 1970, 4).

Industrialization, linked to the commercialization of agriculture and mining and increasingly integrated with the U.S. economy, began in the northern city of Monterrey. Initiated by a small number of northern landholding families, much of this industrialization involved import substitution in consumer goods (Camp 1989, 209). Textile mills took advantage of the raw material produced by the new plantations in henequen and cotton

(Parkes 1962, 3); the new mining communities stimulated demand for such items as food, clothing, and cement while the railways stimulated the domestic production of iron and steel. Foreign and domestic capital established the country's first steel mill, Fundidora Monterrey (Haber 1989, 15). The volume of manufactured goods produced doubled during the Porfiriato (Meyer and Sherman 1970, 444–445), and by 1910, Monterrey had become "the industrial capital of Mexico" (449). Mexico's economic transformation under the Porfiriato was profound: Between 1877 and 1910, the volume of the country's trade increased by nine times (Smith 1979, 31). Silver production quadrupled during the period, and Mexico became the world's second largest copper producer (Miller 1985, 275). When Díaz left office, the public treasury, empty when he took power, was in surplus, and the country had acquired a solid international credit rating (Cumberland 1968, 231).

However, the Díaz modernization drive had a number of problems. The international demand for the country's minerals was more unstable than Chile's, making the country subject to frequent economic downturns: These occurred in 1871, in 1900–1901, and in 1907–1908 (Ayala Espinosa 1988, 69). In addition, some of the features of this initial industrialization phase would haunt industrial development for many years to come.[7] Porfirian industrialization involved the creation of oligopolies, heavy concentration in ownership, the use of capital-intensive methods, and an attitude of disinterest in export markets—all of which restricted the ability of industry to provide employment. This feature arose from a number of government practices, including the legally sanctioned right of firms to operate under federal monopoly concessions. The manufacturing sector quickly developed into a relatively few number of vertically integrated money-losing firms, many owned by Díaz's cronies (Haber 1989, 44). Aside from its negative implications for domestic employment, the entrepreneurial preference for capital-intensive methods made industry highly dependent on imported capital goods and on the foreign exchange earning capacity of a fragile primary export sector. It also put up the costs of production and made necessary the importation of skilled labor to operate machinery (Haber 1989, 36).[8] Compared with Chile, the impact of this initial phase of industrialization on social structure was limited. By the turn of the century, 68.1 percent of the population still worked in agriculture (see Table A-7). Nevertheless, new middle-class groups were beginning to emerge, as was an incipient labor movement in the mines and new factories. Unlike Chile, this early industrial development did not provide a rapid expansion of employment.

The most important drawback of Porfiriato modernization was the dramatic increase in poverty and inequality it created. By 1910, many small landowners and most indigenous communities had lost land, with the consequence that 96 percent of the agricultural population was landless and less than 3 percent of the population owned land (King 1970, 5; Tannenbaum 1968, 140). The real wage of the rural laborer dropped to one-quarter of what it had been in 1800. In the words of one observer, Mexican agricultural laborers during the Díaz regime "survived in a condition of sodden and brutish misery, unmatched by the proletariat of any other country" (Parkes 1962, 261). For the reasons already explained, this dispossessed rural labor force could not find employment in the urban sector, where real wages had also been declining for years. Life expectancy and infant mortality rates, already very low to begin with, deteriorated in the last decades of the Porfiriato (Cumberland 1968, 192). In 1900, illiteracy stood at 75.5 percent of the population (see Table A-6).

Mexico's critical conjuncture spans the period from 1890 until the mid-1920s. The internal upheaval of the Mexican Revolution (1910–1917) constitutes a critically important sequence of domestic events that opened the possibility of substantial redistributive change. The dynamism of the U.S. economy and the integration of the Mexican economy with that of its northern neighbor comprise the other sequence. This development began before the Revolution and continued thereafter. With the Revolution, Mexico once again descended into anarchy that devastated the economy, producing a dramatic fall in mineral production and declines in agriculture and manufacturing (Cumberland 1968, 255). In 1924, the country faced a crushing external debt with people probably much worse off than they had been before the war. The combination of the Revolution and the country's integration with the dynamic economy to the north gave rise to a new group of commercial agriculturalists who would successfully thwart land redistribution. Meanwhile, the new institutional arrangements and policy directions of this postrevolutionary leadership structured poverty and inequality outcomes in powerful ways. However, the Revolution established worker and peasant expectations that would force periodic, though never sufficient, redistributive adjustment. These upsurges from below would, as in the case of Chile, produce reactive consequences (see Figure A-1).

In the aftermath of the Revolution, the establishment of the modern Mexican state faced formidable challenges: strong social forces that vied for political control and strove to shape the direction of development— peasants, workers, middle-class groups, and a propertied class that has survived the Revolution. The peasant struggle had become best known through the war waged by the peasant leader Emiliano Zapata, whose radical social program included the restitution of Indian communal lands. The 1917 constitution incorporated this aspiration, and it would be a persistent and recurrent promise of every postrevolutionary administration until the 1980s.

The postrevolutionary leadership also faced worker militancy and strike activity. As in the Chilean case, the greatest militancy occurred among workers in the foreign-controlled mining and petroleum enclaves—and related activities like railways.[9] Workers had played an important role in the revolutionary struggle, constituting revolutionary units known as "Red Battalions" to fight in defense of labor rights. Given labor's strength, between 1914 and 1923 every revolutionary leader attempted to recruit labor into the internecine struggles among revolutionary groups (Clark 1973, 101). The 1917 constitution also incorporated various workers' rights such as the eight-hour day and minimum wages (article 123).

Other groups had also supported the Mexican Revolution, including members of the middle class along with some wealthy landowners, such as one of the Revolution's best-known figures, Venustiano Carranza, president of Mexico from 1914 to 1920. After the assassination of the first postrevolutionary president (Francisco Madero) in 1913, the struggle for control resulted in the emergence of a predominantly middle-class leadership, people from the legal professions, teachers, and owners of small to medium-sized landholdings, many of whom were from northern Mexico. This group, which would dominate Mexican politics into the 1950s,[10] strongly supported free enterprise and envisioned modern Mexican agriculture very differently than did indigenous and mestizo peasants. Initially, the postrevolutionary leadership supported the creation of a small landowning yeoman class—an image that contradicted the Zapatista notion of agricultural development via Indian communal land ownership (Cline 1961, 195). However, while the new Revolutionary leadership had little interest in the restoration of communal landholdings, the high degree of peasant mobilization forced it to give some attention to this aspiration.

The middle-class revolutionary leadership lost no time in incorporating a portion of the prerevolutionary economic elite to the new order. Because postrevolutionary Mexico faced almost total financial collapse, the new government required the collaboration of the Porfirian banking sector in the reconstruction of the banking system. Hence, the bankers participated in the drawing up of the banking legislation, laws, and regulations and, later, sat on the boards of the government banks, including the Central Bank, where they lobbied for orthodox macroeconomic policies (Hamilton 1982, 37; Maxfield 1990, 59). The northern industrialists had also survived the Revolution and became a force to be reckoned with.

Rivalries among revolutionary leaders, combined with the reluctance of the postrevolutionary leadership to address the demands of workers and peasants, created a situation of political instability—one that saw repeated uprisings and repression through the 1920s. The end to the ongoing upheavals appeared to be in sight when President Plutarco Elías Calles created a new political party, which incorporated state political machines and used patronage to keep violent conflict in check.[11] While the authoritarian nature of these new political arrangements alienated many of the Revolution's middle-class supporters (Loaeza 1983, 418), most of those in leadership positions and their allies now used their increasingly authoritarian control of the state to transform themselves into a powerful new class of commercial agriculturalists, based in northern Mexico. They used the state to further their economic interests, through protecting their lands from confiscation and redistribution, providing their farms with state-funded irrigation works, and granting themselves favorable access to state credit (Cockcroft 1983, 128).[12] This new agrarian commercial class came to see land redistribution and labor rights as contrary to its interests and was successful in pushing the presidency and the political leadership increasingly to the political right. Hence, while an attempt was made to improve the living standards in rural areas,[13] relatively little land redistribution occurred before 1930, and most of the land that was given out was not arable (Sanderson 1981, 17). Nor did organized labor make important gains.

The Great Depression had a devastating impact, producing a high level of social unrest, pushing the regime to the left, and making it increasingly impossible for the government to resist reform. With a younger generation of revolutionaries gaining ground within the ruling party, by 1934 social reform, including agrarian reform, was firmly on the agenda. Meanwhile, foreign control of extractive industries like mining and petroleum, accounting for one-third of national income (Cline 1961, 339), was stoking nationalist fervor against a postrevolutionary leadership that had failed to take measures to curtail foreign capital. Popular pressures from below would soon push the state toward more radically redistributive measures, but those measures would face stiff resistance from powerful propertied interests and from the conservative faction of the postrevolutionary leadership.

The Cárdenas Years (1934–1940): Strong Social Forces and the Failure of Redistribution

General Lázaro Cárdenas came to power with support from the political left of the party and with a strongest social base in the labor movement. While he had an important social reform and redistributive agenda, his overwhelming concern became that of managing the intense pressure from below and balancing that pressure against an increasingly restive propertied class. Unlike General Park, President Cárdenas was unable to control his business class—indeed, he ultimately gave in to its pressure. While his new cabinet contained the architect of the most progressive articles of the constitution dealing with labor rights and land reform, it also integrated a representative from the political right of the party (Parkes 1962, 341). Further, Cárdenas's ability to move the regime in the direction of redistributive and nationalist measures was only possible due to the mobilization of his popular base—one he cultivated to keep the forces of reaction at bay while he carried out social reforms. This base gave the regime sufficient autonomy to push social reforms forward. To this end, he sponsored the establishment of nationwide labor and peasant confederations, created worker paramilitary units, and organized peasant militias, distributing weapons among the latter (Parkes 1962, 342). However, the redistributive moment was fleeting. As in the Chilean case, the redistributive and nationalist measures immediately gave rise to a visceral reaction from the private sector along with fear and alienation on the part of the country's small middle class. This, combined with opposition from the political right of the ruling party, would put a stop to, and reverse this reformist redistributive attempt, setting in motion a reactive sequence.

During the Cárdenas presidency, there was little in the way of economic policy that would stimulate economic growth. Faced with an onslaught of work stoppages during his first two years in power, Cárdenas became captive of popular pressures from below, which, by the end of his administration, he no longer controlled. Worker anger at the better wages and working conditions afforded foreign workers was particularly strong in the foreign-controlled enclaves of mining, petroleum, and railways and was instrumental in Cárdenas's nationalizations in the petroleum and railway industries. The force of the worker mobilization is illustrated by the fact that Cárdenas turned the operation of the country's railways over to the workers and, when the petroleum industry was nationalized, gave workers four of nine positions on the board of directors of the company— thereby giving the labor unions access to sources of wealth through higher-paying jobs and government contracts.

The Cárdenas years are best known for land reform, however. As the first Mexican president who did not come from the north, Cárdenas rejected the northern dynasty's emphasis on private property and on small peasant holdings in favor of the large communal land holdings known as *ejidos* (Cline 1961, 225).[14] Between 1935 and 1940, the government distributed 44 million acres of land, more than twice that distributed by all of the previous governments combined (Parkes 1962, 343). Landless workers declined from 68 percent to 36 percent of the rural workforce between 1920 and 1940 (Hansen 1980, 31; Hewitt de Alcántara 1976, 4; Parkes 1962, 351).[15] By the early 1940s, more than one-half of the rural population belonged to these *ejido* communities, and *ejidos* accounted for more than one-half of total cropland and for 51 percent of farm production (Hewitt de Alcántara 1976, 5). The creation of *ejidos* was accompanied by significant public investment in roads, irrigation works, schools, and medical services. The government increased credit to the *ejido* sector through a bank created explicitly for this purpose. The result was an increase in *ejido* productivity. In addition, Cárdenas spent twice as much on rural education as had any previous president and established regional schools of practical agriculture (Meyer and Sherman 1979, 601). But although his programs improved the daily lives of many of the rural poor, his land reform was not sufficient to alleviate the widespread rural poverty that had been the legacy of the Porfiriato. Over 60 percent of peasants eligible to receive land either did not receive any land or received an inadequate parcel (Cockcroft 1983, 134). Moreover, big landholders retained large farms by registering various parcels of land under the names of different family members.

Other initiatives during the Cárdenas years contributed to an improvement in health and welfare. Between 1934 and 1940, social expenditures increased from 20 percent to 26 percent of total expenditures, reaching the highest point in Mexican history in 1938 (Pardo 2000, 463; Wilkie 1967, 158). Workers made gains in wages and benefits, with government rulings favoring labor (Hansen 1980, 92). However, as happened in Chile, Cárdenas's attempt to expand social security—heath care, pensions, and unemployment insurance—to all was thwarted by the most organized and powerful middle-working-class workers who had gained the most generous social security arrangements. Civil servants won improvements of already generous social security benefits, while the railway and petroleum workers obtained social security packages that were among the best (Mesa-Lago 1978, 214). The vast majority of workers, on the other hand, remained without any social security protection whatsoever.

In some respects, Cárdenas's policies were not radical. He made no move to change the main structural features of the economy. The state would drive economic growth by stimulating a dynamic agricultural export economy. To this end, Cárdenas created the National Bank for Foreign Trade for the purpose of promoting agricultural exports and facilitating merchandise imports (Ayala Espino 1988, 207). While the big commercial agriculturalists were happy to see an end to the inefficient large landholdings, most aspects of Cárdenas's program caused concern. Strikes and other forms of labor unrest that accelerated during the last two years of the Cárdenas administration alarmed business, particularly the northern business interests of Monterrey. Business opposed the nationalizations for foreign companies; the increase in government expenditures, which doubled between 1935 and 1940; and the rise in inflation as the government made increasing use of the printing of money to finance expenditure (Ayala Espino 1988, 188, 197; Meyer and Sherman 1979, 179). The middle class, fearful of the rising level of popular mobilization and profoundly distrustful of the high level of state intervention, was at the center of the anti-Cardenista protests (Loaeza 1983, 433). Middle-class concerns gave rise to the establishment of the Popular Action Party (PAN) in 1939.

Of course, international factors also contributed to the country's economic difficulties, thereby contributing to the strength of the reactive sequence that ensued from Cárdenas's reforms. The fact that Cárdenas's nationalization of the petroleum industry had resulted in the U.S. Department of the Treasury suspending purchases of silver and discouraging foreign governments from buying Mexican petroleum intensified the growing economic crisis, as did the fact that the former petroleum owners lobbied foreign governments not to buy Mexican petroleum (Meyer 1973, 38). The private sector registered its opposition to the regime through capital flight, a tactic it would use repeatedly in the future to discipline the state—with devastating economic consequences. Between 1935 and 1939, an estimated 937 million pesos left the country, 46 million alone in

1934 (Martínez Nava 1984, 103–106). The mobilization against Cárdenas resulted in the end of his radical redistributive experiment and the ascendency of Manuel Avila Camacho to the Mexican presidency in 1940.

1940–1970: The Mexican "Miracle" and the "Perfect Dictatorship"

The Mexican state continued to contend with strong popular social forces in the decades ahead; but, from 1940, it developed political arrangements to contain those forces. Indeed, so effective were these arrangements that the regime has been referred to as a "perfect dictatorship."[16] These political arrangements had their origins in the Cárdenas party reform, which incorporated new organizations representing workers, peasants, and the "popular sector" (middle-class groups, particularly teachers) into the PRI apparatus. After 1940, the leadership (the president and those closest to him) used the party to control workers and peasant organizations, to minimize dissent, and to diminish the likelihood of opposition. It did this by handpicking the official peasant and worker leaders and party candidates and by replacing radical worker and peasant leaders with more acquiescent ones. When some of the most important trade unions threatened to stay outside the official labor organization, the government simply created a new umbrella labor organization (the Labor Congress or CT) in 1966, thereby facilitating centralized control of even the most recalcitrant unions. From the late 1960s, institutions of the state agricultural bureaucracy (marketing boards and the bank serving the *ejido* sector) became the most important institutions containing peasant unrest. In addition, the 1931 labor code, which required labor organizations to obtain legal recognition from the state, allowed the political leadership to favor cooperative labor and peasant organizations and leaders and to marginalize the uncooperative.[17]

The distribution of material rewards in exchange for political loyalty was probably the most important aspect of the system, however. In exchange for opportunities for personal enrichment, labor and peasant leaders quelled dissent and ensured that their rank and file voted for the PRI at election time. Opportunities for personal enrichment were particularly important in the political control of the country's most powerful trade unions in such key sectors as mining and petroleum, where collective agreements provided labor leaders with the ability to dispense housing, loans, and scholarships to loyal supporters. After 1940, the middle class, which expanded with the expansion of state activities, became reconciled to PRI rule, in large part because of the political stability and economic prosperity it provided.[18] Its sectoral organization (the popular sector), officially known as the National Confederation of Popular Organizations, became dominant within the PRI (Gilbert 2007, 61), middle-class individuals controlled the party and public affairs, and its unions, particularly those in the public sector, extracted the most generous social security benefits.

Indeed, concessions to the most powerful unions of the middle and working classes, those most likely to create problems for the administration, were an integral component of the cooptative process and shaped the unequal nature of social welfare protection. Social security benefits (pensions and health care) continued to cover only a minority of the population, mainly state employees and well-organized private sector workers.[19] By 1967, only 22 percent of workers had obtained social security benefits; the figure was still less than 40 percent by 1980. Yet, through the 1970s, the government spent about one-half of total social spending on social security (see Figure 4-1). The substantial state financial contribution to social security exaggerated the unequalizing impact of a system already riddled with sharp inequalities (de Gortari and Ziccardi 1996, 212; Pardo 2000, 470; Ward 1986, 112, 129). The state, for example, provided 44 percent of the financial requirements for the institution providing the most generous social security to public sector workers, the ISSSTE (Ward 1986, 115). The Ministry of Health and Social Assistance (SSA), on the other hand, which was responsible for the provision of health care to the population not covered by social security, was woefully underfunded. Health spending was low in Mexico: Its proportion of social spending at less than 10 percent (see Figure 4-1). In addition, in 1978, probably one-third of the country's population was not served by any health care system whatsoever (Ward 1986, 120).[20] While the proportion of state spending on education (a potentially equalizing social expenditure) began to rise above that for social security by the late 1970s (see Figure 4-1), educational spending remained unequalizing because it went mostly to urban areas and to postsecondary education, used mainly by the children of the middle and upper classes.

The Mexican miracle bypassed rural dwellers. By 1970, Mexico had the highest illiteracy of the three countries, and illiteracy remained substantially higher in rural areas than in urban ones (see Table A-6). While organized labor made some gains, peasants, particularly *ejiditarios,* saw their situations deteriorate. This occurred despite the fact that pub-

FIGURE 4-1. Mexico: Education, health and social/security/welfare, percentage of total social expenditures, 1973–2000. Sources: Data from International Monetary Fund, *Government Finance Statistics Yearbook*, 1985, 1991, 1999, 2001, 2003, 2005.

lic investment in agriculture, at least in the early part of the period, was substantial, averaging 20 percent of government investment per year between 1942 and 1956, producing an agricultural growth rate averaging 7.4 percent annually (Gollás and García Rocha 1976, 415, 416). The state, dominated by the big northern agriculturalists between 1940 and 1950, provided those big landowners with loans and irrigation works—the latter were essential to making the northern arid lands productive (Hansen 1980, 81; Hewitt de Alcántara 1976, 177).

Indeed, the governments of Avila Camacho (1940–1946) and Miguel Alemán (1946–1952), closely linked to the big commercial agriculturalists, were particularly hostile to *ejidal* agriculture and pursued a variety of policies prejudicial to its survival. Poor peasant producers in south and central Mexico, dependent on rain-fed lands, experienced a sharp decline in government loans, while the terms of repayment tightened. In addition, the state fertilizer company favored big farmers and made it difficult for small and *ejidal* farmers to obtain fertilizer (Hewitt de Alcántara 1976, 63). Meanwhile, the government not only stopped creating new *ejidos* but also divided many *ejidos* into individual plots. In the northern state of Sonora, government repression forced the dismantling of local organizations and, by 1954, had forced the transfer of the majority of *ejido* lands to individual peasant holdings (193). The Green Revolution, with its development of new technological agricultural packages, further harmed small and *ejidal* producers. Small and *ejidal* farmers, unable to afford or manage these packages successfully, usually became heavily indebted and then bankrupt.[21] Small farmers sold their land, and *ejiditarios* rented theirs. As big farms mechanized, however, there was less and less need for paid labor, a fact that contributed to the growing problems of rural unemployment and increased rural urban migration.

Big agriculture did, however, experience rapid growth. Between 1938 and 1958, total agricultural production rose 250 percent (Cockcroft 1983, 165; Parkes 1962, 358). By 1970, the country had achieved self-sufficiency in food, while exports of agricultural products (sugar, cotton, henequen, coffee, and cotton) increased (Hansen 1980, 45). Agriculture played an important role in promoting industrial growth in this period because the growth in commercial export agriculture provided the foreign exchange to import inputs that helped industry to expand.

From the mid-1950s, public policy focused almost entirely on industry, withdrawing its support from even commercial export agriculture, a shift in emphasis that reflected the decline in the power of agricultural commercial interests and the increasing power of the industrialists. Before World War II, Mexican industry had advanced considerably: By 1940, the consumer goods industry supplied the bulk of home demand for consumer goods (King 1970, 129). World War II provided an important stimulus to Mexican industry, opening U.S. markets to manufactured goods that were in short supply due to the war effort and to products directly related to the war effort (Meyer and Sherman 1979, 634). Mexico's manufactured exports rose to 25 percent of exports in the immediate postwar years (King 1970, 24). However, the country faced many of the same problems Chile did—inadequate resources to fund government investment programs, a growing public deficit, and inflationary pressure. Unlike those in Chile, Mexico's leaders had the institutional mechanisms to manage the political pressures arising from these economic difficulties. The incorporative and containment nature of the political system played an important role in allowing the state to mitigate the societal (organized working- and middle-class) pressures that contributed to inflation.[22]

Although the Mexican state had a variety of instruments by which it could intervene in industrial development, political pressures from strong social forces prevented the state from producing an effective industrial strategy. The state, through its regulation of the banking sector, could direct commercial banks to move credit into what it considered priority areas. It also channeled large portions of the substantial reserve requirement (funds the commercial banks were required to deposit with the Central Bank) into public investment. However, industrial policy was highly politicized, with policy operating largely in the service of vested business interests. Mexico's state development bank, NAFINSA (Nacional Financiera), invested heavily in infrastructure, provided a substantial portion of the financing going to industry, and invested and established enterprises that could supply inputs to existing economic activities.[23] However, with a board of directors consisting of both government ministers and representatives of the private sector, the NAFINSA board became a forum for lobbying by private sector interests. In addition, as economic difficulties emerged in the 1960s and 1970s, its role became even more explicitly political, as it repeatedly took over companies on the verge of bankruptcy to save jobs. As a result, NAFINSA acquired investments in enterprises in practically every sector of the economy, about one-half of which were enterprises taken over when their survival was in danger (Amparo Casar and Peres 1988, 38). The state enterprise sector became extremely large.[24]

As in the case of Chile, industrialists came to permeate the state with predictable implications for industrial policy. Eager to win the support of the newer industrialists who had arisen with the recent import substitution and were fearful of the resumption of foreign imports, the government acceded to demands for increased protection. It introduced import licenses in 1944 for certain items and established tariff protection in 1947. The government gave industrialists direct representation on the committee responsible for the distribution of import licenses. This arrangement gave already established industrialists the upper hand in securing quantitative restrictions on imports of their products and produced an overly protected industrial sector. The percentage of imports requiring licenses increased from 38 percent in 1956 to 65 percent by 1964, hitting 91 percent by 1976 (Lustig 1998, 114; Vernon 1963, 417). The direct participation of business in industrial policy distorted the industrialization process, producing an industrial structure that contravened the state's objective of encouraging the domestic production of capital goods when easy import substitution industrialization began to run out of steam by the mid-1950s (Aspra 1977, 114). Between 1940 and 1968, imports of capital goods, primary material, and replacement parts increased by a factor of 20.8; that is, much faster than Mexican production (Aguilar and Carmona 1973, 210).

While Mexico industry was to remain heavily dependent on imported inputs and capital goods, capital and durable consumer goods production did begin to expand from the 1950s (Aspra 1977, 114; Solís 1981, 171). These new growth industrial sectors, which included chemicals, steel, the automotive industry, and machinery, were the recipients of a rapid increase in direct foreign investment, which doubled between 1950 and 1960 and again between 1960 and 1968 (Meyer 1973, 43). However, these newer dynamic industries were capital intensive (and therefore not important in employment generators) and were themselves dependent on the importation of inputs and machinery. Because this new investment entered Mexico to take advantage of high levels of protection to sell to the domestic market, it was not export oriented.

Some state bureaucrats were concerned about the low productivity and lack of competitiveness of Mexican industry and pushed for measures to stimulate exports (King 1970, 113; La bastida Martín 1980, 151). Hence, several tentative measures began to emerge. In 1960, special credit facilities were established for manufactured exports produced in Mexico, and in 1963 FOMEX (Fund for Promoting Manufactured Exports) was set up to promote manufactured exports. It provided loans and guarantees against political hazards. The Border Industrialization Program (export processing zones or *maquilas*), introduced in 1965, allowed for the protection-free importation of industrial inputs for products to be exported. Government officials saw this program as important in employment generation. Other policies included the reimbursement of indirect taxes for manufactured exports and financial assistance for manufactured exports and credits. The state did not attempt, however, to identify specific industrial sectors for expansion into export markets nor to tie access to state industrial credits to export performance as South Korean policymakers did.

There are a variety of reasons why a strong push for a different industrial strategy was unlikely to emerge from the Mexican public bureaucracy. Probably the most important reason was that the bureaucracy, which expanded rapidly throughout the period, was closely integrated with the Mexican system of political co-optation. Hence, the state was a major avenue of upward social mobility for the increasingly educated mestizos. As a new president came to power every six years, the incoming government almost completely replaced the bureaucracy, giving the new president and his ministers the opportunity to reward supporters and spread around state appointments among the middle class (Greenburg 1970, 140). This context was discouraging to both the establishment of institutional memory and to the development of an independent bureaucratic voice on issues of economic policy.

Furthermore, unlike Korea, there was not a centralized cabinet-level mechanism to coordinate economic policy. In general, the development of economic policy rested in the hands of the president, the minister of finance, and the head of the Central Bank of Mexico. However, the proliferation of public enterprises eroded centralized authority over economic policymaking as public enterprises became increasingly autonomous. Attempts to mitigate this development failed (Teichman 1996, 40–42). In addition, as in the Chilean case, societal clienteles lobbied ministries and often permeated state institutions, rendering cooperation among ministries very difficult.

Although poverty declined during Mexico's miracle years, that reduction occurred mainly in the urban sector. The neglect of *ejido* and small agriculture, the fact that large farms did not provide sufficient or well-paid employment, and the failure to provide equal educational and other social services to rural dwellers all contributed to the high level of rural poverty. Land ownership had reconcentrated after 1940. By the late 1960s, 2 percent of farm families owned 76 percent of all farmland while 51 percent of farms, with less than five hectares per family, accounted for only 6 percent of all farmland (Cockcroft 1983, 177). Half the rural labor force, who worked as day laborers, saw their wage decline between 1950 and 1967 (Aguilar and Carmona 1973, 208; Hewitt de Alcántara 1976, 133). At the same time, industry accounted for only about one-fifth of the growth of employment, with most of the increase in employment occurring in services. The declining employment opportunities in the rural sector, combined with the failure of industry to expand employment sufficiently, produced an informal sector (disguised unemployment) estimated at between 40 and 60 percent of the economically active population by the late 1960s (Tello 1980, 76). Inequality increased after 1950 (see Table A-2), and there was sharp inequality between regions with greater prosperity and less poverty in the northern and central regions, where industrialization occurred. By the late 1960s, the proportion of national income held by the 10 percent wealthiest households was the highest of the three cases (see Table A-3). Poverty was widespread in the south, where the largest concentration of indigenous population engaged in traditional agriculture was located.

As economic growth stagnated from the mid-1960s, unrest increased on the part of those social forces that had benefited the least from the economic model of the previous twenty-five years. Independent unionism was on the rise, peasant uprisings mounted, and guerrillas began to emerge in parts of rural Mexico. This unrest came to a climax in 1968 with the massacre, by government troops, of some 200 protesting students, who had taken up the cause of the country's workers and peasants. The following administration of Luis Echeverría (1970–1976) attempted to find a new source of economic growth and to provide some redistributive measures, but these efforts ran headlong into an international economic downturn and into tough resistance from the country's ever more powerful industrial and financial business interests.

From "Shared Development" to the Petroleum Bust to Market Reform: More Poverty and Inequality

The presidency of Luis Echeverría (1970–1976) illustrates the growing weakness of the Mexican state. The state was pushed in contradictory directions not only by strong social forces but also by ministries with competing policy prescriptions and distinct societal clienteles. Faced with a serious balance of payments situation and inflation, Echeverría began his tenure in office by following a restrictive program, involving a sharp drop in public expenditures. The minister of finance, Central Bank director, and the private sector were strong supporters of this program. However, under pressure from ministries and agencies of government whose constituencies favored increased state spending, the president switched to an expansion program when the country slid into recession (Teichman 1988, 47). At the same time, concerned about the loss of regime legitimacy occasioned by the 1968 student massacre, Echeverría also sought to address the social justice issues that had given rise to the worker and peasant unrest. His program, known as "shared development," involved a dramatic expansion in state investment, state support for the expansion of exports, and an emphasis on redistributive and social welfare measures, with a particular commitment to improve the situations of small and *ejidal* agriculture.

The state increased investment in agriculture, energy, and heavy-industrial and capital goods and in the state-owned petroleum, electricity, and fertilizer companies (Teichman 1988, 49). It reduced import duties and made direct subsidies available to exporters, whom it also provided with credits at low rates of interest through the newly formed Mexican Institute of Foreign Trade. For the first time since the Cárdenas years, the PRI administration turned its attention to small and *ejidal* agriculture. Spending on agriculture as a percentage of total government expenditure increased from 7.1 percent in 1971 to 14.7 percent by 1975 (Gribomont and Rimez 1977, 786). In addition, the government instituted measures to support small and peasant agriculture, including increased credit. It also increased the number of agricultural schools and guaranteed prices for agricultural products through the expansion of the activities of the National Company of Popular Goods (CONASUPO), a state marketing board. It restored *ejidal* lands to original owners and purchased land to create additional *ejidos*.

A new program sought to expand the social security coverage offered by the IMSS to provide health services to 1.9 million small farmers lacking access to social security coverage (Frenk, González-Block, and Lozano 2000, 359). The administration also initiated the Program for Investment for Rural Development (PIDER) to reduce social tensions and stimulate employment and production in rural regions of extreme poverty, particularly in the south. The National Workers Housing Fund, financed by a tax on business, was set up to provide low-cost housing for workers and the government expanded its milk distribution program. Government social spending increased as a percentage of GDP from 5.3 percent to 7.3 percent between 1972 and 1976 (see Figure A-3).

However, while social improvements occurred, as during the Cárdenas years, Echeverría's redistributive and spending program aroused the strong opposition of the country's powerful private sector, which, as usual, registered its disapproval by means of capital flight from 1973 on. Another reactionary sequence ensued. By 1976, capital flight had assumed disastrous proportions: Over a half billion U.S. dollars left the country over the winter of 1976 (Fitzgerald 1978, 49). The private sector was particularly distressed at the high level of public expenditure, the expansion of the public enterprise sector, and the increased role of the state in the economy. Business also opposed price controls, wage increases, and the government's attempt to control direct foreign investment (Gereffi and Evans 1981, 51). Business defeated four attempts at tax reform, required to provide the revenue for increased government expenditure and investment. These reforms involved increasing the taxes paid by upper income groups and those with substantial assets. Opposition from the private sector produced tax reforms that were either considerably watered down or abandoned altogether (Martínez Nava 1984, 193–195; Solís 1981). Hence, while tax income as a percent of GDP increased, the increases were not adequate to the state's very substantial fiscal requirements and were considerably below Korea's and Chile's tax revenue (see Table A-10).

It was the government's actions on the land reform issue—pressed as it was by the long-time unsatisfied demands of the peasantry—that triggered a dramatic turn for the worse in state–business relations. Faced with a rash of land invasions in the state of Sonora in 1975, the government expropriated 4,387 hectares of irrigated land and distributed it among 433 peasants (Sanderson 1981, 40). This measure was followed by more land invasions in the states of Durango and Sinaloa and the granting of additional lands to *ejidos*. Rural mobilization produced a sharp reaction from business. By that time, entrepreneurial opposition had coalesced in a new peak organization known as the Coordinating Business Council (CGE), an organization that integrated almost all of the country's business organizations. The CGE gave strong support to the country's big commercial farmers' protest against the government land redistribution measures. At the same time, Echeverría's propoor reforms whetted the appetite of the popular classes for whom his reforms had not gone far enough. The pace of peasant land takeovers continued to rise, labor demands for wage increases escalated, and there was a rise in independent union activity (Cockcroft 1983, 249). As in Chile, growing political polarization was the consequence as redistributive measures became more radical.

Echeverría was forced to abandon his redistributive direction. A slowdown in the U.S. economy and increased tariffs ended the country's hopes of increasing exports to the United States. However, it was the 1973 oil crisis that put the final nail in the coffin of "shared development" because it dramatically increased the already pressing requirement for foreign exchange due to the need to purchase petroleum. Increased attention to agriculture had not been able to improve growth in the sector. With declining export earnings, pressing import needs, and an inability to raise revenues through increased taxation, the state relied more and more on foreign borrowing. The foreign debt grew from $4.5 billion (U.S.) to $19.6 billion (Grayson 1984, 54). In October 1976, Mexico was forced to reach a politically unpopular agreement with the International Monetary Fund, and the country returned to a restrictive/recessionary program.

The discovery of vast petroleum reserves in 1972 in Tabasco and Chiapas marked a renewed commitment to a capital-intensive economic model. Under President José López Portillo (1977–1982), the rapid expansion and exportation of petroleum provided revenue to lubricate the patronage network and, for a time, kept the lid on political discontent. A new plan called for the doubling of crude production and refining capacity in six years and for the tripling of the country's production of basic petrochemicals (Teichman 1988, 60). The official announcement of the country's petroleum resources restored business confidence and produced an avalanche of new borrowing opportunities. With capital flowing in, the government paid off loans in advance, and the country embarked on a period of state-led petroleum-based expansion that saw real per capita growth rates averaging 5.5 percent per year between 1978 and 1981 (see Table A-5). The new strategy changed the structure of the Mexican economy: Whereas in 1976 petroleum and its derivatives accounted for 16.8 percent of the value of exports, by 1981 this figure reached 74.4 percent. The state petroleum company became the country's single most important taxpayer, accounting for 25 percent of total taxes collected by the federal government in 1981 (66).

President López Portillo adopted the strategy because he believed it would restore business support for the regime, so severely damaged during the Echeverría years. He received strong backing from the director of the state petroleum, Jorge Díaz Serrano; from the powerful petroleum workers' union; and from other state bureaucrats with business connections to the petroleum industry. Private sector business people who benefited from the expansion of the petroleum industry (particularly the Monterrey business group) were also on board, as were prospending government agencies with societal clienteles (Teichman 1988, 69–74). On the other hand, leftist parties; peasants in petroleum areas; spending ministry officials (such as Natural Resources and Industrial Development), who wanted a more diversified investment program; and Finance and Central Bank officials worried about the impact of borrowing and spending on the public deficit, all opposed the petroleum strategy (10). The critics lost the debate, and so the strategy went forward.

The petroleum export strategy, while successful in terms of economic growth, papered over, but did not solve, the country's most pressing economic dilemmas. Furthermore, it made no long-term contribution to either the alleviation of poverty or the reduction of inequality. In the end, the strategy probably worsened the situation of the urban and rural poor. The rapid growth, and its capital-intensive nature based on petroleum extraction and petrochemicals, increased the country's appetite for imports. Hence, the balance of trade remained in deficit after 1974. With the growth of petroleum exports, Mexico began to suffer from the "Dutch disease."[25] Manufactured products began to loose their share of the value of exports, while agriculture fell into a profound crisis. By 1980, one-quarter of all foodstuffs had to be imported, while the value of food exports declined in absolute terms between 1979 and 1981 (Esteva 1983, 9). The inflow of capital produced by petroleum development was causing inflationary pressures and had produced an overvalued currency that was rendering nonpetroleum exports less and less competitive. Meanwhile, the fact of petroleum wealth and the vested interests it generated discouraged the felt need to give concerted government attention to either manufacturing or agriculture because petroleum wealth could be used to purchase both manufactured goods and food imports.

The decline in petroleum prices in the early 1980s, combined with the increase in interest rates, put an abrupt end to this strategy. Even at its best, it had done little to provide for a generalized improvement of living standards. The petroleum sector, given its capital-intensive nature, was not an important job producer. Although employment grew at an average annual rate of 4.7 percent between 1979 and 1981, its expansion occurred largely in construction and public works, areas that are often not long-term job producers (Székley 1983, 109). Particularly in the later part of the López Portillo years as the economy fell into crisis, social welfare began to lose ground. Social spending as a percentage of total spending declined for most of the López Portillo years and stagnated as a proportion of GDP for most of the period (see Figures A-3 and A-7). From 1980 on, the administration began to abandon the programs for the poorest initiated by Echeverría. The government declared land reform to be no longer the objective of rural policy (Sanderson 1981, 1).

To fuel this rapid petroleum-led growth, the state had borrowed heavily: The public sector deficit as a percent of GDP was 12 percent by 1982 (see Figure A-8). The situation was once again exacerbated by the loss of confidence of the private sector, which engaged in capital flight. Loss of support from the private sector occurred despite the fact that the government had granted the biggest conglomerates subsidies and tax exemptions while new banking legislation allowed conglomerates to unite all forms of banking into one institution, a measure that increased both their profits and their economic power (Quijano 1982, 223; Tello 1984, 59). Neverthe- less, once the economic downturn hit, the private sector, concerned about inflation and hostile to price controls, criticized the growth in government expenditures and the waste of state enterprises. The state proved incapable of grappling with the crisis. At first, it continued its expansionist policies, reduced its petroleum export prices, and resisted devaluation. Then, it de- valued the currency by 60 percent. As chaos ensued, capital flight during the last trimester of 1982 was close to $1 billion (U.S.). It was within this context of rising social unrest, including peasant unrest, and the inability of the state to manage the economic crisis that the president announced the nationalization of the banks on September 1, 1982. Although the deci- sion did little to end the outflow of capital—indeed, capital flight acceler- ated even further—the measure did much to rally public support behind the president. At the same time, it solidified the opposition of the pri- vate sector to the regime—an opposition that subsequent regimes would struggle to reverse.[26]

Conclusions

Mexico was faced with a reality that posed far more difficult chal- lenges to both nation-state building and political stability than existed in either Korea or Chile. Sharp racial and regional divisions, reinforced by social class, made nation-state building a very difficult task. Mexico, un- der the Porfiriato, underwent early modernization and industrialization, involving incorporation into the world economy as a mineral and agricul- tural enclave. This early modernization phase witnessed the incipient for- mation of a powerful propertied class of financial and industrial interests and triggered a rise in rural and worker mobilization that would culminate in the Mexican Revolution. Popular notions of social justice involving land redistribution, state support for *ejidal* communities, workers rights, and rejection of both the sanctity of private property and the capitalist eco- nomic model have their origins here. This legacy increasingly frightened the propertied and middle classes, engendering reactionary sequences that put a stop to redistributive efforts during the Cárdenas and Echeverría administrations.

The leadership of the Revolution was taken over by members of the middle class from whom a new and powerful agricultural class arose—its prosperity and economic success closely linked to the highly successful economy to the north. Its control of the postrevolutionary governments from 1940 until the 1950s slowed and then reversed the land reform of the Cárdenas years, even in the face of mobilized peasant groups. After 1940, public policy discriminated against small and *ejidal* agriculture, and there was a marked bias in service provision toward urban areas, contributing to the poverty of indigenous communities in southern and central Mexico.

The political arrangements put in place by the postrevolutionary leadership were an integral component of the reactionary sequence that arose in response to the high level of mobilization of the Cárdenas years. Those institutional arrangements functioned to contain highly mobilized workers and peasants, effectively restraining dissent, thereby facilitating economic growth with only a slow reduction in poverty and an increase in inequality through the 1960s. These arrangements also ensured that welfare improvements were highly selective, benefiting only the most highly organized sectors of the working and middle class in urban areas and leaving out the majority of the population. Like Chile, the state was heavily permeated by entrepreneurs, producing an industrial sector that was not only uncompetitive but also unintegrated. However, Mexico was also burdened by the legacy of an industrial and agricultural structure that preferred capital-intensive to labor-intensive ones—an important employment-inhibiting ingredient of its economic model. Mexico's bureaucracy was also extremely politicized—part of the panoply of co-optative methods that contributed to the longevity of the PRI regime. Ministries and agencies of government were linked to societal clienteles whose interests blocked the development of economic and industrial policy with an overall vision.

In postrevolutionary Mexico, strong social forces engaged in sharp distributive struggles, involving disagreement on fundamental questions such as how agricultural production should be organized. The process of industrialization and urbanization did not soften social force conflicts. Indeed, divisions were reinforced over time and were further strengthened by the experience of the debt crisis and neoliberal reform, topics explored in Chapters 6 and 7.

5

Social Forces, States, and Distributive Outcomes

THE PREVIOUS THREE CHAPTERS argued that the relative strength of social forces, at various times through history, shaped differing poverty and equality outcomes. In Chile and Mexico, strong and conflictive social forces and weak states were responsible for less successful economic growth outcomes and poorer and more unequal social outcomes compared to South Korea. The critical conjunctures identified in Mexico and Chile generated reactive sequences that had the effect of blocking or reversing attempts at redistributive reform. In Korea, on the other hand, once the state carried out land reform, quiescent social forces allowed a strong state to lead a profarmer and employment-generating economic strategy that reduced poverty and kept inequality low. Inequality remained low in large part because South Korea's critical conjuncture generated a path-dependent sequence that triggered efforts to reduce inequality when it began to rise. In Chile and Mexico, weak states with social bases in propertied groups and in conservative middle classes slowed or defeated land reform and shaped the state pursuit of industrial strategies inadequate to the long-term goal of good social outcomes.

However, to explain fully the sharp compartmentalization of the Chilean and Mexican cases, on the one hand, and the greater integration and homogeneity of Korean society, on the other, it is helpful to combine the insights of the previous three chapters with a closer consideration of the timing and pace of events and with a consideration of the basic political economy realities that characterized the three cases. Doing so will illuminate *why* the Korean state has been able to keep inequality relatively low and steadily reduce poverty even as its economy and social structure were transformed. Compared with Chile and Mexico, Korea's historical trajectory was compressed. It was also an agricultural economy, bereft of important mineral deposits. These distinct attributes were important in contributing to the conditions facilitating state strength and societal commitment to equity. In addition, early and fast-paced modernization induced by Chile's mineral enclave status gave that country a variety of advantages that provided social outcomes superior to Mexico's by the 1950s and 1960s.

The Duration of Colonial Rule and the Formation of Social Categories

The historical legacies of colonial rule shaped critical conjunctures in powerful ways because the colonial experience established the preexisting settings for these conjunctures. The extent and nature of already identifiable social categories with differential access to resources, the degree of exploitive control over disadvantaged social categories, and the precise role of the colonial state in this process were all important in molding the ability of disadvantaged groups to mobilize for redistributive change once the critical conjuncture emerged. Colonial rule invariably involves the creation of sharp inequality between colonial rulers and subject population as it entails political subjugation for the purposes of economic exploitation. Colonial rule also involves the creation of inequality within the conquered population as rulers attempt to create a stratum of domestic collaborators. However, there are, as we shall see, important differences in how profound the impact of colonial rule is. The key difference in colonial rule that has been important in accounting for the distinct contextual conditions that ultimately shaped conjunctures and social outcomes in the three cases was its duration.

The Spanish conquest of the Americas and the colonial orders that subsequently emerged produced in their immediate aftermath searing social and economic inequalities. It was the length of the period of Spanish colonial rule in Chile and Mexico that was most salient in this process: It gave ample time for these original social categories to become established. Spanish colonial rule of Mexico and Chile lasted 300 years (1521–1821) and 277 years (1541–1818), respectively. In Mexico, the conquerors exploited indigenous populations ruthlessly, believing that their use of Indian labor came as a right of conquest. Colonial rule and subsequent racial intermingling eventually created a social hierarchy that involved a white

European–descended elite at the top, a large mixed-blood category in the middle, and an indigenous poor population in the rural areas of south central Mexico at the bottom. In Chile, the absence of a large indigenous population resulted in the emergence of a small white wealthy oligarchy and a mass of mixed-blood rural dwellers. In both of these cases, the Spanish conquerors imposed an elaborately detailed racial caste system that established discriminatory legal rights based on the percent of one's ancestry from the various racial groupings.[1] Independence from Spain did not signal the exit of the descendants of Spanish conquerors—their American-born descendants remained as the new ruling class and monopolized economic wealth and political power.

While independence marked an end to legal distinctions based on race, negative social attitudes toward mixed-blood and indigenous peoples remained firmly entrenched among white elites. High levels of asset inequality, most notably seen in the large *fundos* (Chile) and haciendas (Mexico), and widespread rural poverty coincided with race and were predominant features of postcolonial societies. This social compartmentalization encouraged the perpetuation of elite social attitudes, which saw the rural poor as inherently backward and lazy and unmotivated by wages—attitudes that fostered stereotypes and hindered empathy. Further, such attitudes, at the heart of the *inquilaje* labor system in Chile and debt peonage in Mexico, lingered well into the twentieth-century industrialization and modernization phases. The reinforcement of social compartmentalization over time contributed to the hardening of resistance to redistributive concessions and to the intensity of reactive sequences. In contrast, there is no evidence that Korea's postcolonial rulers held particularly negative attitudes toward the people they governed. Neither General Park nor his close cohorts ever saw the peasantry as a backward, ignorant class, antithetical to modernization and national development. In fact, one of the hopes behind Park's support of the peasantry (admittedly, not entirely realized) was that the peasantry would be an integral part of Korean modernization and that there would be a substantial improvement in their productivity.

In Korea, the much shorter duration of colonial rule made it impossible for that rule to engender the sort of social compartmentalization found in the two Latin American cases. Colonial rule lasted from 1910 to 1945, a mere thirty-five years. Further, the Japanese colonial rulers and landowners did not remain behind as the new ruling class once colonial rule ended but were expelled with their defeat in World War II. Like all colonizers, the Japanese denigrated the culture they conquered and, given their negative attitude toward things Korean, rigid social categories may well have emerged had colonial rule lasted longer than it did. However, history did not give colonial conquest sufficient opportunity to destroy the culture of the conquered people nor the time to create a hierarchy of distinct racial and social class categories. While Japanese conquest was most certainly devastating for Koreans, the threat it posed to Korean culture may have in fact solidified cultural unity and contributed to a more homogeneous society later on.[2]

This fundamental difference in colonial experience and its impact on social categories had implications for the struggle for land reform— that all-important equity-inducing transformation that marks the initial critical conjunctures. In Korea, a homogeneous peasantry, rendered more unified by the widespread loss of land in the face of the expansion of commercial agriculture under Japanese colonial rule, created such high levels of mobilization that land redistribution became irresistible. In the face of rising unrest, the Japanese colonial rulers virtually abandoned their support of landlordism, thereby weakening the landholding class. The nature of Korean landholding arrangements (scattered plots owned by absentee landlords), which prevented landowners from keeping peasants in thrall through the cultivation of dependent and subservient relationships, further facilitated mobilization and pressures for land redistribution.

In Chile, on the other hand, the postindependence expansion of commercial agriculture in central Chile occurred in a context of a rigid social hierarchy involving a white landowning political class and a mixed-blood peasant population. It resulted in the expansion of already large estates and increased the grip of criollo landowners over the mestizo peasantry. The political power of this landed oligarchy ensured state complicity in quelling any signs of rural unrest. From its earliest history, the Chilean rural labor force was, unlike the Korean one, extremely heterogeneous, divided among *minifundistas* (very small landowners), small and medium landowners (located in southern Chile), and the *inquilinos* and wage labor of the large estates of central Chile. Over the twentieth century, these divisions became sharply political ones, reflected in distinct visions of how the rural sector should be organized, hindering a unified peasant project of land reform. Under these circumstances, Chile's critical conjuncture, in which redistributive measures became a possibility, was delayed. The much slower development of peasant mobilization and the lack of unity around what form land reform should take were important obstacles to successful and thorough land redistribution.

In Mexico, as well, the expansion of commercial agriculture, beginning in the last quarter of the nineteenth century, reinforced the social categories created by colonial rule. The communal agriculturalists and small owners who were divested of their land and came to constitute a mass of landless rural dwellers were indigenous and mixed-blood peoples. While the process of land divestiture gave rise to peasant mobilization (the Mexican Revolution), as it did in Korea, the Mexican peasantry was deeply divided—even more so than in the Chilean case. Tillers were divided by their relationship to the land: There were small and medium individual property owners, communal (*ejidal*) landholders, and wage laborers. The peasantry was also divided ethnically between indigenous and mestizos (mixed-blood) rural dwellers. Profoundly different visions of landholding, originating early in Mexican history between indigenous notions of communal land, on the one hand, and private property, on the other, endured throughout most of the twentieth century. As in the Chilean case, lack of consensus over what form land reform should take compounded the difficulty of achieving it, a goal ultimately thwarted by the old and new postrevolutionary propertied groups.

Chile and Mexico: The Curse of Mineral Wealth

While intransigent propertied classes blocked land reform and showed little interest in redistributive measures generally, they were not the only obstacle to the achievement of better social outcomes in Chile and Mexico. The presence of mining enclaves, particularly foreign-owned ones, shaped social force configuration and the ideology that invigorated reactive sequences. The nineteenth century had witnessed the emergence of geographically isolated foreign-owned mining enclaves, especially in Chile but also in Mexico. As we saw, mining enclaves encouraged the emergence of intense anticapitalist and anti-imperialist ideologies among miners. The radical ideologies of miners contributed to the difficulty in obtaining redistributive compromises with propertied groups because these ideologies saw social injustice as rooted in the nature of the capitalist system and therefore rejected the very concept of private property. Chile's foreign-controlled mining enclaves, the motor of its economy in the early twentieth century, gave rise to an increasingly militant labor movement and a Marxist anti-imperialist ideology propagated by the left-wing parties seeking working-class support. Indeed, Chile's political left called for the eradication of capitalism and, as we saw in Chapter 3, once achieving power in 1970, engaged in large-scale expropriations of private property. The heavy foreign presence in Mexican mining shaped the development of the nationalistic bent of the Mexican Revolution and its militant anti-imperialist worker ideology. As in Chile, Mexico's foreign-owned mineral enclaves were the seat of worker radicalism, where unions fiercely challenged the concept of private property ownership, driving the nationalizations of resource and resource-related industries in the 1930s.

In Korea, on the other hand, the intense repression of the political left was instrumental in the eradication of leftist ideology. In addition, however, the division of North and South Korea, at the time of that country's critical conjuncture, removed permanently the material basis on which such ideologies could flourish because the mines and industry were located mostly in the North, leaving South Korea as a homogeneous grain-producing farming region. South Korea, as an agrarian-based economy, lacked the structural conditions that could feed into a radical working-class ideology. The South, of course, did retain intense ideological anticapitalist sentiments among the left-wing leadership, but these were roundly defeated by large doses of political repression. As we saw in Chapter 2, radical working-class ideas did not reemerge until the late 1970s when big firms in heavy industry brought together large numbers of workers in isolated regions of the country.

As detailed in Chapters 3 and 4, in Mexico and Chile, an initial phase of industrialization in the late nineteenth and early twentieth centuries was closely tied to mining development (Chile) and mining and commercial agricultural export development (Mexico). Industry grew up to support the new mining industry and to supply the mining communities and urban export centers with consumer goods. In both cases, these early industrial processes generated powerful industrialists who permeated the state and shaped highly protectionist industrial policies. Early mining development shaped other choices with redistributive consequences as well. Chile's initial success in achieving high levels of mineral exports was yet one more factor contributing to the unlikelihood of improvements in agriculture. Mining's foreign exchange earnings and revenue-generating capacity made it entirely feasible to allow unproductive large landholdings to continue and made greater state financial support for agricultural production less necessary.

In contrast, the fact that Korea was an agrarian-based, largely subsistence economy without preexisting strong propertied social forces with an interest in a particular industrialization model left the nature of its industrialization process undefined. As explained in Chapter 2, strong vested business interests did not permeate the state and mold the industrialization process in Korea. In addition, the absence of a lucrative exportable resource meant that Korea could not rely on a tax on resources for revenue. Hence, the state leadership was much more free to engage in export promotion while efficient tax collection, in the absence of a taxable resource, became a much more compelling priority.

This section has pointed to the importance of early history in shaping the nature of postcolonial societies. As argued in the preceding pages, in the Latin American cases, colonial rule bequeathed deep political and social inequalities, which coincided with racial and cultural differences. Nineteenth-century mineral enclave development further reinforced these differences. The prior creation of distinct social categories and mining enclave status shaped conflictual scenarios involving strong propertied interests, divided peasantries, and profound disagreements over property rights. These factors contributed not only to the possibility that the economically powerful would survive the critical conjuncture but also to the difficulty of reaching a redistributive compromise afterwards.

The following section examines the land reform and private property issues in greater depth. While the early timing and thoroughness of agrarian reform set Korea apart from Chile and Mexico, equally important was the nature of reform because differing visions of land reform affected the potential success of reform initiatives.

Land Reform: A Comparison of Its Timing, Thoroughness, and Nature

As the Korean case illustrates, having land redistribution occur early in the modernization process was crucial to ensuring a balance in the distribution of resources between rural and urban sectors—an important dimension of poverty and distributional outcome. If land redistribution occurs prior to or early in the industrialization phase, then the vested interests that might balk at resources flowing to the agricultural sector are considerably weaker. As we saw in the case of Korea, the early achievement of land reform also contributed to state strength because it eliminated the sort of ongoing destabilizing political conflicts over the land issue that characterized the two Latin American countries. The Korean state, initially unencumbered by a strong industrial and financial business class or by the urban working- and middle-class groups (in notable contrast to Mexico and Chile), was free to support the rural poor and pursue employment-generating industrial growth. It was therefore feasible and, indeed, politically necessary for the state to provide ongoing support to agriculture—where the majority of the population lived. Meanwhile, the weakness of the Korean propertied class meant that it could not block land reform and was malleable during the industrialization phase. This situation allowed the Korean political leadership a breathing space to establish an independent technobureaucracy and strong state institutions that could lead an employment-generating industrialization strategy.

On the other hand, in the absence of an early and thorough land reform in Chile and Mexico, pressure for land redistribution from mobilized peasants confronting powerful landed interests was ongoing throughout the twentieth century. The attempt to carry out land redistribution once industrialization was well under way confronted not just big landowners but also powerful industrial and financial business interests, who became strong allies of big landowners. Recall, also, that representatives of Chile's middle and working classes also made compromises with the oligarchy (under the Popular Front government) that consigned the peasantry to misery. As Chapter 4 documents, elements of the middle class formed the postrevolutionary leadership in Mexico, and both they and the organized working class gained a privileged position within the country's postrevolutionary authoritarian corporatist arrangements that marginalized the peasantry, particularly the indigenous rural poor in southern Mexico. Carrying forward reform, when leaderships were inspired to do so, in support of a smaller and politically weaker peasantry became enormously more difficult under these circumstances.[3] In the context of weak states, political leaders acceded to the demands landed and business interests and of well-organized working- and middle-class groups while they ignored the situation of rural dwellers who remained under the control of big landowners (Chile) or local political elites (Mexico). As industrialization progressed, neither well-organized middle classes nor working classes, who acquired privileged positions, had much interest in the plight of the rural poor.

The early occurrence of land reform in Korea, was not, however, its only noteworthy feature. Land redistribution benefited a much higher proportion of the peasantry and affected a considerably higher proportion of arable land in Korea than it did in Mexico and Chile. While in Korea 75 percent of rural households benefited from redistribution of 80 percent of the land, the corresponding figures for Chile and Mexico were much lower.[4] Furthermore, as we saw in Chapter 2, the Korean state's continued support for small farmers and the equitable expansion of education into rural areas in the decades following redistribution were crucial elements in the perpetuation of equality. Recall that equality in the countryside, a consequence of a thorough land redistribution program, meant that farmers made equitable use of the new opportunities and supports provided by the government.

In Mexico, not only did a smaller proportion of peasants benefit from land redistribution, but also support for the new beneficiaries of land reform lasted only briefly. As explained in Chapter 4, support for small and *ejido* farmers was abandoned in Mexico from 1940. In Chile, where land redistribution was delayed until the 1960s, a large class of small and medium-sized peasant producers (over one-half the agricultural labor force) was ignored by government policy both before and after land reform (see Chapter 3), and land redistribution in Chile between 1964 and 1973 benefited the smallest proportion of rural households—only 20 percent. The Chilean military government privatized the land redistributed under President Allende with a focus on the creation of a new class of agricultural capitalists. Small family farms between five and twenty BIH (basic irrigated hectares) declined. However, given the smaller and declining proportion of the Chilean population in agriculture, the impact of policy neglect of agriculture and the lateness of land reform had less devastating consequences for national poverty figures in Chile than in Mexico.

The fact of conflicting visions of the form of land redistribution made land redistribution an even more distant and unlikely achievement in Mexico and Chile and placed formidable obstacles in the way of the creation of a class of small farmers. Historically, official support for the creation of a class of small farmers had scant support in Chile. As we saw in Chapter 3, in the nineteenth century a radical liberal faction of the propertied class, which had advocated the breaking up of the big estates, was defeated, entrenching propertied-class commitment to the maintenance of the *fundo*. In the 1960s, even among members of the Chilean political center (the Christian Democrats), support for the creation of a small yeoman class of farmers lost out to supporters of communal agriculture, while the Popular Unity government, rejecting the very concept of private ownership, created state-owned farms. The fact that Chile's militant trade union movement also questioned the notion of private property further reinforced the deep schism over how agricultural production ought to be organized. The Chilean left's rejection of private property (demonstrated in nationalizations of private companies and the creation of cooperatives from land taken over from big landowners) was a key factor contributing to the growing fear of the business community and middle classes that led to the 1973 military coup in Chile and the reversal of decades of social gains.

In Mexico, a large portion of the rural peasantry remained committed to communal (*ejidal*) land holdings, a goal that motivated their support for the Mexican Revolution. Furthermore, leaders of the postrevolutionary Mexican state, although initially supportive of the creation of a class of small yeoman farmers, became increasingly opposed to land redistribution after 1940 and were particularly hostile to *ejidal* (communal) farms. In fact, Mexico's big agriculturalists and political elites came to see big commercial agricultural enterprises as the most efficient form of organization and as a more effective foreign exchange earner than smaller farms. Meanwhile, much of the peasantry struggled for communal landholdings for most of the twentieth century. However, reform attempts in this direction invariably elicited virulent reactions from powerful private sector interests (not just landed interests).

The institution of private property was clearly a much more contested concept in Mexico and Chile than it was in Korea, where there was a stronger societal consensus in support of private property. In the former cases, strongly mobilized demands for communal, cooperative, and state forms of land reform made redistributive compromises with strong propertied classes especially difficult.[5] Such popular aspirations caused fearful reactions on the part of the propertied groups and their middle-class allies, generating sharp reactive sequences. In Korea, on the other hand, private individual land ownership, the unambiguous aspiration of the Korean peasantry, could readily provide the foundation of a redistributive pact. The creation of a small farming yeoman class fit coherently with Korea's capitalist growth project, removing from the political scene conflict over property rights that could hamper capital accumulation, investment, and capitalist growth—in sharp contrast to the two Latin American cases.

Understanding divergent social outcomes in the three cases also requires a consideration of the attitudes and strategies of middle and working classes and their relationship to the state. In Chile and Mexico, where industrialization began much earlier, these groups were relatively large and politically important. In Korea, these groups were very small at the beginning of the industrialization drive (early 1960s) but substantial by the late 1970s. As we shall see in the following section, the pace of industrialization had important implications for issues of rural–urban equality, the continuing strength of the state, and public support (from the working and middle classes) for equality-enhancing measures.

The Length of the Industrialization Process

The weakness of powerful propertied interests was an important ingredient in Korea's successful land reform. However, other social groups, which became sizeable and constituted important allies in redistributive struggles, were important in keeping inequality low in the Korean case once modernization was underway. Even as middle- and working-class interests emerged quickly in South Korea, the state remained supportive of small farmers, of employment-generating economic growth, and of mitigating socioeconomic inequality as it began to increase in the 1970s. Unlike Mexico and Chile, attitudes of the political leadership, of the bureaucracy, of a faction of the working class, and especially of the middle class remained strongly supportive of measures to ensure socioeconomic equality. The fast pace of the industrialization process contributed to this outcome. In Chile and Mexico, on the other hand, industrialization was earlier, was more prolonged, and occurred within contexts of weak states. This process reinforced the social categories that had arisen with colonial rule and its aftermath. It reinforced working-class militancy and weak state capacity (faced with strong social forces) and engendered middle-class indifference to issues of inequality. In short, the extended period of modernization in the Chilean and Mexican cases had the effect of contributing to the force of reactionary sequences because it gave time for social compartmentalization to strengthen. In contributing to a lack of empathy for the poor on the part of other groups, particularly the middle class, prolonged modernization reduced knowledge and understanding of the poor, thereby making compromise on redistributive issues less likely.

Prior to its industrialization drive, South Korea's industrial development was well below the level of industrialization in Chile and Mexico.[6] In 1950, 79.4 percent of Korea's economically active population worked in agriculture (see Table A-7); in 1960, only 6.8 percent were employed in manufacturing (see Table A-8). In 1955, Korean manufacturing accounted for only 11.8 percent of GDP, compared with Mexico and Chile at 21.1 percent and 18.8 percent, respectively (see Table A-9). However, by 1980, the proportion of GDP accounted for by manufacturing in Korea had reached 27 percent, considerably ahead of Mexico and Chile, at 23.2 and 21.5 percent of GDP, respectively. Growth rates in Korea, low in the 1950s, were high from the mid-1960s through the 1980s (see Table A-5). By 1980, the proportion of the Korean economically active population employed in agriculture had dropped to 34 percent (see Table A-7). Rapid urbanization accompanied industrialization. At only 28 percent of the population in 1960, the urban population hit 57 percent by 1980 (U.N. Common Database).

These economic changes signified a profound change in the country's social structure. While the working class expanded, of particular importance was the rapid expansion of the middle class. Recall that, by 1980, it constituted 38.5 percent of the population. As Chapter 2 explained, most middle-class Koreans were first-generation entrants to the middle class, and the vast majority had peasant and working-class origins. This fact, in combination with their having gained their new middle-class status via educational achievement (an ingredient that apparently predisposed them to social criticism) (Arita 2003, 204), resulted in a great deal of middle-class sympathy for workers and farmers for many years to come. As detailed in Chapter 2, many among the middle class worked for both democracy and social justice from the 1970s, joining forces with a progressive faction of the working class. Moreover, given their recent middle-class origins, the Korean middle class remained tied to their poor rural kin in important ways not present in the two Latin American cases. The private financial transfers they made to poor relations had a significant redistributive impact, as such transfers accounted for an important proportion of poor family income (see Chapter 2). Equitable access to education for the rural poor and employment opportunities in the cities were essential ingredients that allowed rural migrants, having obtained employment in cities, to make the financial contributions that helped to mitigate rural hardship.

Both the Chilean and Mexican modernization and industrialization processes occurred over a much longer period, as illustrated in Table 5-1. Chilean industrialization spanned a period of at least sixty-five years, beginning with the expansion of industry and even greater growth of the service sector that occurred with mining development in the first quarter of the twentieth century. By 1910, 19.3 percent of the Chilean economically active population was employed in industry (including mining and construction)

TABLE 5-1.   Percentage of economically active population in industry and services: Mexico and Chile, 1910–1980.

Year	Mexico		Chile	
	Industry	Services	Industry	Services
1910	17.2	14.5	19.3	44.5
1930	15.0	14.6	23.0	41.9
1940	15.5	19.1	26.6	35.5
1950	15.9	25.7	29.0	37.9
1960	19.0	26.9	27.9	41.4
1965	21.6	32.0	30.1	41.5
1970	23.1	39.4	28.4	46.9
1980	29.0	Na	23.7	60.0

Sources: Data from: Mexico: 1910–1980: Solís, 1981, 196; Chile: 1910–1950: Mamalakis 1976, 176; 1960–1970: Castells 1974, 51; 1975, 1980: Frías and Ruiz-Tagle 1992, 66.

and 44.5 percent in services. In 1940, on the threshold of Chile's second phase of industrialization, industry (including manufacturing, construction and mining) already accounted for 26 percent of employment, and services 35.5 percent (see Table 5-1). The Chilean middle class had expanded rapidly with the expansion of the service sector during the first phase of industrialization and continued to expand with the second phase.

Recall (from Chapter 3) that while the Chilean middle class supported reformist parties in the first quarter of the twentieth century, it became increasingly conservative over time. As improved benefits for the middle class set its members further and further apart from the working class, it lost interest in social issues. By 1973, the middle class also felt increasingly threatened by the strength of the political left and its radical ideology and sided with the coup makers. Given the two-phased nature of industrialization and its extended period in Chile, intergenerational mobility into the middle class became unlikely after 1940. The inflow into the middle class after that date was not working class and certainly not peasant in origin but, rather, "shorn off segments of the bourgeoisie and their descendants" (Grant 1983, 165). Moreover, until the 1960s, when transportation routes began to expand, the middle class would have had little knowledge of life on the *fundos,* while mining communities, where worker militancy took root, were isolated and located far away from urban centers, in the north (nitrate, copper) and the south (coal).

Political polarization culminating in the 1973 military coup, after which social conditions deteriorated, marked the height of the country's increasingly intense social compartmentalization. The Chilean military, recruited from the lower middle class, had, unlike the Korean military, undergone decades of isolation from mainstream Chilean society. While in the 1920s the military felt that the government was not addressing pressing social concerns and identified with the new social groups that had emerged with Chile's first industrialization phase (Nunn 1970, 43),[7] by the 1970s it lacked both knowledge about, and sympathy for, the Chilean masses. Sharp social compartmentalization, born not of ethnic identity but of a drawn-out period of social isolation, became integral to distributive struggles and social outcomes. Chile became a "country of parallel subcultures that never touched" (Constable and Valenzuela 1991, 140).

Mexico also underwent an early, though less expansive, industrialization process. While the Mexican Revolution caused an important setback in industrial development (the proportion of the population employed in industry declined between 1910 and 1930) (look again at Table 5-1), employment in industry expanded rapidly between 1940 and 1970. This industrial growth produced a sizeable working class, while the country's middle class was considerably smaller than the cases of Korea or Chile, reaching only 13.4 percent of the population by 1980 (Gilbert 2007, 29). Early in Mexican history, workers and peasants had united in their struggle for social improvements.[8] However, from 1938 the official worker organization, the General Confederation of Labor (CTM), was prohibited by law from recruiting peasant organizations. Peasants were given their own official confederation. As in the case of Chile, the lack of sympathy of the Mexican middle class for the plight of the urban and rural poor[9] has its origins in the longer process of its formation. In Mexico, the small size and social and racial compartmentalization of the middle class made it an unlikely force for social change, especially change favoring the country's poorest groups.

As we saw in Chapter 4, Mexico's mestizo middle class gained a privileged position within the party and state apparatus. It was ethnically and geographically isolated from the country's rural indigenous poor of southern Mexico. In addition, the growing distance between it and most of the Mexican working class in terms of income and benefits spawned a lack of interest in social justice issues. As in the Chilean case, import substitution expansion brought very little upward social mobility from the working class into the middle class. According to Gilbert, most upward mobility did not cross the manual–nonmanual labor divide but largely involved movement among manual categories and among white-collar categories (2007, 30). The Mexican middle class, small in size, overwhelmingly mestizo, and many generations removed from rural roots, had little connection with, and generally scant concern for, the plight of peasants or workers. A social hierarchy that placed poor Indian peasants at the bottom, a mestizo working class and a small middle class in the middle, and Europeanized propertied elites at the top, remained firmly entrenched.

Meanwhile, Mexico's popular classes, particularly its rural poor, had developed strong and distinct collective identities of their own during their decades of organized action against the state. These struggles began with the Mexican Revolution, which saw workers fight for workers' rights and peasants struggle for land. For peasants, especially, struggles reemerged after 1940 when faced with the government's abandonment of support for small and *ejidal* agriculture. Hence, Zapata's revolutionary aspirations for a return of *ejidal* communal land lived on, to be invoked repeatedly in future struggles.[10] With this long history of exclusion, struggle, and repression, the Mexican peasantry, particularly indigenous people, developed an identity and opposition to the state that set it apart from the rest of Mexican society.

In Korea, an early and thorough land reform, combined with a fast-paced industrialization drive, ensured an equitable start to modernization and the state strength and social consensus to ensure that equitable growth and favorable social outcomes would continue. State control of trade unions through corporatist arrangements did not need to be supplemented by expensive and corrosive state patronage or special privileges in social security benefits. Because working- and middle-class groups were comparatively weak in the 1960s, state institutions could retain their largely developmental role and did not have to become agencies for the co-optation of working- and middle-class constituencies. Nor did business permeate the state in pursuit of its particular interests.

In contrast, in Mexico, the presence of strong social forces and the need to contain the most powerful among them contributed to the creation of elaborate mechanisms of political containment. Generous social security benefits formed part of the panoply of material incentives designed to maintain the support of the most powerful sectors of organized labor. The unequal impact of social security spending was less detrimental for Chile because by the mid-1970s social security reached over 70 percent of the economically active population. While Korea's formal social spending may have been low, it did not contribute to inequality, and, as explained in Chapter 2, the various government supports provided for the rural population contributed in important ways to poverty reduction. As illustrated in Table 2-1 (Chapter 2), for Korea potentially equalizing education expenditure outweighed the more unequalizing social security spending within formal social spending.[11] In the 1970s, Korean social security and welfare spending constituted less than 1 percent of GDP while it constituted over 3 percent for Mexico and rose from 6 to 9 percent in Chile (see Figure A-6). With weaker worker and middle classes, the Korean state was less subject to the same intense pressures for social security protection. It was also able to direct educational spending equitably between rural and urban areas, while poor educational services for rural dwellers in Mexico and Chile produced lagging rural literacy gains (see Table A-6).

Explaining Better Social Outcomes in Chile than in Mexico before 1973

Thus far, the analysis has compared Korea's success in poverty reduction and the maintenance of low inequality, with the obstacles faced by both Chile and Mexico in achieving such outcomes prior to 1980. However, Chile's better social progress, compared with Mexico during the period, requires an explanation. Relatively low poverty compared with Mexico is especially puzzling given Chile's growing economic problems in the 1950s and 1960s, including stagnant and slow economic growth rates. Chile's propertied interests, particularly landed interests, posed strong resistance to redistribution, particularly improvements for rural dwellers during this period. In addition, as already argued, the country's prolonged period of industrialization appears to have firmly solidified social compartmentalization by the early 1970s.[12]

Although, in general, mineral wealth contributed to social force configurations and industrialization patterns that tended to inhibit equitable outcomes, its very dynamism and early occurrence in the Chilean case created several advantages that produced better social outcomes than in Mexico in the 1950s and 1960s.[13] In Chile, the very success of mineral exports provided the government with revenue that it spent on social improvements. In addition, mineral development gave rise to new social forces—middle-class and working-class groups—which, in the context of electoral competition, were able to pressure for further employment opportunities and better social protection once import substitution was underway after 1940.[14]

Mexico, on the other hand, with a far less dynamic export economy, experienced a modernization process that not only generated less employment in industry and commerce but also divested peasants of their land. In the last part of the nineteenth century, the Mexican state was chronically short of resources, a situation that led to policies, such as land grants to foreign companies, which, in divesting peasants of their land, fueled revolutionary insurgency. Furthermore, the Mexican Revolution (1910–1917) represented a major setback in economic development given the destruction of infrastructure and industry that occurred. Meanwhile, social progress was slow as most government expenditures went into the military (Cortés Conde 2006, 219). Strong and contentious social forces emerged in the wake of the Mexican Revolution, forces that a competitive political system could not contain as it had for many decades in Chile. Hence, after 1940 the postrevolutionary leadership put a political arrangement in place to quell the dissent; had this party–state arrangement been less effective in containing unrest, popular pressure might have propelled more redistributive measures, wider social security protection, and changes in economic policy that could have generated more and better employment opportunities.

In Chile, revenue from mineral exports produced a tenfold increase in government revenues between 1869 and 1895, a development that had a multiplier effect on the rest of the economy. The state invested heavily in infrastructure and government services, particularly in the expansion of education in urban areas (Cortés Conde 2006, 211). Tax revenue as a percent of GDP stood at 12.8 percent in 1935 (Arellano 1985, 40), a level not achieved by Mexico until 1975 (see Table A-10). Expenditure on education increased from 9.7 percent of total government expenditures to 14 percent between 1905 and 1935 (30). By 1907, more than one-half of the Chilean population was literate. By 1930, 73 percent of the population was literate (24), a level not achieved by Mexico until 1970 (see Table A-6).

As we saw in Chapter 3, Chile underwent a rapid process of industrialization between the 1880s and the late 1920s. Indeed, between 1875 and 1907, the percent of the population living in urban centers increased from 27 percent of the population to 43 percent of the population (Godoy Urzúa 1971, 266; Arellano 1985, 24). In 1930, 65 percent of the economically active population in Chile was employed in industry and services, more than double that of Mexico at the time (look again at Table 5-1). For Chile, the rapid process of urban rural migration, and the decline in the agricultural labor force, meant that the focus of government-provided services on urban areas benefited an ever-increasing proportion of the population.

As noted, during the early period of modernization in Chile, middle-class-backed political parties pursued social improvements not just for the middle class but also for workers—although not for the rural poor. The pluralist nature of the Chilean political system was instrumental in allowing these new parties to gain ground. After 1940, pressure exerted by the leftist and centrist parties ensured the continued expansion of social welfare protection, particularly social security, to an ever-larger proportion of the economically active population. Expenditure on education, although focused on urban areas, was much higher than Mexico's.

The emergence of a competitive pluralist political system in Chile, was, however, very unusual in Latin America. Its origins and durability originate in the unity of the country's landholding and mining elite from the end of the nineteenth century. That elite was able to produce a viable conservative party, capable of winning elections.[15] The control that the landed elite exercised over the peasantry and the overrepresentation of rural constituencies in congress were important factors allowing the landed oligarchy to maintain political control. In short, the landed oligarchy tolerated competitive electoral politics because, for many decades, elections did not represent a threat to that political control (Remmer 1984, 71, 219). The oligarchy had no need to employ military intervention in the political process.[16]

Nor did the country's landed and mining elite have the need to construct the elaborate co-optative and clientelist methods that characterized the Mexican case. Although Chilean bureaucrats were often political appointees and acquiesced in the political swings of the day, the state, unlike the Mexican one, was not riddled throughout by clientelism. While an important employer of the middle class, the political leadership did not use the Chilean state as the central instrument of political co-optation that it was in the Mexican case. Hence, even though Chile did not produce an independent bureaucracy that would guide economic growth in the Korean manner, a bureaucratic enclave of expertise did emerge within CORFO, the state development bank.[17] The evolution of the Mexican state after 1940 was the most politicized of our three cases—a consequence of the very highly mobilized working-class and peasant social forces that the state had confronted in the immediate postrevolutionary period. Hence, in the case of Mexico, institutions established for development functions also had equally, and sometimes more important, political containment responsibilities. More so than either of the other two cases, the highly politicized nature of the Mexican state impeded the development of effective bureaucratic enclaves and the development of a coherent industrial policy.

By 1940, Chile had a considerable head start over Mexico. It had more industry, had more government resources, and was more urbanized, and its population was more literate. It had a competitive political system that was gradually allowing middle- and working-class groups the ability to influence policy and obtain greater social protection. After 1940, employment expansion in industry and services continued to occur in Chile, although that expansion was not as dynamic as that of the first industrialization period. However, by 1965, 30.1 percent of the economically active population was employed in industry (more than either South Korea or Mexico at the time) and 41.5 percent in services (look once more at Table 5-1), also more than either Mexico or Korea.

Chile's import substitution industrialization was better than Mexico's at generating employment and therefore better at keeping poverty down.[18] Chilean light consumer goods manufacturers had successfully obtained much higher levels of industrial protection than was the case for Mexico, a reality that protected employment in small employment-intensive activities. The presence of a very large service sector, particularly in the government sector, was an additional source of employment in Chile. Furthermore, the fact that Chilean landowners had been less enthusiastic about replacing labor with capital-intensive methods meant the absence of a large class of destitute landless laborers, and migration to the cities occurred at a pace more amenable to urban labor absorption. All of these factors produced a relatively higher level of formal employment in Chile compared with Mexico. This large formal employment and the fact that social security protection expanded to cover an ever-larger portion of the economically active population (a function, as noted, of the prior emergence of new middle-class and working groups and the country's pluralist political system) explain Chile's relatively better social welfare outcomes during the import substitution industrialization phase despite slow growth.

Conclusions

This chapter started from the premise that early historical features, colonial rule and natural resource endowment, shaped the social configuration that critical conjunctures would confront. Thereafter, the timing and pace of events reinforced path-dependent and reactive sequences. While the strength and resistance offered by landed and business elites was important in blocking redistributive measures in Mexico and Chile, and the weakness of Korea's landowners was important in allowing redistributive measures to go forward, the full story of the distinct outcomes of the three cases is not complete without a consideration of the attitudes and role of the working- and middle-class groups.[19] Their choice of political allies had profound consequences for state policies affecting poverty and distribution.

Korea's historical evolution has been described as "compressed." First, a much shorter colonial period, and the expulsion of the colonial occupiers, mitigated the creation of rigid social categories, contributing to peasant homogeneity and to the strength of mobilization demanding land redistribution. Secondly, land redistribution occurred extensively and prior to the onset of industrialization and set the stage for equitable growth, by creating a nation of equal and homogeneous small farmers. This reality contributed to public expectations that equality was the norm. The remarkably rapid process of modernization and industrialization that followed reinforced a path-dependent sequence that kept inequality low and reduced poverty quickly. While state institutions were able to operate relatively unencumbered by social force pressure for much of the period (until the 1970s), the new groups that arose from this modernization pro- cess, particularly a new middle class with recent rural origins, took actions and exerted pressure that kept inequality low.

Chile's and Mexico's statuses as mining enclaves (and Mexico's as an agricultural exporter) gave rise to an early industrialization process and the emergence of new middle- and working-class groups. By the middle of the twentieth century, the middle class (in Chile) and the middle class and the most privileged sectors working class (Mexico), long separated from rural roots, were uninterested in radical redistributive measures, in- cluding land reform. In general, these groups were not strong advocates of the expansion of social protection to the unprotected portion of the population either. In addition, profound disagreements on the nature of land redistribution, which included disagreement on the sanctity of pri- vate property, were also features of the Chilean and Mexican cases. Con- flicts over private property made distributive compromises very difficult and increased the intensity of reactive sequences.

The fact that Mexico and Chile had important mineral deposits that developed early in their histories shaped their industrialization process in important ways. Unlike the Korean case, industrialization was not open ended: It arose with production oriented to the consumer market and with vested interests (industrialists, workers, and middle-class groups) who strove to maintain the main feature of the model. Industrialists balked at reduction in protection, and workers and middle-class groups strove to maintain and expand employment, benefits, and wage levels. Chile's very dynamic early mineral export growth, however, produced high rates of economic growth and the presence of a unified mining and landed elite that supported a competitive electoral system. This situation allowed Chile's growing middle and working classes the opportunity to pressure for and obtain expanded social protection. Mexico's postrevolutionary leadership, on the other hand, was weaker and, faced with recalcitrant social forces, constructed a highly effective system of political containment that made it much more difficult for popular groups to demand improved social outcomes.

6

The 1980s and 1990s
Economic and Social Outcomes Diverge

IN THE DECADE OF THE 1980S, Korea pulled noticeably ahead of both Mexico and Chile. By 2000, Korea's gross national income per capita at $17,130, was almost double Mexico's ($8910) and Chile's ($8960) (see Figure A-2). In contrast, the debt crisis of the early 1980s devastated the Mexican and Chilean economies, and Mexico suffered additional shocks in 1986 and 1995. Poverty increased in Mexico from 32 percent of households in 1977 to 39 percent of households in 1989; then, with the 1995 peso crisis, poverty increased from 36 percent in 1994 to 52.9 percent by 1996, and inequality remained high through the 1980s and 1990s. Chile's economic difficulties of 1974–1975, combined with draconian structural adjustment followed by the debt crisis, resulted in an increase in poverty from 17 percent in 1970 to 39 percent by 1987. There was also a substantial increase in inequality with the Gini coefficient reaching a high of 0.56 by 1987 (see Tables A-1 and A-2). Beginning in the late 1980s, however, Chile began to make noticeable gains over Mexico in the area of poverty reduction. While Mexico and Chile had similar poverty levels in the late 1980s, by the year 2000, Chile's level of poverty was approximately one-half that of Mexico's (see Table A-1). The election of the center-left Concertación government in 1990 signaled a further decline in poverty for Chile.

Mexico's third critical conjuncture spanned the years 1980–1994, a period characterized by a turn toward radical neoliberalism. In Mexico, commitment to the market model, combined with a powerful propertied class and a legacy of weak popular social forces, produced a set of policies that exacerbated inequality and poverty. Chile's second critical conjuncture, which spanned the period from 1973 through the debt crisis, encompassed the failure of the radical market model so vigorously pursued by the Chicago boys, a consequent alteration in the social base of the state and an invigoration of state measures in support of export-led growth. A weakened trade union movement and civil society and a powerful private sector, combined with the legacy of authoritarian institutions, however, stalled adjustments that could have mitigated inequality.[1] Meanwhile, in Korea, strong popular forces, weaker propertied classes (compared with the two Latin American cases), and a continued central role for the state, bolstered by past successes, ensured continued growth with equity until the 1997 financial crisis hit.

From Military Rule to Electoral Democracy: Export-led Growth with Poverty Reduction in Chile

International circumstances were instrumental in exacerbating the depth of the economic crisis faced by Chile in the early 1980s. The country's terms of trade declined by 30 percent between 1981 and 1982 as copper, the most important export, dropped to its lowest price in a century (Edwards and Cox Edwards 1987, 196; Estategia 1994, 196). As world interest rates skyrocketed, Chile faced a sudden halt of capital inflow from abroad. In 1982, the country's foreign debt stood at 17.2 billion (U.S.), 80 percent of which was in the hands of its private sector. In 1983, the banking system collapsed, and the government took over nine key banks and financial houses. Between 1981 and 1984, the average GDP growth rate was negative, with a negative growth rate of 16 percent in 1982 alone (see Table A-5). By 1982, unemployment had risen to 26 percent, and real wages and salaries had dropped 40 percent (Foxley 1987, 16). Political repression and the loss of labor rights made it impossible for labor to defend its interests, contributing to the socially ruinous impact of the crisis. Economic and political inequality would be intractable legacies of the period of military rule.

As observed in Chapter 3, the country's powerful conglomerates were closely integrated with the Pinochet regime and were enthusiastic adherents of market liberalization, particularly financial liberalization. The removal of all restrictions on how much Chilean banks and firms could borrow had produced a binge of reckless foreign borrowing. Most of the debt had been acquired by the big conglomerates, with the country's two biggest (BHC and Cruzat-Larraín) by themselves accounting for over one-half of the country's external debt (Petras and Leiva 1994, 27). Meanwhile, export competitiveness was declining, in large part due to a fixed exchange rate policy, implemented from 1979 to help control inflation. A speedy government response, in the form of the devaluation of the country's currency, might have moderated the devastating impact of the crisis. However, the close alliance between the top technocratic policymakers and conglomerate executives, whose firms had become so highly indebted that devaluation would spell certain disaster, precluded such a move (Silva 1996, 155).

The 1981–1983 economic crisis triggered an important change in the entrepreneurial basis of the state and, in so doing, encouraged stronger state support for the new export economic strategy based on nontraditional agricultural exports. With the radical neoliberal economic model on the brink of disaster, the state now cast aside its close ties to a few conglomerates and incorporated a wider cross section of business interests into policy discussions (Silva 1996, 177). Under fierce criticism from the bulk of the private sector, the state now abandoned the radical neoliberal model, taking a more pragmatic and interventionist approach to economic policy. Hence, Fundación Chile, for example, a semipublic agency providing support for the export sector, initiated the cultivation of salmon in 1982 and engaged in the first commercial production of salmon in 1986–1987. By the 1990s, salmon had become one of Chile's major exports (Ffrench-Davis 2002, 148). PROCHILE (Program for the Support of Chilean Exports) stepped up its promotion of business associations engaged in developing new export activities. Such an association of firms was instrumental in the tomato and wine industries (Agosín 1999, 96; Pérez-Alemán 2000, 50). Expanding employment in nontraditional agriculture and related activities became the key element in poverty reduction as employment expansion in the fruit and vegetable industries expanded to reach 18.6 percent of industrial employment in 1985–1992 (Pérez-Alemán 2000, 42). Thousands of employment-generating enterprises arose to produce for the large agroindustrial export firms. The increase in international copper prices after 1987 was, however, also an important factor in Chile's economic recovery (Estrategia 1994, 141).

Employment generation, even after the return to civilian rule, was the primary reason for poverty reduction.[2] However, the jobs being created were usually low-paying precarious employment in the nontraditional food sector (especially fruit and vegetables), rather than in increasingly sophisticated manufactured goods. As rural labor unions declined, a consequence of both political repression and the replacement of full-time by temporary employment in the new export sectors, the rural poor became increasingly vulnerable and open to influence by both agriculturalists and the political right (Kurtz 2004, 149–150). There was a retrenchment in social spending, which declined sharply as a percentage of GDP and as a percentage of total public expenditures from 1982 (see Figures A-3 and A-7). However, the government did establish a temporary work program, a means-tested mother–infant program, and food programs for the very poorest. This increased attention to the welfare of the country's poorest 10 percent, however, was at the expense of the less and medium poor who saw their access to social expenditure drop and their living standards decline (Tironi 1988, 177).

Chile's political transition, a pacted one led by the leaders of the opposition political parties, was important in accounting for the fact that the government was not more successful in addressing inequality in the first decade after the return of civilian rule. Initially, widespread popular protest suggested a central role for civil society in the Chilean transition. However, by the end of 1986, the participation of the middle class in the protests was declining, and mobilization became dominated by the urban poor, especially the youth (Puryear 1994, 78, 80, 105). The regime increased the level of repression, especially against poor neighborhoods. At this point, the center-left party leaders advised civil society to desist from further efforts at mobilization and took over the transition, focusing attention on a campaign to drive Pinochet from power through winning a constitutionally mandated plebiscite that would require an election in 1989. By accepting the military government's constitution and timetable for transition, however, the opposition party leaders accepted a variety of institutional restrictions, including nine Pinochet-appointed senators, that constrained the government's ability to address poverty and inequality.

In addition to these formal institutional constraints, however, Chile lacked a strong national consensus on reducing inequality. A significant percentage of the Chilean public regarded socioeconomic inequality as acceptable. According to a public opinion survey carried out by the Fundación Ideas and the University of Chile in 2000, 47 percent of those surveyed believed that social inequality was necessary to the functioning of the economy, and 49 percent believed that people are poor because they make no effort to extricate themselves from poverty (Worthington 2003, 15).[3] Measures to enhance inequality also clashed with the interests of the country's powerful business community. Business representatives quit President Frei's National Commission for Overcoming Poverty, established to build a societywide consensus on how best to reduce poverty and inequality, because of its opposition to increased labor protection and measures to reduce inequality (Teichman 2009, 76).

The Concertación, an alliance of left-center parties that includes the Christian Democratic Party (PDC), the left-leaning Socialist Party (PS), and the Popular Party for Democracy (PPD), struggled to balance the conflicting pressures of the powerful private sector, on the one hand, and its popular electoral and party base, on the other.[4] It had been voted into power by a promise of "growth with equity," understood as the need to address the legacy of social needs bequeathed by the years of military rule. The rank and file of the leftist parties in the Concertación coalition pressed for strong measures to address social justice while a now-weakened trade union movement[5] demanded a revision of the military-designed labor code. During the early years of the return to civilian rule, the Concertación was especially concerned about business confidence. Hence, it instituted further trade liberalization and expanded privatization to include airlines, mining, electricity, and ports—this latter, a key business demand, was especially useful in increasing business confidence. The new civilian rulers also gave the private sector privileged access to the policy process through such mechanisms as working commissions on economic policy and monthly meetings with the head of the Central Bank (Silva 1996). Direct personal access to the president and cabinet ministers continued to be important as well (Teichman 2001, 92). The Concertación took care to assuage business fears that the return of civilian rule would produce fiscal disequilibrium by, among other things, maintaining a budget surplus every year until 1999 (see Figure A-8). However, the Concertación leadership itself had become supportive of the new economic model.[6] Hence, the administrations of Alywin and Frei remained cautious, at least until the last few years of the Frei administration, in social spending. Between 1990 and 1996, social spending as a percentage of GDP remained stable at between 12.0 and 12.8 percent. Only in 1998 did it begin to creep up, reaching 15.3 percent by 1999 (see Figure A-3). As a percentage of total government expenditures, social spending increased moderately (see Figure A-7).

Powerful path-dependent institutional legacies, arising from the period of military rule, were an important part of the story. Social spending was, in part, constrained due to the difficulty in securing tax increases. Opposition from the political right and business community, bolstered by the strength of the political right as a consequence of the appointed senators, inhibited the sort of tax reform the government saw as necessary to properly fund social programs. Faced with an alliance between the political right and the appointed senators, the government could not get its proposed tax reform passed by congress. It was therefore forced to negotiate its reform with the congressional right wing. The consequence was a tax reform that failed to provide a permanent increase in the corporate tax on profits from 10 to 20 percent. Instead, it provided for an increase in the tax on profits of 15 percent for a limited four-year period, and the regressive reform of an increase in the value-added tax from 16 to 18 percent (Boylan 1996, 9; Muñoz Gomá and Celedón 1996, 197).

The political right's control of congress also played a role in the defeat of the government-proposed revision of the labor code, a reform that labor regarded as necessary because the existing labor code undermined its inability to improve the living standards of workers. Labor conditions are particularly poor in the rural sector where, as one study shows, existing labor law, which outlaws collective bargaining and prohibits strikes by temporary workers (mostly women), locks in low wages and the lack of benefits. Owners in the fruit and vegetable export sector impose temporary work contracts even when full-time ones are warranted to avoid collective bargaining, with its troublesome negotiations and the possibility of strikes (Berg 2004, 59). For Kurtz (2004, 134), the very process of market economics in the Chilean countryside, involving community fragmentation due to out-migration to take up temporary employment without benefits, produced high levels of dependence and vulnerability and created almost insurmountable obstacles to collective action.

In the face of fierce resistance from business, the government carried out a timid reform in 1991, regarded by labor as woefully insufficient because of continued restrictions on collective bargaining above the firm level (Haagh 2002, 90). A more generous labor reform bill was proposed in 1995 but was blocked by the business community and by the political right in the senate, including opposition from the appointed senators. Despite strikes and demonstrations through the 1990s, along with growing criticisms from rank-and-file members of Concertación, particularly from members of the Socialist Party, a third attempt at reform in 1999 also failed in the face of stiff opposition from business and the political right.

The improvement of social conditions after 1990 occurred largely due to employment expansion and wage increases. Wages for low-skilled workers crept up because of government legislated minimum wage increases. In an effort to expand employment through stimulating economic growth, the Alywin and Frei administrations pursued a series of bilateral trade agreements. In addition, both administrations expanded support for that all-important employment-generating sector, small and medium-sized companies. One of CORFO's main functions became the financing of new small and medium-sized enterprises, especially for those wishing to enter export markets. In 1993, the government established a new program, "Projects of Promotion" (PROFOS), to promote exports in sectors such as textiles and footwear that the economic model of past decades had so adversely affected. By 1997, there were 305 PROFOS involving 3,400 small and medium-sized enterprises (Pérez-Alemán 2000, 49, 50).

However, while policies designed to support the expansion of small and medium-sized companies may have been responsible for some improvement in the country's manufactured-goods export profile, the change does not appear to have been substantial. Minerals, especially copper, and nontraditional agricultural products (the export strategy that had germinated within CORFO in the 1960s and came to fruition under military rule) continued to account for most of the value of exports. In 1996, mining accounted for 46 percent of the value of all exports (see Table A-13), while most exports classified as "industrial" were processed and semiprocessed agroforestry products. Meanwhile, between 1994 and 2000 the proportion of exports accounted for by small and medium-sized firms, which provided 77.3 percent of employment, dropped, settling at 3.94 percent in 2000 (Goldberg and Palladini 2008, 12). The Chilean economic structure remained highly concentrated; it continues to be characterized by the ownership of many firms by a small number of conglomerates or "groups." The second wave of privatization, occurring between 1985 and 1989, was instrumental in contributing to the pattern in concentrated ownership that continued after the return to civilian rule (Agosín and Pastén H. 2003, 2). Indeed, Chile emerges as the country with the highest degree of economic concentration of the three cases. In 1998, the largest business group controlled 23 percent of the total assets of all publicly traded corporations, up from 14 percent in 1994 (Lefort and Walker 2000, 18). In that same year, the ten largest groups controlled 70 percent of total assets (18). Through the 1990s, eighteen firms generated an estimated 60 percent of Chilean exports (Díaz 1997, 162).

Chilean civil society organizations were weak during the 1990–2000 period. This weakness stemmed from a variety of factors. With the return to civilian rule, many activists who had been involved in civil society organizations went to work for the political parties or for the government. In addition, international financial support for civil society organizations declined, and most civil society organizations became financially dependent on the government's Social Solidarity and Investment Fund (FOSIS). This financial dependence involved them in the delivery of government programs, thereby diverting attention from political issues and mobilization. At the same time, however, the Concertación leadership was resistant to civil society and labor involvement in policy. Given the experience with popular mobilization during the Popular Unity years and the severity of the reaction of those who felt most threatened, the leadership feared the destabilizing impact of pressures from below and was, therefore, predisposed to a closed policy process—including insulation from the rank and file of the alliance's constituent parties (Teichman 2009). A skewed policy access, which allowed business privileged access but tended to exclude other groups, was reflected in policy outcome: a vigorous pursuit of market liberalization and new markets, on the one hand, but slowness in addressing many of the concerns of labor, civil society, and the Concertación left on issues of equality and labor protection, on the other.

However, by the end of the decade of the 1990s, civil society organizations were becoming increasingly restive on the issue of the inequality of services. Health services were highly unequal, with the private health system offering the middle and upper classes significantly superior service. The private health system was also a drain on the public one insofar as individuals enrolled in the private system often used the public system if their private insurance did not cover a particular ailment or if there was no service close by. Additional pressure on the public system also occurred because it continued to provide care for the elderly, while the private system did not. The educational system also entails significant inequalities. Complaints about such issues were on the rise but would not have an impact on policy until after 2000 (the subject of Chapter 7).

The path-dependent processes triggered by Chile's second critical conjuncture, involving the social force configuration and institutional arrangements left behind by the military regime, weighed heavily on the new regime's ability to institute tax and labor reform and to address inequalities in social service provision. Heavily concentrated economic power, involving a business sector that expected past arrangements to continue, a weakened labor movement, and a weak civil society, were important ingredients in explaining the Concertación's approach in the first decade after the return to civilian rule. The political leadership itself was concerned about business confidence and fearful of political mobilization and so was reluctant to proceed more forcefully. It chose instead to pursue employment-expanding measures, which it did with some success, though not as successfully as the Korean case, as we shall see later in this chapter.

Mexico: Market Liberalization, Economic Crisis, Poverty and Inequality

As we saw at the close of Chapter 4, Mexico's plunge into economic crisis in the early 1980s was precipitated by the decline in the international price of petroleum, the country's main export commodity. The binge of foreign borrowing of the late 1970s and early 1980s produced a foreign debt of $84 billion (U.S.) by 1982. Economic growth was negative or stagnated through the 1980s as petroleum prices continued to slide and poverty increased (see Table A-1).[7] Hence, the years 1980–1994 involved a profound alteration in the structure of the state and in the governing alliance.

By the mid-1980s, Mexico's rulers enthusiastically embraced the market reform model. Two administrations, that of Miguel de la Madrid Hurtado (1983–1988) and Carlos Salinas de Gotari (1989–1994), oversaw the implementation of market-liberalizing reforms, while President Ernesto Zedillo (1995–2000) presided over the 1995 peso crisis and its aftermath. Beginning with President de la Madrid, the social base of the state shifted increasingly to the country's big conglomerates—the main beneficiaries of the market reform process, who now became close allies of the country's radical market reform technocrats. When the debt crisis hit, those technocrats in the upper echelons of the Finance Ministry and Central Bank, trained in economics (usually with graduate degrees from top-ranking U.S. universities) and with contacts in the multilateral lending institutions (the International Monetary Fund [IMF] and the World Bank), rose to predominance. Their expertise and contacts now seemed to make them indispensible to the process of debt negotiations and economic restructuring (Centeno 1999). As the country's economic difficulties continued into 1985, the de la Madrid administration completed trade liberalization while the Salinas administration carried out the major privatizations. The continuing economic deterioration through the

1980s reinforced the economic recommendations of these technocrats and discredited the old statist import substitution model.

Mexico's rulers were particularly preoccupied with cultivating the support of the private sector given that the 1982 bank nationalization had deeply alienated the country's bankers, as had a variety of issues including price controls, the rise in the public deficit, and the failure of the government to return the nationalized banking sector to private hands quickly enough. In his efforts to bring the private sector onto his side, President de la Madrid made the country's largest companies the main beneficiaries of his export promotion program, providing them with preferential credit and tax relief treatment (Heredia 1996, 249). In deals of questionable transparency, the big business interests closest to President Salinas became the purchasers of the privatized public companies with the consequence that, by 1992, the country's most important financial and industrial activities were in the hands of only four conglomerates (Teichman 1996, 187). Asset concentration (1991) among the top nine conglomerates remained high (although not as high as for Chile), accounting for 55.1 percent of the assets of publicly traded companies (Garrido 1998, 412). Big business became closely intertwined with the country's political elite, making enormous election campaign contributions to the PRI.[8]

Meanwhile, the country's economic reform program further marginalized the southern indigenous population. With the aim of stimulating investment and export competitiveness in the agricultural sector, the 1992 reform of Article 27 of the constitution declared the end of land redistribution and effectively put an end to the *ejido,* the collective landholdings of much of the country's peasantry.[9] This reform had a devastating psychological impact on the *ejiditarios,* who concluded that the PRI had abandoned them (Harvey 1998, 188; López Monjardin 1996, 444). Meanwhile, southern poverty deepened as the state withdrew technical assistance and marketing boards (such as the state coffee marketing board, INMECAFE). The state also eliminated guaranteed farm prices for all products except corn and beans and abolished protection for most agricultural products (Martínez and Fárber 1994). Several observers have linked the worsening situation of many indigenous communities in the south to the dismantling of state supports and protection for agricultural products (Harvey 1998, 177–183; Lustig 1998, 205, 209; Serrano 1997, 84).

At the same time, the retrenchment of already inadequate social protection also contributed to the socially devastating impact of the debt crisis and its aftermath. Social expenditures as a percent of GDP, already low in 1980 at 6.5, dropped to 5.6 percent by 1990 (see Figure A-3). The resumption of economic growth in the first half of the 1990s produced an improvement in social expenditures, but they remained low by international standards (Laurell 2003, 344). From 1985, many of those covered by social security, who lost their jobs with the economic crises and the subsequent structural reforms, lost what social protection they had and joined the ranks of the informal sector, which swelled during the difficult years of the 1980s (Cortés 2000, 38, 49; Lustig 1998, 78). While there were new targeted social programs, these could not compensate for the reduction in social support and expenditures and usually did not reach the poorest.[10] The agricultural support program, PROCAMPO (Program of Direct Support to Rural Areas), which provided subsidies to agricultural producers to compensate for the reduction in price supports, mainly benefited larger farmers having more than five hectares of land, while subsistence farmers with fewer than five hectares received only 8 percent of PROCAMPO payments (Corbacho and Schwartz 2002, 44). The program provided no benefits to the landless.

While Mexico's highly effective mechanisms of co-optation and control played an important role initially in ensuring popular quiescence (Middlebrook 1995, 277), the growing recognition that cooperation would no longer generate benefits caused rank-and-file workers and peasants to abandon support for official labor organizations and the PRI. In particular, the jettisoning of tariff protection on agricultural imports and the abandoning of other rural supports, combined with the privatization of the *ejido,* caused peasants to join independent peasant organizations and, particularly in the south, to join insurgent movements (Harvey 1998, 177–183). The 1985 earthquake, and the public perception that the government had failed to respond adequately, was especially important in triggering the emergence of civil society as a more independent social force. Meanwhile, the regime remained an authoritarian one. The PRI regime resorted to electoral fraud in the early 1980s and did not hesitate to use repression, including repression by the military, against labor unions that resisted massive layoffs, drastic revisions of labor contracts, and privatizations (Teichman 2001, 173).

Given that Mexico had regular elections, combined with the fact that the political leadership used electoral fraud to maintain power, the political transition became focused on the ability to remove the PRI from

power by electoral means. The large-scale electoral fraud that characterized the 1988 election was particularly important in invigorating the
pressure for clean elections.[11] Securing clean elections to defeat the PRI
became the driving goal of almost all opposition groups, including those
that had been primarily concerned about social issues. Hence, in the process of democratization, social issues became of secondary importance.

The lack of focus on social issues occurred despite the fact that the
new economic model embodied a package of policies that demonstrated
scant concern about social welfare. Public statements indicate that the
pursuit of free trade agreements, particularly the 1994 NAFTA with the
United States and Canada, was supposed to expand employment through
stimulating increased investment (*Mexico and NAFTA Report,* April 15,
1993, 4c). However, the government took little in the way of concrete action
to ensure that this would be the consequence. The leadership allowed no
role for small and medium-sized enterprises, the important employment-
producing sector, in the NAFTA negotiations, while it gave its big-business
allies the opportunity for ongoing direct input into free trade discussions
(Kleinberg 1999, 127–151; Thacker 2000, 162). Unlike Korea and Chile,
neither the administration of de la Madrid nor that of Carlos Salinas concerned itself with industrial policy.[12] In fact, there was a fundamental shift
toward the explicit abandonment of industrial policy because now even the
few sectoral programs that the country had were dropped, as were credit,
tax subsidies, and trade protection. Instead, the government favored the
streamlining of administrative procedures. The country's neoliberal technocrats assumed that economic growth and employment expansion would
follow on the heels of market reforms and the consequent trade and investment flows facilitated by NAFTA. Foreign investment (chiefly American)
would expand employment. However, foreign companies that engaged in
investment in Mexico sought to involve Mexico in only a single stage of
any given production process. Indeed, Mexico now pursued a foreign investment strategy that involved the separation of production processes and
integration of the Mexican economy with the American one through the
creation of cross-border productive chains.

The Mexican economy had barely resumed growth in the first half of
the 1990s (growth during that period averaged 1.9 percent per year) when
the peso crisis hit (see Table A-5). In 1995, the growth rate of real GDP
per capita declined by 8 percent, the biggest decline since 1932 (González
Gómez 1998, 52). Poverty shot up, and inequality remained high. Rural

poverty hit 62.8 percent of households in 1996 and was still high at 54.7 percent in 2000 (see Table A-1).

As in the Chilean crisis of the early 1980s, the tight integration between radical neoliberal technocratic policymakers and business conglomerates made the economic crisis worse than it needed to be. Financial liberalization had encouraged the newly privatized Mexican banks to borrow heavily in dollars to take advantage of lower interest rates and to lend out in pesos at higher rates. This aggressive lending produced a dramatic rise in nonperforming loans and a banking sector with a high level of bad debts. Meanwhile, appreciation of the peso not only harmed Mexican exports, but it also produced a rapid rise in the private sector's foreign debt (ISLA, March 1995, 53, 79; Feb. 1995, 39; July 21, 1994, 7). All of this rendered the Mexican economy highly vulnerable. Two political assassinations, including that of the PRI presidential candidate, combined with the insurgency in Chiapas (the latter related to the decline in support for agricultural producers), triggered a reversal in short-term capital inflows, precipitating growing pressure on the peso. Mexican officials resisted devaluation, in part due to pressure exerted on them by banking interests holding debt in dollars (Teichman 2001, 148–149). When devaluation finally occurred, the value of the peso dropped 50 percent against the dollar.

Like Salinas, President Zedillo integrated top businessmen into his policy team. The extent to which the big conglomerates continued to be favored by government policy, in a very personal way, is perhaps best illustrated by the bank rescue operation. Bankers each made separate deals with the government, with some, particularly those with closest links to the PRI, obtaining considerably more advantageous terms than others (López Obrador 1999, 32–34, 60). By 1996, the government had spent $16 billion (U.S.) to stave off the collapse of the banks (*Mexico and NAFTA Report,* June 13, 1996, 5).

Although the middle class had begun to abandon the PRI from the early 1980s, the 1995 peso crisis, given its devastating economic consequences for this group, was the crucial event in the shift of their support from the PRI to the center-right PAN (Gilbert 2007, 79, 94). As the middle class recovered from the 1995 crisis, the income gap between it and the popular classes began to increase. Hence, middle-class concerns were not social justice ones but involved demands for democratic freedoms, women's rights, the environment, and management of the economy (78, 83).

With the economic crash of 1995, sharp fissures became apparent over the issue of market reform, and the poverty issue became increasingly to the fore as an important problem, although it would not become front and center as a public issue until after 2000. Inequality, however, was scarcely mentioned. Social justice and redistributive issues remained largely confined to the leftist political party (the PRD, the Party of the Democratic Revolution) and a number of civil society organizations concerned specifically with poverty. While trade unions, for so long under the tutelage of the state, fiercely apposed market reform policies, they generally confined their concerns to wages, working conditions, and the maintenance of privileged social security benefits. Indeed, the increase in unemployment that came with the 1995 peso crisis encouraged labor quiescence (ISLA April 1995, 49).

The 1995 economic crisis once again made the containment of government spending a top priority among the political leadership. That leadership became particularly concerned about eliminating what it regarded as "waste" in social programming. Hence, an important redistributive shift now occurred in government spending, from the moderately to the extremely poor, with the removal of subsidies on basics consumed by the poor generally, such as corn and tortillas. The government transferred this subsidy, which mostly benefited the urban poor, to a new program, PROGRESA (Program of Education, Health and Food), designed to benefit the poorest rural dwellers in the south (Scott 2003, 27).[13] The new program identified the poorest families within poor communities, offering cash payments to female heads of households who brought their children regularly to health clinics and kept them in school.

Mexico's ongoing economic difficulties, which had produced a decline in employment and wages, also gave rise to increasing government interest in privatizing the country's two social security institutions (IMSS and ISSSTE) because these institutions were facing serious fiscal difficulties (Laurell 2003, 325). Mexico's technocratic market reformers perceived pension privatization, following the Chilean model, as a way to increase domestic savings. The government was also under pressure from the private sector, which demanded a reduction in social security contributions, claiming that such obligations were harming its ability to compete with Asian products (Dion 2006, 3). Due to stiff political resistance from the trade unions, however, the government was unable to reform the public sector social security system (the ISSSTE), managing, in 1997, to reform only the pension system overseen by IMSS, the institution providing social security to private sector workers.[14] This system was transformed to a defined contributory scheme operated by private sector pension funds (Retirement Fund Administrators, or AFORES). The reform displayed the major drawbacks of the Chilean privatized system: The transition costs to the federal government are high, estimated at 1 to 1.5 percent of GDP per year for six decades (Laurell 2003, 329). In addition, the new system has high administrative costs, and the qualification for pensions are more onerous. This means that fewer people would qualify, and pensions were likely to be lower—estimated at between 16 and 37 percent of a retiree's salary (Laurell 2003, 331).

Meanwhile, health care spending, low as a percentage of GDP (see Figure A-5) remained highly unequal. In the mid- to late 1990s, expenditure per capita on health in the social security system was 3.9 times that spent by the secretary of health for those without social security (Frenk et al. 2000, 351). A study carried out in the late 1990s found that 17 million people lived in rural areas with no health care unit (OECD 2005, 65). There are also sharp regional differences, with the southern poorest states spending considerably less than wealthier states.

Between 1982 and 2000, then, Mexico slid further behind Korea and Chile—in terms of economic growth rates, employment generation, and poverty levels. A thorough market reform program, pushed forward by radical technocratic reformers with powerful conglomerate allies, was pursued on the assumption that economic openness and foreign investment would result in steady economic growth and job creation. It did not. Mexico's past shaped these developments. The 1980–1994 critical conjuncture was characterized by an ongoing economic crisis that gave rise to a new powerful alliance. The economic crisis discredited the old statist economic model and opened the way for a new economic direction that would stand firmly against state activism in the economy. Meanwhile, authoritarian arrangements and a powerful business class shaped a market reform process that benefited the already rich and powerful and was particularly harmful to the rural indigenous poor of southern Mexico. The PRI's corporatist arrangements, though in decline, helped propel market reform forward. Those arrangements had left a legacy of a weak labor movement and a weak, though strengthening, civil society, unable to effectively challenge the new economic model.

South Korea: The Persistence of the Developmental State and Expansion of Social Protection

Like Chile and Mexico, South Korea had borrowed extensively on the international market. Its external debt, of $20.3 billion (U.S.) in 1979, surged to $46.7 billion by 1985, making it the fourth-largest debtor after Brazil, Mexico, and Argentina (Cooper 1994, 125; Woo 1991, 180). However, the debt crisis had far less devastating consequences for South Korea. Path-dependent processes were important in this result. A solid base for export-led economic growth, a continued relatively strong and effective role for the state, and a sound fiscal situation facilitated rapid recovery, job creation, and the expansion of resources to address poverty and inequality. International factors, however, reinforced this virtuous circle of events. The decline in the price of crude oil from 1985 (a factor that sent the Mexican economy into renewed crisis) and the depreciation of both the won and the Japanese yen stimulated exports (Kong 2000, 102).[15] The current account surplus arising from the country's export performance between 1985 and 1987 was important in ensuring the continued access to foreign loans (Collins 1994, 236; Haggard and Collins 1994, 100)—unlike Mexico and Chile, which faced severe foreign borrowing constraints once the international debt crisis hit.[16]

The Korean state played a crucial role in maintaining the country's export performance. The administration of Major General Chun Doo Hwan (1980–1987), brought to power by a military coup in a context of rising unrest, signed two standby agreements with the IMF covering the periods 1980–1982 and 1983–1985. However, these agreements did not signify a descent into recession, as they had for Mexico and Chile, but ushered in a prompt resumption of economic growth. Korean business interests, less powerful than their Latin counterparts and with more confidence in state intervention, stood aside as the political leadership took swift action to secure continued export-led growth. An immediate devaluation increased exports and ensured sufficient confidence to maintain foreign borrowing. The Chun government reorganized the heavy and chemical industrial sector through forcing private sector firms to merge to raise overall competitiveness (Jwa 2002, 23). Moreover, the bank privatization, initiated by the Chun government, kept the *chaebols* from controlling the privatized banks by restricting the size of minority stakes and by retaining the government or its agency as a major shareholder (An, Bae, and Ratti 2002, 5). Hence, the state continued to control decisions on policy loans and on who should receive credit. Although economic growth declined by 6 percent in 1980, it resumed in 1981, averaging 10 percent in the 1985–1989 period (see Table A-5). Strong economic growth continued until the 1997 crisis. While the resumption of economic growth in itself helped keep unemployment rates down, the government took additional measures to expand employment in

1984–1985. It increased credit to that important employment-producing sector so consistently ignored by the Mexican government—small and medium firms (Haggard and Collins, 1994, 93, 95).[17]

While the Chun regime was strongly antilabor, purging top labor leaders and restricting the right to strike, real wage rates dropped only 1 percent in 1981 but experienced a period of average annual increases of 10 percent per year thereafter (Koo 2007, 115; Kwon 1993, 84). In addition, the debt crisis coincided with an expansion in social programs. The erosion of regime legitimacy arising from a government massacre of workers in the city of Kwangju in southwestern Korea in 1980,[18] along with fear of the rise of independent unionism, prompted President Chun's announcement that his government would support the establishment of a Western-style welfare state (Gray 2008, 47; Kwon 1999, 3; Song and Hong 2005, 180). While economic difficulties at the time precluded such a goal, the government initiated new social programs and expanded existing ones. It placed some 1,600 community health practitioners in rural areas (Kwon 1993, 233), repeatedly increased the number of workers covered by the health insurance program, and, although there were some oscillations, after 1982 spending on health increased through the decade, both as a proportion of GDP and as a proportion of social expenditures (see Figure A-5 and Figure 2-1 in Chapter 2). The government followed the 1985 announcement of a national pension system and a minimum wage law with an expansion of the benefits provided under the public assistance program (Kwon 1999, 80, 85). Social spending at 4.6 percent of GDP in 1980 rose to 6.0 percent in 1982 before leveling off (see Figure A-3).

The public's perception of high levels of inequality produced a skyrocketing demand for measures to mitigate it (Kwon 1993, 36)—pressures that neither the military government nor the elected civilian governments that followed it could afford to ignore. These concerns were raised by activists among the country's large middle class, a class estimated at 45.7 percent of the population by 1990 (Arita 2003, 204),[19] and from an increasingly vociferous faction of the labor movement. By the 1980s, more than 3,000 students had taken up jobs in factories, mostly in medium-sized firms in major industrial centers, for the purpose of raising worker political consciousness and organizing union activity (Koo 2007, 113). By 1984, the middle-class prodemocracy movement had come together in the Council of Movement for People and Democracy, an organization integrating a variety of social movements.[20] The council called for a more independent national economy, social justice, and the reunification of Korea (S. Kim 2000, 83).

At the same time, as industrialization progressed through the 1980s, a radical faction within the labor movement (the precursor to the Korean Confederation of Trade Unions or KCTU),[21] based in small and medium-sized industry, emerged as a rival to the pro-state labor federation, the FKTU. Accounting for one-quarter to one-third of union membership, this new organization of trade unions called for a comprehensive and redistributive system of social welfare protection. It joined with the Council of Movement for People and Democracy and with other popular organizations (including peasants) to form a national movement for democracy. The prodemocracy opposition was also strongly anti-*chaebol*—indeed, all groups saw reining in the power of the *chaebol* as an important task of democratic government.

The years 1987 to 1993 marked South Korea's political transition. During this period, urban and rural unrest pushed the state toward both the election of the president and policies that would improve living standards. Widespread popular protest in 1987 compelled the government to agree to allow the election of the president in the upcoming presidential election. Highly competitive elections in 1988 brought Roh Tae-woo, a former army general, to the presidency (1988–1993).[22] The election was highly competitive, revolving around the promises of social reform (Kwon 1999, 128). Given the narrowness of his victory, combined with ongoing pressure from labor and civil society, Roh remained sensitive to public opinion, pursuing policies conducive to employment expansion and improved social welfare. The results of a national survey, carried out shortly after he took power, which showed respondents listing income inequality as their number-two concern after law and order, no doubt spurred his social agenda (Buzo 2002, 167). President Roh supported two sectors, either harmed or largely ignored by economic policy in our other two cases—farmers and small and medium-sized enterprises. Debt relief operations for farmers, begun in 1987, were increased (Kim and Mo 1999, 81). Among the support instruments provided to small and medium-sized enterprises were funds to assist in technological development and tax exemptions (Bąkiewicz 2008, 56). The share of employment accounted for by small and medium-sized enterprises increased from 49.6 percent to 69.2 percent of all enterprises between 1980 and 1996, while their proportion of exports increased from 31.2 percent to 41.8 percent (47). With pressure and agitation from the labor movement, wages improved at the average annual rate of 20 percent per year after 1987, while the minimum wage increased by over 25 percent in 1989 alone (Kim 1994, 209; Kwon 1993, 1984).

The Roh administration also expanded the coverage provided by both the national health scheme and the national pension program (Woo 2004, 77). Under pressure from civil society organizations and the progressive trade union movement, Roh took the first steps toward unifying the country's health care system. That system had begun to develop the kinds of inequalities characteristic of Mexico and Chile because of a 1981 amendment to the health insurance law that allowed for the establishment of separate health funds (Kwon 1993, 258; 1999, 93). By the late 1980s, there were some 400 separate health insurance funds. An attempt by the National Assembly to establish a National Health Fund that would allow financial transfers between funds was, however, vetoed by the president, due to strong opposition to financial unification from some sectors of the middle class, from the upper class, and from the conservative FKTU. The bill passed in 1990, but by stipulating that the merger would occur over a long period of time it effectively delayed the redistributive intent of the original bill (Kwon 1999, 66, 95).[23] Tax reforms were also progressive. In 1990, the government instituted a tax reform that lowered the tax rate for wage and salary owners and increased taxation on high-income groups by strengthening capital gains tax and implementing a new tax on excess land profits (Kim and Mo 1999, 81). Taxes increased as a proportion of GDP; by 2000 Korea was the most effective tax collector among our three cases and did not depend for those taxes on volatile mineral or petroleum prices (see Table A-10).[24]

The fact that top-level political leaders and most members of the bureaucracy were not themselves enthusiastic converts to radical economic liberalization in the 1980s was important in the avoidance of policies that might have deepened social hardship. South Korea thereby escaped the sharp ruptures that occurred in Chile and Mexico. While radical neoliberal technocrats rose to top-level positions with the debt crisis and had some influence early in the Chun years (Haggard and Collins 1994, 79, 91; Moon 1999, 6) their policy preferences were overridden by other technocrats and top policy makers, who were unwilling to allow major bankruptcies and layoffs and who were apparently unimpressed with the roller-coaster experience that had been Chile's (Kong 2000, 244–245). The Roh administration continued the trade liberalization, initiated under President Chun. However, unlike Mexico, both President Chun and President Roh resisted pressure for agricultural liberalization (Kong 2000, 134)—thereby protecting small farmers from certain bankruptcy and social hardship.

While economic liberalization of the Korean economy went forward under the administration of President Kim Young Sam (1993–1997), policies continued to be supplemented by efforts to stimulate employment expansion. Policies to stimulate industry included a new (1995) Capital Goods Industries Promotion Plan that aimed to promote high-value-added capital goods industry. Support for small and medium-sized enterprises, particularly those involved in exporting, saw a doubling of financial support in 1994 alone (Kim and Mo 1999, 81). Banks and secondary financial institutions were required to allocate 45 percent of their annual loan increases to small and medium-sized firms, while local banks were required to allocate 80 percent of loan increases to this sector (Mo and Moon 1999, 15). In 1996, the Kim government established the Agency for Small and Medium industry. In 1997, small and medium-sized industry accounted for 69 percent of employment and 42.9 percent of exports (Bąkiewicz 2008, 45). The government increased investment in research and development. The ratio of research and development to GDP increased from 2.0 percent in 1992 to 2.6 percent in 1997 (Mai 2006, 157, 159). In the face of increasingly restrictive international rules, the old direct export subsidies (loans, tax benefits) were replaced by indirect measures to stimulate exports such as the Export Insurance Fund and duty drawback, measures that did not contravene WTO and OECD guidelines (Mai 2006, 159, 162, 164).

By the mid-1990s, the growing strength of social forces, particularly of the *chaebols,* was apparent. Although by 1995, the top ten *chaebols* accounted for 39.5 percent of assets, the concentration of ownership remained below that of the two Latin American cases (You 2005, 32). The fact that the *chaebols'* collective economic leverage was considerably less than in the two Latin American cases meant that the collective pressure they could put on the government was less. However, it is also the case that the greater legitimacy of state intervention, a consequence of its success, also accounts for the ability of the state to maintain its economic leadership role. Nevertheless, by the mid-1990s, the *chaebols'* increasing influence was apparent. Government favoritism toward the *chaebol* may even have become more nefarious during the Kim Young-Sam years as subsidies to these big businesses were increasingly given on the basis of personal connections rather than on the basis of successful performance (Kong 2000, 212). Under pressure from the *chaebols,* who argued that the high cost of labor was rendering them uncompetitive, the state began to take steps to secure greater labor flexibilization.[25] In 1996, the government established a Tripartite Committee to secure business and labor agreement on reform of the labor laws. Agreement proved impossible as business opposed the unions' demand for termination of restrictions on union activity. When the government attempted to push its own bill through the National Assembly, the labor movement responded with a massive general strike. Although blocked momentarily, the bill would be resurrected once the 1997 financial collapse hit.[26]

Nevertheless, there were gains in the expansion of social protection as a consequence of the heavy lobbying by the KCTU and civil society organizations (Gray 2008, 92; Woo 2004, 87). The government expanded the national pension plan to cover farmers (Song and Hong 2005, 186) and, in 1995, introduced unemployment insurance to cover full-time workers in companies with thirty or more employees (Moon and Yang 2002, 145).[27] We see a marked expansion in state expenditure on social programs: Between 1992 and 1997 social expenditures increased as a percent of GDP and as a proportion of total spending (see Figures A-3 and A-7). However, probably the most extensive improvement in social welfare provisioning in the 1990s occurred with the expansion of company welfare, an expansion that the state was responsible for given that it provided corporate tax concessions and subsidies in exchange for company welfare (Woo 2004, 82).[28] Indeed, the importance of extragovernmental welfare support is indicated by the fact that when all extrastate expenditures are taken into consideration (household purchases of education and health services, enterprise welfare, and private transfer between households), the proportion of social spending of GDP in 1997 reached 22.4 percent (Gough 2004, 179). Family income transfers appear to have been particularly important. There is some disagreement as to how much family income transfers contributed to poverty reduction and the mitigation of inequality. However, there is a consensus in the literature that, during the 1980s and 1990s, private transfers between upwardly mobile members of the middle class and poorer kin were more effective than state social programs in achieving poverty reduction and low inequality (Kim 2002; Kim and Son, 1995; Son 1999).

The 1997 Korean financial crisis had many of the ingredients of the earlier Latin crises. Although triggered by the Thai financial crisis that produced a sudden reversal of capital flows, the Korean crisis was closely linked to the *chaebols'* excessive borrowing from foreign banks made possible due to financial liberalization (Gray 2008, 39; Kim and Park 2006, 439). Within a year of the crisis, ten banks and 284 financial institutions closed (Kim and Park 2006, 439). The year 1998 saw a negative growth rate of 9 percent per capita and a threefold increase of the poverty rate (see Table A-1). The crisis allowed the IMF and domestic technocrats unprecedented influence and opened the way for market reform and labor flexibilization.[29] The country, however, recovered quickly. By 2000–2003, economic growth had returned, and unemployment was at an acceptable 3.5 percent (Kim and Park 2006, 443).

Conclusions

In the 1980s, the three countries began to diverge significantly, but this divergence was heavily shaped by much earlier political and economic developments and institutional legacies. In Mexico and Chile, the debt crisis of the early 1980s hit hard and occurred in contexts of preexisting high levels of socioeconomic inequality. In Chile, the dramatic failure of the radical neoliberal model in the early 1980s precipitated a change in the social base of the military regime. The regime abandoned its tight alliance with the conglomerates and incorporated a broader cross section of business interests, opening the way for a resurgence of state economic activism (a defeated alternative that had survived within the Chilean bureaucracy),[30] which produced employment-generating export-led growth in nontraditional agricultural products.

In Chile, the continuing power of the business sector and the comparative weakness of labor and civil society groups in a context of a particularly authoritarian military regime were important factors in accounting for the deepening of inequality and poverty during that period. The high concentration of ownership in a few economic groups and the critical importance of these groups in the export-led growth model meant that the government felt it had to pay close attention to the wishes of the most powerful business interests and resist pressures from labor and civil society that business interests might not favor. The legacy of Chile's second critical conjuncture (1973–1983) meant that reducing inequality in the 1990s was a particularly difficult challenge for the civilian government that took power in 1990. The pacted nature of the country's political transition produced an institutional legacy that bolstered the power of the political right. Hence, the Concertación pursued poverty reduction by means of state-stimulated, employment-generating export-led economic growth. However, the leadership itself believed in the neoliberal model and, given its commitment to the maintenance of business confidence, was reluctant to move forcefully on issues such as labor reform. Aspirations among civil society and labor groups for greater equality persisted, however, and produced demands that would require redress after 2000.

In the 1980s and 1990s, Mexico's technocrats were enthusiastic adherents of a radical market reform program—and continued this adherence even in the face of the 1995 crisis. The failure of the import substitution model and the petroleum export strategy discredited these forms of state-led growth and opened the way for the technocratic proponents of the new neoliberal model to push forward their economic vision. With the reform process triggering the dismantling of the old corporatist and clientelist mechanisms of PRI control, the radical reform technocrats now allied with the country's powerful conglomerates.

Mexico's conglomerates became the major beneficiaries of economic reform. Their economic importance no doubt gave them considerable leverage as the country's technocratic reformers sought out companies with export potential. However, additional factors included the private sector's history of sanctioning policies it did not like through capital flight, an action that had particularly reprehensible consequences for economic growth. The country's market reform regimes, therefore, took care to court conglomerate support for market reform policies. More importantly, perhaps, and in sharp contrast to the Korean case, state interventionist policies were widely viewed as having failed. The fact that the very notion of state action in the economy suffered a profound loss of legitimacy in the Mexican case further strengthened the power of the conglomerates.

At the same time, however, powerful path-dependent processes in industrial development continued to be at work in the Mexican case. Like past economic schemes (import substitution and petroleum export growth), Mexico's market reform model lacked a domestic industrial strategy capable of generating adequate employment generation. While the failure of industry to generate sufficient employment has long historical roots, with the signing of NAFTA that problem now acquired new, modern features that involved the incorporation of Mexican firms into international production chains. Alongside these economic difficulties, there was retrenchment in already inadequate social protection system and the turn to more targeted programs that involved a shift of resources from the moderately poor to the extremely poor.

With a political transition concerned primarily with ousting the PRI from power through the electoral process, consideration of social issues was not a primary concern during this period. Moreover, neither labor nor civil society was capable of securing a political commitment to improved social welfare. The Mexican labor movement, so long under state tutelage, was further weakened by the market reform process, a process characterized by both repression and large-scale layoffs. Civil society organizations, now just beginning to emerge, were weak. The country's small middle class demonstrated little interest in social issues, and many of its members moved over to the opposition PAN with the 1995 economic crisis. As the country with the highest level of preexisting poverty, along with lower educational achievements, Mexico's repeated economic crises had a severe social impact. In the absence of sufficient employment generation, poverty reduction was slower and reversed when economic crisis hit. Those on the edge of poverty, with the least assets (such as education), were in the worst position to defend themselves and so fell into poverty. The most disadvantaged group continued to be the southern rural indigenous population.

Korea faced the debt crisis of the early 1980s with a set of features that enabled it to recover quickly without a sustained increase in poverty or inequality. Powerful path-dependent processes stemming from earlier historical experience played a central role in shaping outcome. The success of Korea's past export-led growth secured the legitimacy of an activist state among policymakers, the *chaebols,* and the public. Even though the power of the *chaebols* increased relative to the state, the Korean state remained considerably more powerful than its Chilean and Mexican counterparts, as illustrated by the restructuring measures it was able to carry out in the wake of the economic crisis of the early 1980s. The state continued to successfully pursue a variety of measures to stimulate export-led economic growth, and many government bureaucrats remained skeptical of economic liberalization, which the country pursued only gradually. The state paid particular attention to the support of employment-generating small and medium-sized enterprises. In response to intense pressure from a fraction of labor and civil society, the Korean state also began to expand its social programs, introducing new ones and expanding existing ones. Civil society organizations, drawn to a considerable extent from the country's large middle class, in alliance with a progressive sector of the labor movement, were much stronger than in the other two cases and were important actors in pushing the state in this direction.

7

Social Conditions and Welfare Regimes in the Twenty-First Century

SINCE 2000, THE WELFARE REGIMES and economic strategies of our three cases have continued to diverge despite the fact that the pressures of economic globalization have created some important similarities in labor markets. Although the South Korean state has weakened, it continues to play an important role in employment-producing economic growth, and the country has continued to move formally, at least, toward the development of a welfare state where the main policy instruments for modifying income distribution are taxes and income transfers. Chile's export-led growth has continued to be the main factor in poverty reduction while the role of social programs continues to be less important.[1] Inequality finally began to fall from 2003, and there have been improvements in unequal social service arrangements. Mexico's economic growth is the most sluggish of our three cases, averaging only 1.8 percent per year between 2000 and 2009 (see Table A-5). While poverty in Mexico declined between 2000 and 2005, it increased by 3.3 percent after 2006. Inequality remains high and is comparable to that of Chile's (see Tables A-1 and A-2). Meanwhile, Mexico's welfare regime remains heavily segmented.

In all cases, social forces have continued to be important in shaping distinct social welfare regime outcomes. In Chile, the path-dependent legacies of military rule, arising from that country's second poverty and inequality-inducing critical conjuncture, have waned while civil society mobilization propelled measures bringing about greater equality in service provision. In Mexico, on the other hand, path-dependent processes (an unintegrated and capital-intensive industrial structure, the legacies of PRI rule, and the neoliberal transformation of the 1982–1994 period) arising from all three critical conjunctures continued to block more equitable outcomes and greater success at poverty reduction. In South Korea, powerful path-dependent processes were responsible for the continuing important, although eroding, role of the state and for the ongoing concern of civil society groups, particularly those of the middle class, for social protection.

Despite these important differences, however, by 2000 labor market flexibility, present in all three cases, was an important ingredient in labor precariousness, inequality, and lack of social protection. Contrary to its early proponents, evidence that labor flexibility would have a positive impact through, for example, employment stimulation is sparse. A 1999 OECD (Organisation for Economic Co-operation and Development) study concluded that employment protection legislation had little or no effect on overall unemployment (1999, 88). In addition to employment generation, the pursuit of labor flexibility in Latin America also stemmed from a belief that greater equality would result from changes in legislation ending the expensive privileges of the formal labor sector in labor protection (Marshall and Adams 1994, 168). However, a mounting body of literature has associated labor flexibility with increasing labor market inequality, wage deterioration, increased job insecurity, and the loss of health, pension, and other benefits on the part of those who lose the standard protective features of formal employment. Indeed, particularly when it has been part of a broader restructuring process, as is the case for the three countries considered in this study, observers have linked labor flexibility to high social costs (Atunes 2000; Standing 1999, 181, 187). Although failure to fully address the social costs of labor flexibility characterized all three cases, there were important differences in the extent to which governments have moved to address negative social outcomes.

South Korea: Adapting to Globalization and Moving toward the Welfare State?

While the 1997 crisis did produce an increase of poverty and inequality, South Korea's economic recovery was widely regarded as remarkable. Its average annual growth rates have been the highest of our three cases—averaging 4 percent since the year 2000 (see Table A-5). Korea remains leagues ahead in terms of equality, poverty levels, and employment. Nevertheless, the financial crisis did accelerate the process of neoliberal transformation. While the Korean state pursued social welfare measures with even greater vigor after 1997, a number of observers have pointed to a deterioration of social conditions not fully compensated for by the new social programs. The proliferation of nonstandard or irregular employment—meaning the increasing proportion of the labor force accounted for by temporary, short-term contract, and daily workers—has produced a powerful challenge to equitable social welfare provision.

South Korea's dual transition, democratization (including demands for social justice), and gradual neoliberal reforms produced contradictory tendencies. While civil society and labor organizations secured greater freedom politically, market reform resulted in the *chaebols* gaining ever-greater market power. This increased market power rendered the *chaebols* more independent of the state—and signified a weakening of the state's ability to mold their behavior. However, the continued operation of powerful path-dependent processes mitigated the potentially long-term socially harmful impact of the 1997 economic crisis. Already established export capacity provided a basis on which future export success could be built while civil society activism continued to be a driving force, pressing the regime to expand social protection.[2]

The 1997 financial crisis now catapulted to prominence Korea's highly educated neoliberal technocrats, who, like their Mexican and Chilean counterparts, blamed their country's economic difficulties on interventionist state practices (Amsden 1994; Choi 1996; Lim and Jang 2006, 446). The fact that Korea signed an agreement with the IMF, which stipulated a restrictive monetary policy, the removal of the ceiling on foreign investment, trade liberalization, deregulation, privatization, labor flexibilization, and a close watch on public spending to reduce the deficit, reinforced their policy prescriptions. However, the fact that Korea's most profound economic crisis occurred in the late 1990s, and not in the early 1980s, buttressed domestic pressure for increased social protection because by this time there was widespread recognition, including among officials of the IMF and the World Bank, of the importance of social protection during times of economic adjustment. Indeed, in their negotiations with Korean authorities multilateral officials were attentive to social welfare issues, even relaxing their conditionalities on fiscal austerity to ensure that social welfare was addressed (Moon and Yang 2002, 154).

While market reform went forward after 1997, the state continued to have an important economic role stimulating exports in employment-generating sectors. The government of President Kim Dae Jung (1998–2003) now resolved to give even greater support to the small and medium-sized enterprise sector (Bąkiewicz 2008, 61). His administration established a number of programs for the sector, including an export promotion fund of half a billion U.S. dollars to, among other things, help small and medium-sized enterprises with the development of technology and marketing. In addition, the government selected ten new industries to target for government support to lead economic growth while it continued to support, largely through the provision of infrastructure, the information technology industry (Chun 2008, 13, 14). Hence, after 2000, exports expanded in high value-added sectors, particularly telecommunications, sound recording, reproducing apparatus, and equipment (see Table A-12). By 2006, small and medium-sized manufacturing firms (defined as firms with 300 or fewer employees) accounted for 87.5 percent of employment in manufacturing and continued to retain an important, though declining share of exports—at 35.6 percent in 2004 (Bąkiewicz 2008, 47).

The immediate impact of the 1997 financial crisis was the discrediting of the *chaebols,* whom the Korean public blamed for the crisis (Kong 2000, 222). Hence, in the immediate aftermath of the crisis the government took decisive measures to improve industrial efficiency, such as requiring *chaebols* to concentrate on core industries. The government also passed regulations obliging *chaebols* to sell unproductive firms and to reduce the debt ratio of firms (Song and Hong 2005, 194). However, the increasing power of the *chaebols* was now evident in their ability to resist state directives. *Chaebols,* for example, transferred key industries within rather than outside of the conglomerate to circumvent the directive to divest from noncore activities (Kong 2000, 230). The government's attempt to strengthen measures restricting intra-*chaebol* industrial investment confronted the emergence of complex conglomerate governance structures involving in-house financial institutions, which made it possible to evade such restrictions (Lee 2008, 443).

The *chaebols'* support for labor flexibility increased with the financial crisis (Lim and Jang 2006, 447). The fact that labor reform was one of the conditions that the IMF included in its bailout loans bolstered their demand for this reform (Kim and Park 2006, 439). Hence, for the second time, the government brought together labor (both the independent KCTU and the progovernment FKTU) and business leaders in what would now turn out to be a successful attempt to reach a consensus on reform through a Tripartite Council. The 1998 agreement, the Tripartite Accord, called for the introduction of labor flexibility, including the immediate introduction of layoffs. In exchange, however, the government guaranteed the expansion of social welfare programs. It promised to ease eligibility requirements and to extend the duration for unemployment insurance payments, to expand unemployment insurance coverage to firms with fewer than five employees and to temporary and part-time workers, to expand health insurance coverage, to financially integrate health funds into one system, and to provide more job training and more jobs in the public sector. In addition, the agreement gave teachers and civil servants the right to establish trade unions, and it allowed trade unionists to engage in political activities (Gray 2008, 133, 233; Koo 2007, 124; Woo 2004, 105). While the KCTU, faced with the rejection of the accord by its rank and file, withdrew, the agreement held.

The agreement weakened labor. The government declared most strikes after 1998 illegal and frequently used the policy to dissolve strike activity (Kalinowksi 2008, 6). While in theory the new agreement promised to strengthen labor because it gave it the right to engage in political activities, it weakened labor's ability to exact concessions because firms now had the right to replace striking workers. Most importantly, the labor flexibilization agreement produced a rapid rise in irregular employment because it allowed layoffs due to "urgent managerial needs." Firms were now able to reduce costs by laying off highly paid workers and by hiring cheaper and more easily dismissible new employees. Hence, the rapid decline in unemployment following the 1997 crisis was achieved largely through this increase in nonstandard or irregular employment contracts (Kim and Park 2006, 443). By 2002, irregular employment reached an estimated 58.4 percent of the labor force, declining to 47.6 percent by 2006 (Kim and Park 2006, 444; Shin 2008b, 73). Over 60 percent of irregular workers are now women who earn approximately one-half of what men earn, and most are not covered by the social welfare protection (Kim and Park 2006, 444–447). Therefore, while poverty declined between 1998 and 2003, short-term and precarious employment now came to characterize a growing proportion of the workforce.

Even as neoliberal economic reforms created greater vulnerability, civil society and the progressive wing of the labor movement mobilized to push the government to expand social welfare. President Kim Dae Jung (1998–2003), whose main base of support was in the lower middle and working classes, was a supporter of participatory politics, and, while head of the opposition party, he had formed an alliance with civil society organizations. His government provided civil society organizations with grants, and his openness to their participation in social policy resulted in an increase in their role and impact (Lee 2005, 1; Lim and Jang 2006, 449). Probably the most important of the civil society organizations pressuring the government for social welfare expansion in this period was the PSPD, People's Solidarity for Participatory Democracy (Chun 2008, 42), a coalition of hundreds of civil society organizations.[3] For the PSPD the notions of participatory democracy and social justice, defined as a "decent life" for "hardworking people," were indistinguishable (PSPD 2008). Meanwhile, the KCTU became an ever-stronger advocate for social justice, demanding the expansion of unemployment insurance and pension coverage, the financial unification of the health care system, the protection of irregular and independent workers, and a general increase in social welfare spending (Gray 2008, 133). The KCTU also attempted to organize temporary workers and the unemployed (Koo 2007, 127).

Civil society groups and the KCTU faced tough opposition from the Ministry of Finance and Economy, various business federations, the conservative labor federation, the FKTU, and some middle-class civil society organizations. These groups favored a fragmented private–public pension arrangement in line with World Bank recommendations and closer to the Chilean model.[4] They also supported the continued separate financial operation of health care funds rather than their unification. Business leaders and government officials were concerned about the impact on the fiscal health of the state (Woo 2004, 111). However, as detailed in the following discussion, with the support of officials in the Ministry of Health and Welfare, the progressive vision of welfare reform won out despite the fact that the World Bank was pressuring Korean authorities for a Chilean-type pension and health care reform (Moon and Yang 2002, 155).

Social spending as a proportion of GDP rose from 5.9 percent in 1998 to 10.7 by 2004, dipping and then rising to 9.4 percent in 2008 (see Figure A-3). Program coverage expanded, and the government introduced new programs. Most important, however, was the solidarity and redistributive aspects of programs. In 1998, the government, with the support of labor and civic organizations, passed the National Pension Act with a unified redistributive structure and expansion to include the self-employed and the unemployed. In the year 2000, the financial unification of the health care system was finally achieved, a process initiated a decade earlier (see Chapter 6). The financial merger of all of the health care funds into one single payer, the National Health Insurance Corporation (NHIC), signified the establishment of a system that involved redistribution among income groups, particularly between middle- and upper-income employees of the government and large companies, on the one hand, and farmers and irregular sector workers, on the other.

The government also expanded unemployment insurance to cover all the regularly employed and a limited number of short-term and part-time workers, the duration of benefits was lengthened, and the qualifying period was shortened (Gray 2008, 17; Woo 2004, 105). The National Basic Living Standards Act, implemented in the year 2000, also came about largely because of pressure exerted by civil society organizations and by the KCTU. The PSPD played a particularly important role in developing the bill and in pressuring congress (Park 2002, 280, 286). With this piece of legislation, the Korean state recognized the obligation to guarantee a basic livelihood (a social right) as a right of citizenship because recipients are not selected by the state but may apply at their local municipal office (Lomeli 2008, 14). The new program provides a stipend for households below a minimum income regardless of the age or work capability of household members (Gray 2008, 136). It also provides a variety of other benefits such as housing, medical care, education, and self-help. Despite strong opposition from the Ministry of Health and Welfare, the PSPD secured presidential agreement for civil society representation on the Central Livelihood Security Committee, the highest decision-making body for the program (Lee 2005, 12). Finally, in 2007 there was an attempt to mitigate the harmful effects of labor flexibilization, when pressure from labor and civil society organizations secured legislation in 2007 requiring employers to offer irregular workers regular employment after two years. However, the new law ran headlong into the 2008 economic crisis, which precipitated large-scale layoffs of irregular workers (*The Korean Times* 2009).

However universal the aspirations of Korean social policy may have been, most programs fell considerably short of their goals. There are generally significant gaps in coverage and a variety of other weaknesses, leading some to question whether the Korean state is actually moving toward a welfare state model (Gilbert 2004; Holliday 2005).[5] Only a small percent of the unemployed, for example, receive unemployment benefits, due, in part, to strict regulations (Chun 2008, 42). Due to the low participation of the self-employed, the unemployed, and the retired in the pension system, only 62 percent of the population between eighteen and sixty years of age pay into the national pension system (Lomeli 2008, 13; Mishra 2004, 315). According to the Korean Development Institute, 78 percent of people sixty years of age and over do not receive national pension benefits (Dong-A-Ilbo 2006). In addition, the average pension is very low—two-thirds of the minimum wage (Chun 2008, 42). Critics have maintained that the universal health plan also has limitations. While the National Health Service offers universal health insurance, co-payments at the time of use are high (Gray 2008, 143).[6] In addition, the health plan does not cover some illnesses with high care costs, such as cancer (Lomeli 2008, 10). Criticisms of the National Basic Living Standards Act include its underfunding by the government with the result that an estimated one-third of those living below the poverty line do not receive this assistance (Mishra 2004, 317).

The most important reason for the low coverage of most social programs, despite their universalistic aspirations, is the high proportion of irregular workers. Although the government has gradually expanded social protection schemes (health care, pensions, unemployment insurance) to include more irregular workers, many are still not legally entitled to benefits. Part-time workers working fewer than eighty hours per month or eighteen hours per week, daily workers employed for less than a month, workers over the age of sixty-five, and nonwage workers in atypical employment relations are all legally excluded from unemployment insurance (Lomeli 2008, 13).[7] In addition, even regular employment does not necessarily generate access to the various new social protection measures because there are strong motivations for both employers of precarious firms, who do not want the extra expense, and employees who wish to see a higher net pay to evade payment and therefore benefits to avoid joining the system. Hence, for example, for workers legally entitled to unemployment insurance, the actual compliance rate by employers in making social contributions was estimated at 73.4 percent in 2004 (Gray 2008, 142, 145). The figures for coverage for irregular workers for pensions and health insurance are low at 15.2 percent and 17.6 percent respectively (Shin 2008a, 23). According to one estimate, the National Pension Plan covered 58 percent of all wage earners (regular and irregular); health insurance, 59 percent; and unemployment insurance, 50 percent, in 2003 (Kim 2006, 21). Moreover, private transfer from family members are still more important in poverty reduction than government transfers among low-income and unemployed households, although their importance shrank significantly once the National Basic Livelihood Act went into effect (Hong 2002, 75).

Korea's achievements in social welfare remain substantial, however. While income inequality increased following the financial crisis, it declined thereafter and, although it has inched up since 2000, remains considerably below the levels found in Mexico and Chile (see Table A-2). In the year 2000, the ratio of the wealth of the country's billionaires to GDP was 0.01, considerably below the figures for Chile (0.09) and Mexico (0.05) (Guerrero et al. 2006, 7). Indeed, compared with late 1980s, the control of national wealth of the top 10 percent of households remained about the same in the year 2000 and considerably below the income of the top 10 percent in Mexico and Chile. The bottom 40 percent of Korean households continued to account for twice the national wealth compared with the bottom 40 percent in Mexico and Chile (see Tables A-3 and A-4).

However, intraclass inequality has increased in Korea. The middle class has become polarized between those able to improve their fortunes and others who have slid into a poorer and much more precarious existence (Koo 2008, 4). Labor flexibilization affected middle-class employees, and fully one-half of those who became unemployed with the 1997 crisis and who found new employment later did so at lower levels of remuneration (7). Meanwhile, a small number among the middle class benefited from increased salaries as wage systems in big corporations shifted to merit (versus seniority-based) systems. These people have come to constitute a new upper middle class, now differentiated from other members of the middle class by their consumption of expensive imported and domestic goods and services (8). Inequality has also increased within the working class with more generous wages and benefits received by workers in large firms with strong unions as opposed to workers in small and medium-sized firms with weaker or no unions (Chun 2008, 27; Koo 2007, 125).

However, while Korea's experience of labor flexibilization implies erosion of social conditions in certain respects, the role of the Korean welfare regime has been expanding. Nevertheless, Korea's better social outcomes, compared with those of Mexico and Chile, continue to have more to do with employment-generating economic growth combined with income transfers among kin than with the country's expanding social welfare role. At the same time, although the reach of Korean welfare reforms is below the aspirations of their critics, and even of their supporters, redistributive and universalistic principles have driven these reforms. The success in getting expanded welfare protection into legislation has been closely linked to the agitation of civil society and a progressive faction of labor.

Chile: Confronting Neoliberalism and Striving for Equality

An average annual per capita growth rate of 2.9 percent per year—better than Mexico's, but not as good as South Korea—has allowed Chile to continue to reduce poverty, which declined from 20.2 percent to 11.3 percent of households between 2000 and 2006 (see Tables A-1 and A-5). While the Chilean state has played an important role in economic growth, it has been considerably less effective than the Korean one. After 2000, distributive struggles occurred over reform of the labor code, pensions, education, and health care. These struggles pitted the business community and the political right against civil society organizations and organized labor. In this phase, while business and the political right remained powerful, their influence was now increasingly challenged by the electoral base of the center-left Concertación and, since 2006, by the rise of civil society activism. In this period, the institutional legacies of the military period were finally dismantled. However, other path-dependent processes instigated by critical conjunctures were still keenly felt.

One of the most important of these was the country's industrial structure, which continued to bear features of the country's import substitution phase despite the fact that economic policy has promoted new export activities. Policies have not generally been effective at mitigating the unintegrated nature of industry. This fact accounts, in part, for Chile's less successful performance in economic growth, employment creation, and levels of remuneration compared to Korea. Unlike Korea, small and medium-sized firms play little role in the export sector, accounting for less than 4 percent of exports (Daly and Muzart 2007, 5). A number of observers have identified this feature as a significant contributor to socioeconomic inequality because of the low remuneration per worker in small and medium-sized firms that provide the bulk of employment (Infante and Sunkel 2009, 136; Larrañaga 2009, 23; OECD 2009a, 33). One source estimates remuneration per worker in small and medium-sized firms at between one-fifth and one-sixth of wages in high-productivity large exporting firms (Infante and Sunkel 2009, 143). Small and medium-sized firms also have poor working conditions and rising job insecurity (133).

Recognizing the problem, the Concertación continued to pursue policies to support small and medium-sized exporters. The Lagos administration (2000–2006) initiated the Integrated Development Program, which brought CORFO-supported training, innovation, and technical support to small and medium firms outside the Santiago area. It also established the "Emprende Chile" program, which sought to increase the competitiveness of small and medium-sized firms (Goldberg and Paladini 2008, 14; Tan 2009, 5). While these and earlier measures to support small and medium-sized enterprises have had some success for a relatively small number of firms, improvements have taken considerable time, and the gains have not been widespread (Tan 2009). To encourage the creation of better jobs, in 2001 the government also introduced a new strategy of seeking high-technology investors with the objective of establishing Chile as the Latin American center for centralized services (such as accounting or financing), for call and contact centers, and for software development. However, this program does not appear to have been particularly successful; nor is there evidence of linkages and dynamism with other economic sectors. Finally, it is important to note that, with the rise in the price of copper, it now overwhelmingly leads Chile's export growth. By 2008, copper accounted for 60 percent of the value of all exports while the proportion accounted for by industry (mainly processed livestock products) has declined (see Table A-13). In marked contrast to Korea, industrial manufacturing accounted for a small proportion of the value of exports (perhaps 11 to 12 percent) by 2008.

The rise in the number of informal workers,[8] given their low incomes and precariousness, is also an important contributor to income inequality. According to one estimate, informal employment, defined as including employees without an employment contract and not contributing to social security, and the self-employed, also not contributing to social security, constitutes about 33 percent of the economically active population in Chile (OECD 2009a, 47). As in Korea, the growing use of temporary workers and subcontracting arrangements, a feature of a flexible labor force, is the key reason for the rise of precarious employment and involves a disproportionate share of female workers (Gideon 2007, 8; OECD 2009a, 44). Most informal workers are not covered by formal social security arrangements (OECD 2009a, 33).

Chile's highly flexible labor regime has been instrumental in the increase in precarious employment. This regime was a product of military rule and is an arrangement that labor did not negotiate. In seeking the alteration of a labor law firmly entrenched for decades, the Chilean labor movement has faced a much more challenging situation than would be the case if it were simply defending existing arrangements. Chilean labor faced a powerful business sector, fiercely resistant to any changes in the labor law that would grant unions more bargaining power. Under President Lagos, two attempts to arrive at a consensus on labor reform through tripartite discussions within a Council of Social Dialogue failed. When labor secured some provisions it viewed as representing a significant advance in providing for labor protection, business demanded the resignation of the labor minister (*La Tercera,* September 21 and November 15, 2001).[9] Subsequent labor reform initiatives seesawed between an attempt to placate business and an effort to improve labor protection. A bill to ease regulations restricting the length of the working day produced a hostile labor reaction in the form of a general strike in 2003. This strike coupled labor opposition to the proposed legislation with a rejection of the country's neoliberal model that, labor charged, was producing poor-quality, precarious employment and a small number of very wealthy people. Then, in 2004, as economic growth returned and business profits shot up, the government introduced a new labor bill that it claimed would distribute the benefits of economic growth more equitably by reducing the working day and regulating overtime pay (*La Tercera,* September 5, 2004). This initiative, negotiated only with labor representatives, angered business.

Labor unrest continued during the following regime of President Michelle Bachelet (2006–2010), with labor leaders again linking their demands for labor reform to a rejection of neoliberalism and to charges that the political system was not democratic (*Santiago Times,* 2007). Finally, some mitigation of flexibility was achieved in 2007, with regulation of subcontracted and temporary labor that allowed subcontracting only for jobs that are separate from the contracting firm's own work process and the use of temporary workers from agencies only for periods of no longer than three to six months in situations of "urgency" (OECD 2009a, 73). However, while the hope had been that the new legislation would encourage firms that had previously subcontracted to hire more workers, a 2007 survey showed little had changed (73). In addition, the new legislation will be difficult to enforce.

Civil society organization agitation for changes in social policy and equitable access to social services heated up. The demands of civil society met with a fair degree of resistance until the election of President Bachelet in 2006. Under pressure from civil society, President Lagos had promised civil society consultation and even set up a new civil society consultative mechanism, the Citizens' Council, for this purpose. However, by 2003, the work of the Citizens' Council ended when the government ignored the council's recommendations for measures to strengthen civil society and failed to provide promised funding. Civil society leaders felt excluded from social policy (Teichman 2009, 72). The case of Chile Solidario, a program set up to address extreme poverty, illustrates government resistance to civil society consultation. Unlike the Korean government's response with regard to civil society input for its Basic Livelihood Program, the Lagos administration refused the request for civil society participation in its program—despite the fact that civil society organizations had received World Bank funding to do so. However, unlike Korea, most of the civil society leaders who were pressing for greater involvement in poverty policy also directly challenged the neoliberal faith in the market as the mechanism that would solve most poverty (77, 78).

President Lagos did begin to address at least one of the country's pressing inequality issues: inequality in health services. However, the institutional arrangements of the health system and the vested interests it had created made change much more difficult that in Korea. Recall that the Chilean health care system remained sharply divided between an underfunded and low-quality public system serving about 85 percent of the population (served by the National Health Fund, FONASA), and a well-funded private system serving the upper 15 percent of the population.[10] The Lagos administration introduced AUGE (the Guaranteed Universal Health Access Plan), a plan that aimed to ensure that all those suffering from a particular disease receive the same standard of care. However, business and the political right succeeded in having the final bill, passed in 2005, revised such that the proposal was gutted of its redistributive component—the Solidarity Fund. To bolster the financial base of the public system to enable it to provide equitable and speedy treatment, the government would require both the public and private health care systems to provide financial contributions to the Solidarity Fund (*Estrategia*, 2002; *La Tercera*, November 15, 2001). The elimination of the Solidarity Fund from the bill not only removed the redistributive component from the plan but also jeopardized its survival by excluding an important source of increased funding. Given the absence of adequate funding, the fear is that the plan will probably introduce a new set of inequalities with an underfunded system providing privileged care in accordance with particular diseases (Borzutksy 2006, 161).

Given the power of the private sector and the government's fear of an adverse reaction from the political right to its management of the economy, both the Lagos and Bachelet administrations remained cautious about government spending, including social spending. Legislation introduced in the year 2000 required a structural budget surplus of 1 percent of GDP. Hence, between 2000 and 2008, the country had only one year (2002) with a small public deficit of −0.4 percent of GDP. Social spending as a percent of GDP slipped from its high of 15.4 percent in the year 2000 to a low of 12 percent of GDP before rising slightly to 14 percent in 2008 (see Figures A-8 and A-3). Big business and the political right were persistent critics of government social policy, constantly exhorting the government to do more with less. Indeed, a small group of technocrats in the Finance Ministry and their private sector allies initially saw the Chile Solidario program as a way to help streamline public social expenditures (Teichman 2008, 452). Although, in the end, the program provided the poor with much more than just handouts,[11] it does not provide this support as a right of citizenship; rather, participants are selected by government-administered household surveys. Critics claim the impact of the program is minor given the smallness of the cash payment and that it has little impact in helping the poor enter the labor market (OECD 2009a, 131).

While Lagos's health care reform and Chile Solidario were limited in their impact, the rise in civil society activism in the early years of the Bachelet administration (2006–2010) propelled forward policy changes in pensions and education that would be more substantial. Between 2006 and 2010, as mobilization rose, the administration moved increasingly toward a welfare regime that is best described as unequal near-universalism with targeting.[12] The ability to make some inroads into the alleviation of inequality in service provision was possible because in 2005 constitutional reform removed most of the institutional impediments (such as appointed senators) to policy change. In addition, a strong showing in the 2006 elections gave President Bachelet a (brief) majority in the Chamber of Deputies. Hence, unlike her predecessors, she faced far fewer problems with congressional obstruction of her reform bills.[13]

Chronic inequalities in the pension system had arisen from the privatization of the system that occurred under military rule (see Chapter 3) and from the fact that a declining portion of the population was covered. Pensions were also low for most people. A drop of formal, permanent full-time employment since 1989 meant that an estimated 50 percent of Chilean workers did not belong to the privatized pension system and did not enjoy its benefits (Taylor 2003, 31). Even for those with formal employment, periodic unemployment and lapsed contributions meant that fewer and fewer workers could fulfill the twenty-year contribution requirement for a guaranteed minimum pension (Riesco 2007, 127).[14] Hence, the existing system provided reasonable benefits only to a minority of the workforce with stable and highly remunerated employment who were also able to make frequent and significant contributions.

The Bachelet administration's first response was an immediate 10 percent increase for those receiving the minimum pension. She followed this measure with her 2008 pension reform, which established a new non-contributory pension covering 85 percent of the population. The reform provides a basic pension for those with no private pension contributions and tops up the pension for those whose private pensions are low. However, critics point out that the reform did not reinstate employer contributions (an important feature of the Korean system). Nor did it tamper with the very costly and inefficient individual capitalization system run by the private pension companies. Unlike the Korean pension plan, however, the Chilean plan does not require formal sector employment, with the consequence that *all* citizens have access to some pension income. However, while President Bachelet's pension reform provided notable improvement, it left the system of private pensions intact, rejecting civil society demands for a solidarity-based redistributive pension system that would provide redistribution between social classes.

Reforms also occurred in the country's highly unequal educational system under President Bachelet. Here again, institutional arrangements inherited from the military period have been difficult to change. Due to reforms carried out during the period of military rule, Chile's system came to entail sharp inequality between private and private–publically subsidized schools, on the one hand, and entirely publicly funded schools on the other. While poorer children attend the latter, which are of lesser quality, the children of the middle and upper classes, able to pay tuition fees, attend the former, which are of higher quality (Taylor 2003, 36). The first three Concertación presidents addressed this problem largely through increased spending on schools in poorer neighborhoods, but the results were disappointing in terms of reducing the duality of the system (Riesco 2007, 58). At the same time, however, the fact that the Concertación allowed privately run state-subsidized schools to charge a supplementary co-payment for each student reinforced the inequality of the system because it allowed these schools to acquire extra resources while further limiting their intake from the lower classes (Taylor 2003, 35). Indeed, the subsidization of private education by middle- and upper-class families represents a very important part of educational expenditure in Chile. According to one estimate, middle-class families pay about one-third of the cost of educating their children in private state-subsidized schools while upper-class families, whose children attend schools with no state subsidy, spend even more (Driabe and Riesco 2009, 23). Hence, the proportion of family expenditure on education in Chile is very high, constituting 46.3 percent of total expenditure on education, in contrast to Korea, where the figure is 39.1 percent (Riesco 2007, 80). At the same time, for most of the 1990s, Chile's educational spending as a percent of GDP was lower than Korea's (see Figure A-4), while Chile put considerably less of its total educational spending (14 percent versus 33 percent) into postsecondary education than did Korea (82). The proportion of the population with a secondary education diploma is, not surprisingly, low in Chile. In fact, it was lower in 2005 than in 1974 (27 percent in 2005 versus 30 percent in 1974) (59). These differences in state support for education have produced substantial differences in educational outcomes. According to the 2009 OECD PISA (Program for Student Assessment) data, Korea ranked second and fourth in mean scores in reading and math out of the sixty-five countries surveyed. Chile ranked forty-third and fiftieth, respectively (OECD 2009c).[15]

In 2006, the Chilean government was faced with over a million protesting high school students engaged in street mobilizations, sit-ins, and school takeovers, protesting the educational law passed during the military dictatorship, which had privatized the educational system and privileged middle- and upper-class students. President Bachelet established an advisory commission for educational reform with some eighty-one members, including students, teachers, and parents. However, the group was unable to reach a consensus. Students, teachers, and parents resigned and rejected the final report, demanding an end to the decentralization of education and to profit-making schools sooner than recommended in the report. Students returned to the streets to protest (Seymour-Jones 2007).

Although the new educational law did not satisfy everyone, Bachelet's General Education Law did address many of those aspects of the education system most harmful to the poor and working classes. Among other things, the new law created a new system that allocates more funds to serve poor families, doubled the resources directed to poor students, created an agency to monitor the overall quality of education, and provided a four-year deadline for schools to become nonprofit (Fábrega 2010).

The law also prohibited discrimination in student selection (only up to the ninth grade, however) in an attempt to eradicate discrimination against lower-class applicants.

Growing civil society pressure has brought important improvements in pensions and educational reform, although the basic structures of the old systems remain intact. Unlike Korea, Chile has been unable to bring about systems based on solidarity and redistributive principles. Chile's industrial strategy has also been less successful in integrating employment creation with its export strategy. The inadequacies of Chile's industrial sector in providing sufficient and well-remunerated employment pose a serious challenge to the ability to mitigate inequality in the future. Strong social forces still create difficulties for the Chilean state, which struggles to balance conflicting and often still-polarized demands. We see this difficulty most dramatically in the fact that civil society and labor groups have often coupled their demands with a rejection of neoliberal model to which the business community and the middle class is firmly committed.

Mexico: Exclusionary Export-led Growth and Welfare Dualism

Since 2000, Mexico's rulers have been strong supporters of the free market and have viewed the market as the primary mechanism for improvements in living standards. Like Chile, Mexico's welfare regime is fragmented and characterized by a sharp duality—but that duality is even more marked with a much higher proportion of the population lacking access to adequate social protection. The Mexican welfare regime is currently making the transition from a welfare regime providing generous social protection to less than one-half the population to a regime characterized by a dualism in which the state is privatizing the old state-supported social security arrangements while extending minimal state-supported programs to the unprotected population. The absence of sufficient employment creation is the outstanding feature of the Mexican case and has been instrumental in the failure to achieve better poverty and inequality reduction. An estimated 65 percent of the economically active population is in the informal sector today (OECD 2009a, 45). Even though Mexico has successfully expanded its exports of industrial products—by 2008 these represented 82 percent of exports—this expansion has failed to produce sufficient employment expansion (see Table A-11).

The social forces backing the PAN, the party of the country's two presidents from 2000 to the present, Vicente Fox (2000–2006) and Felipe Calderón (2006–2012), has included big conglomerates, the general business community, state technocrats, the middle class, and elements of organized labor. Business interests have been at least as close to the post-2000 administrations as to their PRI predecessors—probably closer. As a consequence, Mexico is a deeply divided polity. The PAN candidate, Felipe Calderón, won the 2006 election only very narrowly.[16] In this election, the free market, business, and the middle-class-supported PAN Party competed against the left-wing, antineoliberal alliance of López Obrador, whose supporters included the rural and the urban poor, the working class, and a portion (about one-third) of the middle class. The political clout of the country's big business sector has been greater than Chile's in the past decade partly because individual businessmen have received a variety of government, including ministerial, appointments (Teichman 2002, 505). There has been no pretence of attempting to balance the interests of the country's capitalists with those of labor and civil society. Although President Calderón appointed long-time traditional PAN Party loyalists, his administration has also had its share of people who have moved in and out of the business community.[17]

The commitment to free trade, in the absence of an industrial strategy, has exacerbated this challenge of creating sufficient employment. For the most part, Mexico's industrial sector, like Chile's, displays both lack of integration and dualism. In Mexico, about 300 big export firms provide little employment and produce for the U.S. market, while small and medium firms that produce for the domestic market provide the bulk of employment (Moreno-Bird, Santamaría, and Valdivia 2005, 1107). Trade liberalization harmed employment in the small and medium-sized enterprise sector because many of these firms, including ones that had produced for the big export firms, could not compete with imports and went bankrupt (Moreno-Bird, Carpizo, and Bosch 2009, 162). Meanwhile, the employment-generating capacity of the *maquilas* (export processing zones), which provided employment to only about 5 percent of the workforce to begin with, declined through the 2000s due to the shift of many *maquila* firms to lower-wage areas in Central America and China. Between 2000 and 2003, the sector lost 240,000 jobs. Although employment in the *maquilas* began to recover after 2005, wages began to fall (*Mexico and NAFTA Report* November 2004, 12, 13, 15). Trade liberalization has worsened the problem of lack of industrial integration because of the close ties between export firms and their foreign suppliers. The failure of exporting firms, which are entirely dependent on imported inputs, to stimulate the rest of the economy through purchasing those inputs from domestic firms is an important ingredient impeding employment growth. With the economic downturn in the United States beginning in 2007, Mexico's heavy integration with and dependence on the U.S. economy has brought further harm to Mexican manufacturing and employment (September 2007, 9). Market liberalization also brought about significant job losses in agriculture. According to one estimate, agricultural trade liberalization linked to NAFTA was the single most important factor behind the loss of agricultural jobs, resulting in an estimated loss of 1.3 million agricultural jobs by the end of 2002. Although with NAFTA the restriction on the importation of maize was to be phased out gradually, in fact the Mexican government allowed tariff-free imports of this grain substantially above the formal allowable quota (Polaski 2003, 15, 20). Full liberalization of maize, beans, sugar, and milk products occurred in 2008 (Scott 2009, 12).

Meanwhile, Mexican popular social forces have been ill equipped to protect their interests through independent and united political action due to a historical legacy of corporatist and clientelist control. This legacy not only left a fractured labor movement unaccustomed to independent action but also bequeathed legal instruments of labor control. Labor has faced increasing demands by business and government leaders for greater formal labor flexibilization.[18] President Fox initiated talks on reform of the country's labor code with the new umbrella labor organization, the National Union of Workers (UNT), an organization uniting unions wanting an alternative to the traditional official trade union organization that operated under the PRI. The UNT proposed the dismantling of the 1931 labor code—one of the key features of PRI labor control (see Chapter 3). The government rejected the proposal, preferring to keep most of the restrictive features of the law in place to be able to marginalize recalcitrant unions through refusing them official recognition and by denying approval for strike action of recognized unions. In fact, the Fox administration's proposal for labor reform increased the requirements for holding a legal strike and called for a variety of measures discouraging to the establishment of new independent unions (Human Rights Watch 2005).

In addition, organized labor has not been able to protect past social protection gains. Rising unemployment and a consequent decline in social security enrollment and payments worsened the fiscal difficulties in the social security institution for public sector workers (the ISSSTE). The Calderón administration achieved pension privatization in the ISSSTE, thwarted by labor opposition during the Fox years, in 2007. This reform involved the dismantling of the limited (intrainstitutional) distributive aspect of existing arrangements and the establishment of private accounts for the provision of pensions to be run by a new Pension Fund (*Mexico and NAFTA Report* April 2007, 11). The new system raised the minimum retirement age and increased pension premiums as well as the number of years subscribers must pay into the fund (July 2008, 4). Because the old pension arrangements were part of a social security regime that excluded half of the population, this reform might be seen as a step in dismantling the segmented nature of the old system. However, the reform did not aim to achieve the creation of a state-supported unified redistributive system that would have been far more effective at addressing inequality in pension access.

Indeed, the significant improvement in social spending in recent years, which reached a high of 12.3 percent of GDP in 2008 (higher than Korea), is misleading (see Figure A-3) because it belies the highly unequal nature of social protection arrangements, which continue despite some recent improvements. Superior benefits and services are available to those (the minority) with formal sector employment and social security protection, who live mostly in Mexico City and in northern Mexico. The remainder of the population must make do with poorly funded government services. Rural dwellers in south and central Mexico are likely to be excluded from services due to difficulties of access. The fact that in 2002 social security organizations accounted for 66 percent of total public social expenditures illustrates the high degree of inequality in social spending (OECD 2005, 39).

Extreme inequality exists particularly in pensions with very low public spending on pensions outside of the formal social security institutions, making pensions in Mexico an important contributor to income inequality. Mexico did not provide any public pension until 2005 when the federal district (municipal) level introduced a basic universal old age pension for those seventy and older. In 2006, a federal noncontributory program linked to the antipoverty program Oportunidades was introduced in rural communities, while in 2007 a more generous rural plan was introduced (Scott 2009, 23, 24). Of our three cases, Mexico is characterized by the most profound inequalities in the provision of health care services—once again, between the insured (formal sector workers) and the uninsured, a fact that is obscured by figures showing Mexican health spending to represent a higher percent of its GDP than Korea's (see Figure A-5). Furthermore, out-of-pocket payments made by Mexican patients constitute over one-half of total health care spending (OECD 2009b, 57). Indeed, the share of total health spending provided by public sources in Mexico was 44.9 percent in 2002 compared with 52.1 percent for Korea (OECD 2005, 40). One of the consequences is that a significant proportion of the population (the bottom two quintiles) faces catastrophic or impoverishing health care expenditure.[19]

In 2004, the government of Vicente Fox instituted the System for the Social Protection in Health, a program aimed at providing health coverage for all those not currently covered by social security. Financed by contributions from the federal and state governments, along with a small income-based family contribution, the program resulted in health coverage increasing from around 40 percent of the population in 2004 to around 65 percent by 2008. But spending on health still remains regressive, with public health spending on the insured 50 percent higher than on the uninsured (OECD 2009b, 76, 77; Scott 2009, 21). As in the Chilean case (and unlike the Korean one), the system remains a dual nondistributional one, deprived of the contributions of middle- and upper-income groups and one that is therefore likely to be faced with resource difficulties.[20]

Profound inequalities also characterize Mexico's educational system. According to one observer, despite recent improvements, Mexico "presents one of the largest absolute schooling gaps between rich and poor in the Latin American and Caribbean region" (Scott 2009, 11). Public spending in basic education is progressive largely because of its low quality, which causes it not to be used by high-income groups (20). Moreover, because both presidents Fox and Calderón have feared alienating the powerful teachers' union (National Union of Education Workers, SNTE),[21] much of Mexico's public educational spending continues to go directly to it rather than to the improvement of education. The union uses these funds to provide teachers with parallel careers within the union bureaucracy, for scholarships and for other perks. The union also allocates teachers to schools and approves promotions (*Mexico and NAFTA Report* August 2007, 2; December 2006, 10; June 2008, 7). Hence, while President Calderón's 2008 educational reform (Alliance for the Quality of Education) sought to, among other things, improve teaching standards and performance, it faced strong and effective resistance from teachers, and there is little indication of improvements (OECD 2009b, 89).

However, the Fox administration did expand the previous administration's antipoverty program, PROGRESA. Renamed Oportunidades, the program was extended by the government to include urban areas and to cover not just elementary students but also junior high and high school students. Fox also created a number of spin-off programs for youth, one of which provided a savings account during the last three years of high school to defray the cost of a university education. However, government claims that the program can have an important role in poverty reduction have been disputed (Moreno-Bird et al. 2009, 166). Remittance payments from Mexicans who have migrated north of the border have probably been more important in poverty reduction between 2000 and 2005 (Esquivel 2009, 5; Polaski 2003, 23).

Despite some shift toward social spending to benefit the lower classes, the persistence of regressive social programs means that, on balance, social spending in Mexico does relatively little to mitigate inequality. Agricultural subsidies, established to compensate farmers for the reduction in state support with economic liberalization, remain among the most regressive programs implemented in Mexico. Most of the benefits go to the top 10 percent of producers (Scott 2009, 15). At the same time, generalized consumption subsidies have grown during the Calderón years, as the government has sought to protect the middle-income consumer from increasing prices. In 2007, the Calderón government froze the prices of tortillas, petroleum, gas, and electricity, measures that largely benefit the middle class (Guererro et al. 2006, 40; *Mexico and NAFTA Report* June 2008, 9). The antipoverty program, Oportunidades, on the other hand, saw its budget reduced from 51 percent of the Social Development Ministry's budget during the Fox years to 33 percent under Calderón (*Reforma* 2008). Given the share of fiscal resources allocated to the country's many regressive programs, Scott concludes that the latter effectively cancel out the propoor impact of the progressive ones, producing a slightly regressive global distribution of public spending (Scott 2009, 31, 32). The top decile's share of total transfers is almost twice that of the lowest.

Attempts to reform the tax system to generate more resources to provide improved social protection continued to face tough political obstacles. Early in his election campaign, President Fox's proposal for a tax on wealth to raise funds for social programs was dropped in the face of stiff resistance from the private sector and replaced by a proposal to expand the 15 percent value-added tax (VAT) to cover basic food and medicine. The private sector supported this proposal, but Congress defeated it. Congress then produced a tax reform bill that increased the VAT on luxury goods, including telecommunication services, soft drinks and cigarettes, the auto industry, and the telecommunication sector—a proposal that was challenged in the courts (*Latin American Weekly Report,* January 2, 2002, 3). President Calderón succeeded in instituting a new business tax on gross operating profits despite business opposition. However, the new tax has generated less than one-half the revenue projected (*Mexico and NAFTA Report* October 2008, 11). The recent increase in Mexico's tax income, 35 percent of which comes from taxes paid by the state petroleum company, is due to the increase in the international price of crude petroleum (see Table A-10). The inability to ensure a more stable tax base has meant that increases in social spending have often come at the cost of lower spending in other areas such as infrastructure (Guerrero et al. 2006, 32).

The Mexican government's weaker efforts at expanding social protection and enhancing equality in social service provision and its continued efforts toward formal labor flexibility are linked to a weaker civil society, strong business resistance, and the opposition of post-2000 government leaders to civil society involvement in matters of social policy. A substantial number of civil society organizations and social policy experts have favored universal redistributive arrangements, but these groups have been relatively weak and have faced a political leadership resistant to their involvement in policy and to their demands. Despite the fact that, in the period leading up to the 2000 election, Fox's transition team carried out an extensive consultation of civil society organizations on social policy, in the end his administration ignored the recommendations of civil society groups. These recommendations included a call for civil society participation and evaluation of social programs, the establishment of universal programs in health and education, and beefed-up infrastructure and productive investment programs to provide employment (Teichman 2009, 73). His government's 2004 Law for Social Development rejected NGO participation in social policy in favor of a technical committee, composed of academics and government officials. Finally, the state firmly resisted pressure to open Oportunidades to civil society participation (82).

Two consecutive right-wing regimes, with strong faith in the market, closely linked to powerful business interests and supported by the middle-class and privileged sectors of organized labor, have had little interest in the expansion of a truly redistributive social protection regime. However, given that the political left represents a strong electoral challenge, the government has expanded health coverage to an ever-larger portion of the uninsured population and has begun to institute pensions. Nevertheless, the system involves a sharp dualism, with superior services available to the formally employed. The poor indigenous population of southern Mexico remains the most excluded from economic benefits and social services. Legacies of the authoritarian period allow control from above and shape the effectiveness of pressure from below. The main factor, however, in failure to alleviate poverty and inequality is the nature of the country's export model—its failure to provide sufficient employment.

Conclusions

There is a certain degree of convergence among the three cases. Labor flexibility is now a common feature—long a legalized feature of the Chilean case, it has been a de facto reality of Mexico for some time and has now been established in Korea. Labor flexibility has meant a rise in an irregular and informal work force, the weakening of labor as a political force, greater labor precariousness, less labor protection, and a declining share of the population with social security protection. Economic liberalization has resulted in the most powerful economic groups increasing both their economic and political power.

However, there are substantial differences in the role and ability of the state to encourage and support employment-generating growth and in the nature of the emergent welfare regimes. In Korea, a long and successful legacy of state-led export growth, and a historically weaker business class, rendered the state capable of continuing the pursuit of employment-generating export-orientated growth. What stands out in the Korean case is the successful and continued incorporation of small and medium-sized firms into export activities. However, this success built on earlier policies and practices and on a historical legacy of industrial integration that was largely absent from the other two cases. Mexico stands out for its failure to achieve export growth with sufficient spin-off effects for employment generation. Again, however, the historical development of Mexico's industrial base, its use of capital-intensive methods, and its ties to the U.S. economy involves a long-entrenched set of features that would have been extremely difficult to overcome, even had the political leadership the will to do so. Adherence to the new market model within the context of NAFTA has reinforced this earlier failure to enhance employment.

The expansion of Korea's welfare regime in the direction of a model that is universal and redistributive among social classes is its most outstanding feature. I have argued that civil society activism and the pressure exerted by a sector of the labor movement have been instrumental in this achievement. A comparatively weaker business class and a middle class with redistributive concerns were important in this development. Korea stands out for its ability to build distributive principles into its pension and health care systems. However, it is important to bear in mind that economic growth, job creation, and extrastate transfers remain the most important factors in low levels of poverty and inequality in Korea.

While many civil society organizations and politicians in Chile have universalistic and redistributive aspirations for their social welfare regime, Chile has confronted much greater impediments to achieving these goals. Institutional impediments, particularly the social service arrangements inherited from military rule, and the vested interests to which they have given rise, have been important in offering effective resistance to change. However, a recent upsurge in civil society activism is forcing some mitigation of inequalities in education and pensions. Mexico's legacy of unequal and exclusionary social protection, combined with, and closely linked to, the legacy of PRI rule, left a weak labor movement and civil society. This has meant less pressure from below for improvements in social protection. However, a powerful business class, a political leadership committed to the market model, a middle class, and privileged sectors of labor unconcerned with broader societal distributive issues have also been key ingredients in accounting for the entrenched dualism of the Mexican welfare regime. At the same time, the fact that the political left has substantial electoral support—recall that the 2006 election was very close—has likely been important in encouraging the government to expand social protection, at least minimally to the large unprotected population.

Economic globalization, which in these cases involved support for labor flexibility to improve competitiveness, created a pressing need to expand social protection. However, because labor flexibility, in creating an increase in the numbers of temporary and part-time employees, reduces the opportunities and incentives to contribute to social protection programs, it creates difficulties for the expansion of social protection to those workers and employees whose employment is precarious. Hence, not only is there continued, or even increased, inequality among workers, irregular workers are also at high risk of slipping into poverty should there be an economic downturn. The difficulty of incorporating these workers into social protection schemes is therefore a major challenge for all three countries.

8

Conclusions

THIS STUDY HAS SOUGHT TO EXPLAIN differing achievements in poverty and inequality outcomes through the examination of explanatory variables found deep in the historical experience of each country. It has focused on the role of social forces and their interaction with states. I have chosen not to employ a critical juncture framework because of its strong association with path dependency. As this study has demonstrated, reactionary sequences, because they stalled or worsened poverty and inequality, were instrumental in poverty and inequality outcomes in Chile and Mexico. While institutions play an important role in my explanation, I have avoided a mainly institutional approach because of the need to account for the destruction of institutions and the constitution of new ones. Reactionary sequences in Chile and Mexico produced the alteration or even destruction of old institutions. In these cases, entirely new institutional arrangements were produced in the wake of the destruction of the old ones, and these new institutional arrangements, as we saw in the cases of Mexico after 1940 (with the operation of the PRI), and Chile after 1973 (with the new institutional arrangements imposed by the military dictatorship), contributed to the worsening of inequality. While in Mexico poverty declined only slowly, in Chile it worsened substantially. My starting point, therefore, is a consideration of the relative weight and alliances of social forces and their impact on institutions and state policy. The interaction between social forces and state institutions was ongoing. Social forces shaped institutions, but institutions, once established, molded poverty and distributive outcomes.

I have employed the notion of critical conjuncture to indicate the possibility of both reactive and path-dependent sequences following a profound rupture from past arrangements and practices. Indeed, as this analysis has demonstrated, both reactive and path-dependent sequences are responsible for the distinct social outcomes in the two Latin American cases. While reactive sequences involving mobilization from below and strong oppositional reactions from propertied and middle-class groups account for alterations in political arrangements that worsened or failed to improve social outcomes, powerful path-dependent arrangements in such areas as industrial structure had profound implications for employment and therefore for poverty reduction. While welfare regimes may play a role in social outcomes, they are only a relatively small part of the story, and their nature and efficacy stem from wider political and economic developments.

Across the three cases, the variables (social forces) that constitute the main actors in the causal chains are significantly different in size, political weight, and ideological predisposition. Moreover, the explanation of outcomes arises not just from the intrinsic features of social forces, their interactions, and impact on the state but also, and perhaps more importantly, from when and under what circumstances they emerged and acted. Issues of timing, sequence, and duration are of critical importance. Taking a long view of history with attention to when social forces arise and why institutions are created and destroyed allows a more complete understanding of *why* actual social outcomes differ so profoundly in the three cases. The remainder of this chapter treats these issues in more detail and offers some final remarks on the implications for addressing inequality in countries where it continues to be an intractable problem.

Path-Dependant, Reactionary Sequences and Social Outcomes

Recall that critical conjunctures, characterized by the intersection of two separate sequences, involve a profound rupture from past practices during which the struggle among social forces gives rise to a new ruling alliance and a new institutional framework. The distinctive features of the Korean case arise, to a considerable degree, from the fact that Korea's critical conjuncture (1930–1953) was by far the most transformative of the three cases. It involved several profound and transformative events that were compressed in time: a high level of peasant mobilization, the expulsion of the Japanese, foreign (American) occupation, and a war leading to the division of North and South Korea. These events not only swept away the old landowning class (both Japanese and Korean) but also ushered in a thorough land reform that set the stage for equitable growth. The creation of a homogeneous small farmer class established the first step in a reinforcing sequence that would ensure poverty reduction and a relatively high level of equality into the future.

Beginning in 1961, a regime with its social base in the peasantry pursued measures that ensured rural social welfare and created employment through export-led industrial growth. The identification of the political leadership with the poor (the peasantry) and its goal of poverty reduction resulted in policies to support rural dwellers and an industrialization program that included employment creation as one of its goals. Indeed, the regime's political survival hinged on its ability to appeal to the deeply felt popular aspiration of poverty reduction. While left ideology, which had played an important role in worker agitation and in peasant mobilization, had been severely repressed during the American occupation and thereafter, the concern for poverty survived as a "past repertoire" that shaped agricultural and industrial policy. Hence, a variety of farm supports, not included in formal social spending, improved the living standards of rural dwellers. Measures were taken to mitigate inequality as it rose in the 1970s. Indeed, general public concern for equity, bereft of class ideology, survived long after the defeat of the left, and it was therefore politically necessary for the leadership to address these aspirations. Furthermore, the fact that Korean social forces were weak at the initial moment of industrialization allowed for the emergence of a strong economic state leadership role and the emergence of institutions, practices, and expectations that kept inequality low. State institutions and practices fomenting employment-generating export-led growth became powerfully entrenched and, as we saw in Chapters 6 and 7, withstood pressures for their complete dismantling.

In Mexico and Chile, critical conjunctures produced reactive oppositional sequences that increased inequality and reduced poverty only slowly (see Figure A-1). In addition, as detailed in Chapter 5, these ruptures were preceded by historical events (colonial conquest and miscegenation) that created new social categories—social forces that became internally tightly interconnected with a consciousness of distinct interests. The reactive sequences following critical conjunctures produced institutions and practices that reinforced this social compartmentalization. Three hundred years of colonial rule involved the subjugation of a large indigenous and mestizo peasant population (Mexico) and a large mestizo peasantry (Chile), under the control of a white criollo landholding elite. Political independence, the expansion of trade, and early industrialization did not assuage this condition but instead reinforced it. The short duration of Japanese colonial rule, on the other hand and the expulsion of the Japanese colonial rulers at the end of World War II contributed to a starting point characterized by the absence of sharp social compartmentalization. Indeed, the demise of the Korean landowning class and the departure of the Japanese ensured the survival of a homogeneous Korean identity.

The timing and duration of events were crucial. In Korea, the occurrence of land redistribution prior to the onset of the country's industrialization drive meant that worker- and middle-class groups were not available to block important equalizing government support for the small farming sector. With fierce repression of the political left, and in the absence of a mining enclave or significant industrialization (all lost with the division of North and South Korea), ideological polarization was virtually eliminated. The more prolonged process of industrialization in Chile and Mexico, beginning at the end of the nineteenth century, produced more complex social structures. Mexico's first phase of industrialization was interrupted by its first critical conjuncture—the Mexican Revolution—a conflagration that involved a very heterogeneous group of revolutionary participants, from indigenous and mestizo peasants and small landowners, to workers, to members of the country's middle class of school teachers and professionals, to some members of the large landowning class. The heterogeneity of the revolutionary participants, a reflection of the fact that Mexico had already begun to modernize, increased the complexity of the struggle among social forces vying for leadership of the Revolution. This new postrevolutionary ruling alliance, some members of which became big landowners, had little interest in land reform or in other redistributive measures. This intransience on the part of the postrevolutionary leadership set the stage for reactionary sequences beginning with increasing peasant and worker mobilization under President Cárdenas (1934–1940). The fear ignited by the intensity of mobilization from below resulted in the construction of a highly efficient party–state apparatus of political containment. This political arrangement structured the differential incorporation of social groups and the highly unequal distribution of benefits and rewards, setting the stage for a rise in inequality and only a slow decline in poverty. *Ejidal* peasants and small landowners experienced adverse incorporation—highly controlled involvement in state–party institutions and decreasing benefits from the system. The hope of land reform, however, ensured that much of the Mexican peasantry continued to support the PRI for many years. An increasing level of mobilization in the late 1960s opened the way for a brief redistributive interlude that generated stiff reaction from propertied interests. Mexico's final critical conjuncture (1982–1994), occurring in response to the international debt crisis and a deepening political crisis, produced a rise in poverty and continuing high levels of inequality.

Chile's early modernization phase, beginning at the end of the nineteenth century, which was based on periods of high demand for mineral exports, was particularly dynamic. Hence, Chile achieved an extensive and earlier industrialization process in the first part of the twentieth century than did Mexico and saw the early emergence of sizeable working- and middle-class groups. Political institutional arrangements—a pluralist electoral system that allowed for the rise of reform parties—were instrumental in allowing for social improvements for urban middle- and working-class groups. Chile's early reformist political parties lobbied for, and obtained, important social improvements for the urban working and middle classes. These gains, however, were highly unequal, with the most organized gaining the highest wages and most generous benefits. Meanwhile, the peasantry remained mired in misery under the control of big landowners, who retained firm control of the state until the rise of the Popular Front in 1938. These circumstances delayed Chile's initial critical conjuncture, which did not occur until the Great Depression rocked the economy and Chilean voters elected the Popular Front. When the Popular Front, originally a coalition of left-center parties, abandoned the peasantry in exchange for congressional right-wing support for state-led industrialization, a reactive sequence ensued, involving increasing repression of workers and the Communist Party and increased mobilization from below. These developments ultimately culminated in the disintegration of the political center, rising political polarization, and the election of Salvador Allende in 1970, an event that triggered a new critical conjuncture, involving the final reactive event, the military coup of 1973. This episode was followed by a sharp rise in poverty and inequality. In both Mexico and Chile, the failure of their less transformative critical conjunctures to sweep away the old propertied classes made reactive sequences likely.

In addition, an important distinction between Mexico and Chile, on the one hand, and Korea, on the other, involved the notion of private property. Land reform became even more difficult in Mexico and Chile because its advocates pushed for land redistribution projects that rejected the notion of private property. Land redistribution proponents in Mexico and Chile did not seek to establish a class of small farmers, as was the case in Korea—a scenario compatible with property rights and capitalist economic growth. Land reform schemes that rejected the notion of private farm ownership invariably spurred the entire propertied sector and often large swaths of the middle class against land reform—and against other redistributive reforms. In this way, rejection of the notion of private property contributed to the intensity of the reactive sequences and made compromise with propertied classes impossible.

The presence of foreign-dominated mining export enclaves in Mexico and Chile also contributed to the difficulty of reaching distributive settlements. Mining enclave status contributed to the complexity of political struggles during critical conjunctures. It also reinforced the strength of propertied classes and contributed to the militancy of labor, thereby adding to the intensity of reactive sequences that blocked or reversed redistributive improvements, including land reform. The presence of foreign ownership of mines in isolated mining communities produced radical left anti-imperialist ideologies that rejected the institution of private property. Indeed, the extent of worker militancy made containment (co-optation and control) of working-class organizations a pressing political necessity in Mexico. In Chile, a militant left-wing ideology, articulated by the leftist parties whose social base was in the mining communities, was a main feature in the political polarization of the 1960s and early 1970s.

Path Dependency and Industrialization

Critical conjunctures, while giving rise to reactive sequences, simultaneously generated powerful path-dependent processes that had important implications for social outcomes. The most notable case where this occurred was in industrial policy. The origins of industrialization in Mexico and Chile were heavily shaped by the circumstances of mineral enclave development and by the specific interests of industrialists. The first industrialization phase arose largely to provide the new urban centers with consumer goods—it was not export oriented. In the Mexican case, this early state-led modernization had involved the creation of domestic government-protected industrial monopolies, granted to cronies close to Porfirio Díaz. This very early industrial development drive, using capital-intensive (not employment-generating) methods, would become a permanent feature of Mexican industrialization (Chapter 4) and one of the root causes of continued poverty. In addition, import substitution industrialization in both Chile and Mexico, as we saw in Chapters 3 and 4, involved the penetration of states by business interests who directed the course of industrialization in powerful ways by using their positions on various commissions to obtain generous protection for their own products while making it easier and cheaper to import needed inputs. Hence, while the international demand for minerals initially shaped the nature of industrialization, once industrialization was underway, state structures were organized in ways that would serve to reinforce the direction and nature of industrialization to serve the vested interests of already established industrialists. The failure of the import substitution industrialization drives in Mexico and Chile to incorporate the goal of poverty reduction through an explicit commitment to job creation reflected the concentration of political power in the hands of propertied interests. In addition, state penetration by business interests shaped an unintegrated industrial development pattern that has persisted into the twenty-first century. This feature made it impossible for those sectors experiencing economic growth to dynamize other industrial and economic sectors and expand employment throughout the economy.

However, after the mid-1980s, Chile embarked on an export-led growth strategy that contributed to the reduction of poverty due to its employment-generating capacity. Recall that, with the 1973 military coup, the left was repressed and much of the old import substitution model dismantled. However, the belief in the efficacy of the state's economic leadership role survived within the country's state development bank. This impulse lay dormant until the crisis of the early 1980s forced the military to abandon both radical neoliberalism and its ties to the big conglomerates. Once the administration decided to broaden its entrepreneurial base, it moved to a more pragmatic position on state intervention, thereby allowing the new emphasis on nontraditional agricultural exports to take flight. The emergence of this past repertoire was crucial to employment expansion and poverty reduction after the mid-1980s in Chile.

In Korea, industrial policy became the most important ingredient in poverty reduction because propoor industrial development was both integrated and oriented to export markets. These features equipped it to provide expanded employment. Unlike the Latin American cases, given that there was very little industrialization of any kind in the early 1960s (South Korea having been left with little industry following the split between north and south), the state was free to decide what sort of industrialization to pursue. Furthermore, the absence of lucrative resources that could be exported to obtain foreign exchange earnings was a strong incentive to develop an export-oriented industrial base and an effective tax base. The success of the model and the presence of industrial promotion institutions made the Korean export-led model "sticky" in the face of pressures during the 1980s and 1990s to adopt market liberalization.

The presence of a state initially free of penetration by particular business interests appears, therefore, to have been essential for successful employment-generating industrial development in Korea. Under General Park, policies encouraged the domestic integration of industry through state-directed creation of backward and forward linkages (Chapter 2). While, in both Chile and Mexico, some state bureaucrats and even political leaders became aware of the pitfalls of having their respective industrial programs driven by the interests of domestic industrialists, stiff political resistance from business prevented policies that might have improved industrial efficiency and export performance.

Korea's relatively stronger state, combined with the fact that it was committed to employment expansion and the generation of foreign exchange earnings, also made possible the country's adaptation to the decline in the international demand for light consumer goods so that export-led economic growth could continue. Faced with stiff competition from countries with lower wage rates, in the 1970s Korea made the transition to the production of new products, such as shipbuilding and automobiles, which would soon become important exports. Meanwhile the inadequacies of Chilean and Mexican industrialization eroded the legitimacy of state-led industrialization and opened the way for radical neoliberal reform. In Mexico, various attempts had been made to adapt the old import substitution model—first through engaging in redistributive reforms in the early 1970s and increased investment and then by means of the petroleum export strategy. However, repeated economic crises between 1980 and 1986 ended the legitimacy of state-led development and opened the way for the new market model. As we saw, in both Mexico and Chile, the move to radical neoliberalism exacerbated problems of inequality and poverty.

In the Korean case, the success of the state-led industrial growth model kept that model in place through the debt crisis of the early 1980s and even, in a reduced form, following the financial crisis of 1997 (Chapters 6 and 7). Most political leaders, state managers, and the public, given the past success of the model, were unwilling to engage in its wholesale abandonment. One of the distinguishing features of the Korean case was strong and successful state support for the participation of small and medium-sized firms in exports, critically important because most employment is in small and medium-sized firms. Support for these firms and, in particular, support for their integration into export activities, was key to the linking of export growth to employment expansion. While, after 1990, the Chilean government made various efforts in this direction, small and medium-sized firms have been largely ignored by Mexican policy.

The Role of the Middle Class and Distributional Outcomes

While, in Korea, instituting land reform prior to the industrialization drive was an important ingredient in keeping inequality low initially, inequality began to rise with the process of industrialization, particularly with the turn to heavy and chemical industry in the 1970s. As we saw, however, the regime took measures to mitigate rural urban inequality (Chapter 2). After 1980, socioeconomic inequality declined and remained low in Korea while poverty continued to diminish. From the 1980s, we also see growing popular pressure for Western-style forms of social protection.

In Mexico and Chile, on the other hand, higher levels of inequality emerge early in history and fail to decline; in the case of Chile, inequality increased markedly during the period of military rule. Welfare regimes in both countries developed in a highly segmented and unequal manner despite universalistic aspirations. The economic crises of the early 1980s signaled retrenchment in social spending, and, in the aftermath of the debt crisis, the aspiration toward the universalistic and solidaristic principles of the Western-style welfare state has also been discarded.

An important part of the explanation for this divergence lay in differences in the length of the modernization and industrialization drives—differences that shaped social force configuration and attitudes. In Korea, public resistance to increased inequality was enhanced by the fast pace of the Korean industrialization process (a mere twenty years), a period that saw the rapid rise of the working class and the emergence of a large middle class. These groups, migrants from the countryside, retained strong ties to rural kin, empathy for the plight of rural dwellers, and commitment to the maintenance of low levels of inequality. Private transfers between members of the Korean middle class and their poor kin are of crucial importance; such transfers, even into the 1990s, have been more important in Korea's poverty and equality achievements than have government transfers. Rapid and successful industrialization produced a substantial and brisk rise in urban incomes, and recent rural migrants who took up urban jobs and became new members of the middle class retained ties to poorer kin. In addition, Korea's earlier history, which bequeathed a more homogeneous population without substantial socioeconomic divisions and without cultural or ethnic differences, also facilitated such transfers.

Indeed, members of the Korean middle class became instigators for the expansion of social protection. As early as the Park regime, middle-class professionals formed an organization that lobbied for expanded social welfare programs, including universal ones. By the 1970s, members of the middle class were involved in raising labor political consciousness and, by the 1980s, through the formation of civil society organizations, demanded both democratization and social justice. Middle-class civil society organizations were instrumental in securing the expansion of social welfare programs, with universalistic and redistributive principles through the 1990s and into the twenty-first century. A faction of the labor movement has also been active in pressing for expanded social protection.

The much longer processes of modernization, industrialization, and urbanization in Mexico and Chile, combined with sharp social compartmentalization, produced middle classes who were several generations removed from rural life. This context was not conducive to the kind of general intrakin financial transfers that occurred in Korea. Chilean and Mexican middle classes were not generally advocates for the rural and urban poor and the working class. Recall that, in the case of Chile, although middle-class-supported reformist parties emerged early in the twentieth century, none of them spoke for the rural poor. Moreover, these parties soon lost interest in social reform. By mid-twentieth century the Chilean middle class identified largely with the country's propertied classes (Chapter 3). In Mexico, the middle class took over the political leadership following the Mexican Revolution. They became the major beneficiaries of economic growth after 1940 and gained privileged representation within the party-state apparatus. Like their Chilean counterparts, they were generally not concerned about the plight of workers and peasants. By the end of the century, the country's middle class had largely shifted support to the center-right Popular Action Party.

The World Economy, Globalization, and Power Relations in Distributional Outcomes

International factors—markets, the geopolitical and economic interests of the United States, and pressures from multilateral lending institutions—were all integral factors contributing to the distinct outcomes in the three cases. Indeed, the processes producing distinct poverty and inequality outcomes were, in many respects, inseparable from various international processes and opportunities.

Integration into international markets interacted with domestic processes to shape the domestic evolution of social forces. Such an interaction occurred with the impact of commercial export agriculture that had distinct implications for the mobilization propensities of the peasantry in the three cases. In Korea, commercial export agriculture loosened the grip of big landowners and nurtured increasingly high levels of political mobilization. In Chile, it increased the grip of the big landowners over the peasantry, making mobilization impossible, while in Mexico it produced large-scale landlessness, a result that was instrumental in peasant involvement in the revolutionary struggle that would follow (see Chapters 2, 3, and 4). The importance of mineral enclave status, a feature of resource endowment that determined demand from the international market, gave rise to an ideologically militant working class with, as already noted, implications for the intensity of political conflict, reactive sequences, and redistributive settlements.

The Korean state's success in leading employment-generating export growth required a receptive international market. The leadership's decision, for example, to produce light consumer goods for export responded to its knowledge of market opportunity. Korea's transition to heavy and chemical industries (HCI) production occurred in response to the belief that it was no longer competitive in light consumer goods. The attempt by Mexico in the mid-1970s, when faced with growing economic difficulties, to make inroads into the U.S. market for its manufactured goods, faced a world economic downturn and growing U.S. protectionism. In addition, pressure from the United States and related issues of a geopolitical nature reinforced South Korea's path-dependent sequence, while such pressures strengthened Chile's and Mexico's reactionary ones. Recall that the United States reacted negatively to land redistribution and the nationalizations in Mexico and Chile in ways that contributed to economic instability and to the anger and fear on the part of the political right and propertied interests.

While the governments of the three countries have handled export growth strategies differently, all three have faced pressures to maintain or increase labor flexibility with important implications for social welfare and social protection. Pressure for labor flexibility has arisen with new technologies that made it possible to spread production processes across the globe. Labor reforms have also responded to the belief that greater labor flexibility would contribute to employment expansion. While labor flexibility makes it easier to hire and fire workers and has been associated with an increase in temporary and part-time employment, this development does not have to mean an increase in economic precariousness and a decline in social welfare protection. In some European countries, such as the Netherlands and Denmark, workers working under flexible labor regimes are provided with adequate social protection in the form of income security/unemployment insurance benefits, social insurance, safety standards, and retraining (Bronstein 2009; 12; Van Eyck 2003, 34, 39).

However, in all of the cases dealt with in this work, labor flexibility does appear to have contributed to labor precariousness. Flexibility in labor regimes has not mitigated inequalities within the labor market in the Latin American cases and has produced them in the Korean case (Chapter 7). Although the Korean case shows universalistic aspirations in social welfare protection, policymakers have not successfully combined labor flexibility with social protection that reaches most of those subject to irregular employment. Recall that pensions, health care protection, and unemployment insurance still do not reach many of those in irregular employment. Indeed, the pursuit of high-skilled employment-generating sectors in the case of Korea does not appear to have mitigated growing labor precariousness. Meanwhile, in Chile, despite the substantial achievements in poverty reduction, rural workers remain subject to temporary labor contracts with limited benefits and without the right to bargain collectively.

Although Korea remains considerably ahead of both Chile and Mexico in poverty and inequality indicators, there is, nevertheless, a certain convergence in the area of labor flexibility and social welfare protection. In Korea, as in Mexico and Chile, a substantial portion of the labor force engaged in precarious employment is without social benefits.

Despite the strong commitment to equity on the part of much of the Korean public and the enormous pressure exerted by civil society and part of the labor movement, social welfare protection is not yet universal in practice. Chile has mitigated some of the worst consequences of its du-alist welfare arrangements, with the greatest progress having been made as a consequence of civil society mobilization during the Bachelet years. While Mexico has moved to confront the exclusionary nature of its wel-fare regime, the system remains highly dualistic, with social spending now slanted to the advantage of the middle class.

This study has demonstrated that ongoing poverty and inequality stem from power inequalities. A weakened landowning class and a mobilized peasantry set the stage for land redistribution and equitable development in Korea. Powerful landed and propertied classes blocked land redistribu-tion in Mexico and Chile. Large-scale mobilization was effective in securing redistributive measures in the two Latin American cases, but it also trig-gered reactive events that stalled or reversed social gains. More recently in Chile, civil society activism has produced some improvements in unequal service provision. In Korea, pressure from middle-class organizations and a faction of the labor movement has been instrumental in recent welfare gains. Hence, as the case of Korea illustrates, mobilization needs to occur not sim-ply among those who find themselves socially excluded but also (and perhaps more importantly) among an important proportion of the more privileged members of society (particularly, the middle class) who, in the case of Korea, came to hold equality and poverty reduction as important values. Middle-class support for equality-enhancing measures helped forestall reactive ac-tions by propertied groups who may have seen their interests threatened. The Korean case also illustrates the importance of a having broad societal com-mitment to reduce the economic power of the wealthiest members of society. Recall that the popular drive for expanded social protection also involved fierce criticism of the *chaebols* and demands that their power curtailed.

The comparative analysis presented here indicates that there is no easy remedy to the problem of high levels of inequality and insufficient poverty reduction. The high levels of inequality found in the two Latin American countries were the product of a long and complex historical experience that entrenched institutions and attitudes and created vested interests fiercely resistant to change. Hence, institutional reforms and changes in policy will be ineffective unless accompanied by a fundamental alteration in societal attitudes, among the more privileged social groups.

Korea had the luxury of a period of weak social forces during which the state could address the problems of the rural poor and lead industrial development relatively unencumbered by the pressure from propertied and working- and middle-class groups. Such an opportunity did not and will not occur in countries like Mexico or Chile—or indeed, in many other global south countries faced with similar social and redistributive challenges. In societies such as these, where there has been a long history of sharp social compartmentalization, redistributive compromise settlements are likely to be especially difficult to achieve.

Redistributive improvement requires a state capable of orchestrating a societal compromise. Indeed, Chapter 1 suggested that the optimal situation for good redistributive outcomes (northern Europe) was a situation in which strong states mediated compromise settlements among strong social forces. But this condition is absent in all of the cases dealt with in this work. Even in the case of Korea, social forces, especially propertied interests, have been strengthening while the state's ability to lead development has been weakening in recent years. Hence, the Korean state's ability to secure distributive settlements that keep equality low may become increasingly problematic. The Chilean case under President Bachelet illustrates the difficulty the state faces in orchestrating a new redistributive compromise when propertied interests have a long history of shaping economic and social policy to their liking. Even though events in Chile suggest an awakening of civil society, labor remains weak. Mexican labor and civil society are weak, a legacy of its particular form of authoritarian rule. Its propertied class, which backs the state, is also very powerful.

Hence, a significant and long-term improvement in distributional outcome is a daunting political task. It involves the building of a strong societal consensus on the importance of the reduction in inequality, one that compels political leaders to make difficult policy changes. In countries with histories of reactionary sequences it is an especially tricky political undertaking. Mobilization from below is required, but rhetoric must be moderate so that a compromise solution is not threatened by fear on the part of the propertied and middle-class groups. The incorporation of middle- and working-class groups, who have hitherto confined their political activities to the protection of their particular interests, is especially important. As noted in Chapter 1, lowering inequality is crucial to economic growth and to mitigating political and criminal violence. Hence, however difficult the attainment of such redistributive settlements may be, their achievement is an urgent imperative.

Reference Matter

Appendix

TABLE A-1 Poverty Rates: Percentage of Households below Poverty Lines, 1963–2007.

Year	South Korea			Mexico			Chile		
	National	Urban	Rural	National	Urban	Rural	National	Urban	Rural
1963/5*	41.4 (1965)	54.9	35.8	55.9 (1963)	—	—	—	—	—
1970	23.2	16.2	27.9	34.0	20	49	17.0	12.0	25.0
1976-1977	14.6	18.1	11.7	32.0 (1977)	—	—	—	—	—
1984	—	—	—	34.0	28	45	—	—	—
1987-1989	9.5 (1988)	9.3	9.8	39.0 (1989)	34	49	39 (1987)	38	45
1990				36.0			33		
1992							28		
1994	—	—	—	36.0	29	47	23	23	26
1996	—	—	—	52.9	46.1	62.8	23.2	22.0	30.4
1997	4.0	—	—	—	—	—	—	—	—
1998	12.0	—	—	46.9	38.9	58.5	21.7	20.7	27.5
2000	5.7 (2003)	—	—	41.1	32.3	54.7	20.2	19.7	23.7
2005	—	—	—	35.5	28.5	47.5	18.7	18.5	20.0
2006	—	—	—	24.6	—	—	11.3	—	—
2007	—	—	—	27.9	—	—	—	—	—

Sources: Data from South Korea: 1965, 1970, 1976, 1988: Kwon, 1993, 96; 1997 and 1998: Koo 2007, 2; 1999 and 2003: Kim and Park 2006, 451. Mexico: 1963: Székely 1998, 10; 1970, 1977, 1984, 1989, 1992, 1994: Wilkie 1999, 428; 1996, 1998, 2000, 2005: ECLAC 2007, 299-300; 2006, 2007: CEPAL 2009, 87; Chile: 1970, 1987, 1990, 1992, 1994: Wilkie 1999, 428; 1994: 1996, 1998, 2000, 2005: ECLAC 2007, 299-300; 2006: CEPAL 2009, 86.

Note on Poverty Lines: Poverty figures for Mexico and Chile are from ECLAC/CEPAL (United Nations Economic Commission for Latin America and the Caribbean) and sources using ECLAC. ECLAC bases figures on the cost of a basic food basket for each country. South Korean secondary sources obtained their data from the Korean government which follows a similar procedure for establishing its poverty line. Independent Mexican academic sources generally put Mexican poverty figures considerably higher than indicated here.

TABLE A-2.   Inequality (Gini coefficient),* 1950–2008.

Year	South Korea	Mexico	Chile
1950	—	.52	—
Early 1960s	.45 (1960)	.54 (1963)	.46 (1960) (urban)
1965	.34	—	—
1968	.36	.59	.46
1975	.39	.50 (1977)	.47
1980	.39	—	.52 (1980)
1984	.35	.49	.56
Late 1980s	.32 (1988)	.52 (1989)	.56 (1987)
1996	.29	.54	.55
1998	.31	.55	.56
2000	.32	.54	.55
2004	.34	.50	.55 (2003)
2006	.34	.51	.53
2008	.33	—	.52

*The Gini coefficient is a number measuring inequality that ranges between 0, where there is perfect equality, to 1, where one person has all of the income. There is considerable variation in South Korea inequality figures. See Peng 2009, 8, 42.

Sources: Data from South Korea: 1960: Koo, 2006, 60; 1965, 1975, 1980: Song 2003, 200; 1968: Yoo 1990, 377; 1984,1988: UN-WIDER Data base; 1996–2006: Jomo 2006, 7–8; 2008: The Hankyoreh, May 22, 2009; Mexico: 1950, 1963, 1968, 1977, 1984, 1988, 1996, 1998, 2000, 2004, 2006: UN-WIDER data base; Chile: 1960, Thorpe 1998, 352; 1968, 1975, 1980, 1984, 1987, 1996, 1998, 2000, 2003: 2000, 2003: UN-WIDER data base; 2006: Larrañaga 2009, 7; 2008, CEPAL 2009, 91.

TABLE A-3.   Share of national income, top 10 percent of wealthiest households.

Years	South Korea	Mexico	Chile
1965–1968	25.78	51.70	34.80
1987–1989	25.14	41.67	45.34
2000	25.4	42.28	45.29

Source: Data from UN-WIDER data base; 2000: Korea: Song 2003, 200.

TABLE A-4.   Share of national income, bottom 40 percent of households.

Years	South Korea	Mexico	Chile
1965–1968	19.34	9.8	13.4
1987–1989	20.50	11.21	10.1
2000	20.3	10.62	10.77

Source: Data from UN-WIDER data base; 2000: Korea: Song 2003, 200.

TABLE A-5.   GDP per capita average growth rates, five-year periods, 1950–2009.

Years	South Korea	Chile	Mexico
1950–1954	.40	.65	3.0
1955–1959	1.8	1.0	3.0
1960–1964	2.6	3.2	4.3
1965–1969	7.5	2.4	2.7
1970–1974	6.4	.2	3.4
1975–1979	7.7	1.4	3.2
1980–1984	4.3	–1.8	.5
1985–1989	10.1	4.0	–1.0
1990–1994	7.3	5.3	1.9
1995–1999	3.6	4.1	1.1
2000–2004	4.8	2.6	1.2
2005–2009	3.3	3.2	2.5

Source: Data from South Korea, Chile Mexico, 1950–2004: Calculated from Heston, Aten, and Summers 2002. Korea, 2005–2009: World Bank 2010a, 78; Chile, 2005–2006: Index Mundi, 2010; 2007–2009: World Bank, 2010, Mexico: 2005–2009: Inter-American Development Bank, Database.

TABLE A-6. Illiteracy rates, 1900–2000.

Year	South Korea National	South Korea Rural	Mexico National	Mexico Rural	Chile National	Chile Rural
1900	—	—	75.5	—	56.5	—
1940–1945	78	—	53.9	—	27.1	—
1960	29.4	—	34.6	—	16.4	—
1970	12.4	10.0	25.8	39.7	11.0	25.6
1980–1982	12.0	—	17.5	—	8.9	21.9
1995	3.1	—	10.5	—	5.1	—
2000	2.3	—	8.8	—	4.2	—

Source: Data from South Korea: 1945, 1980: Mason et al. 1980, 349; 1960 and 1970 national rates: The World Bank 1983, 51; Rural illiteracy rate, 1970, Ban et al. 1980, 312; 1995 and 2000: U.N. Common Database (UNESCO estimates); Mexico: National figures, 1900, 1940, 1960, 1980, 1995: Thorpe, 1998, 354; rural and national, 1970: Wilkie, 1999, 215; 2000: U.N. Common Database (UNESCO estimates); Chile: 1900, 1940, 1960: Thorpe 1998, 354; 1970, national and rural, 1970 and 1982: Wilkie, 1999, 214; 2000: U.N. Common Database (UNESCO estimates).

TABLE A-7. Agricultural labor as a percentage of total employment, 1907–2007.

Year	South Korea	Mexico	Chile
1907–1910	—	68.1	37.7
1950	79.4	58.3	32.2
1960	65.9	55.1	30.5
1965	58.6	50.2	26.4
1970	50.5	45.2	22.6
1975	41.9	40.3	20.9
1980	34.0	35.6	19.2
1985	24.9	NA	20.2
1990	17.9	22.6	19.3
1995	12.4	23.8	15.7
2000	10.6	17.6	14.4
2005	7.9	14.9	13.2

Sources: Data from South Korea: 1950–1974: Mason et al. 1980; 1975, 1980: World Bank1983, 51; 1985–2005: World Bank: *World Bank Indicators*; 2009, Asian Development Bank 2010, 140. Mexico: 1910, 1950: Hansen 1980, 22, 43; 1960–1980: World Bank, 1983, 63, 1990–2005: World Bank: *World Bank Indicators*; Chile: 1907, 1950: Chile: Mamalakis 1976, 11, 129; 1960–1980: World Bank, 1983, 63; 1985–2005: World Bank: *World Bank Indicators*.

TABLE A-8.   Employment in manufacturing as a percentage of total employed, 1940–2000.

Year	South Korea	Mexico	Chile	
			Manufacturing and construction	
1940	—	11	20.9	
1950	—	12	24.0	
			Manufacturing	Construction
1960	6.8	14	17.8	5.6
1965	9.4	15	19.3	7.0
1970	14.3	17	19.0	5.9
1975/6	21.3	18	17.2	4.5
1980	21.7	19.5	16.1	4.6
1985	—	—	13.8	—
1990	26.9	19.1	16.0	6.4
2000	20.1	NA	—	—

Source: Data from South Korea: 1960, 1965, and 1970: Kim and Roemer 1979, 64; 1976, 1980, 1990, 2000: Song 2003, 136; Mexico: 1940–1980: Mexico: Cockcroft 1983, 183; 1990: Calculated from Banco de México 1995, 209; Chile: 1940, 1950: Mamalakis 1976, 11; 1960, 1965, and 1970: Castells 1974, 51; 1975, 1980, 1985, 1990: Frías and Ruiz-Tagle 1992, 66.

TABLE A-9.   Manufacturing as a percentage of GDP, 1940–1980.

Years	South Korea	Mexico	Chile
1940	—	16.6	19.7*
1945	—	18.8	22.1*
1950	—	20.6	16.7
1955	11.5	21.0	18.8
1960	13.7	23.0	20.9
1965	18.0	21.0	23.9
1970	20.0	23.6	25.5
1975	26.0	23.3	20.2
1980	27.0	23.2	21.5

Sources: Data from South Korea: World Bank 1983, 103–104; Mexico and Chile, 1940, 1945: Thorpe 1998, 162; Mexico and Chile, 1950, 1955, and 1960: Furtado 1976, 132–133; 1965–1980: World Bank 1983, 36–37, 122–123.

*Includes construction.

TABLE A-10.   Tax income as a percentage of GDP, 1950–2008.

Year	South Korea	Mexico	Chile
1950	—	7.5	16.7
1960	—	7.1	16.5
1970	—	7.9	22.6
1975	16.3	12.6	23.7
1980	17.2	—	24.3
1985	16.4	—	23.8
1990	18.9	11.8	15.9
1995	18.6	10.6	16.7
2000	22.6	18.5	16.4
2005	23.9	18.1	22.6
2008	26.6	20.4	21.4

Source: South Korea 1975–2008: OECD 2010; Mexico: 1950, 1960, and 1970: Thorpe 1998, 170; 1975: Padilla Aragón 1981, 134; 1990, 1995: World Bank: *World Bank Indicators*; 2000, 2005, 2009: OECD 2010; Chile: 1950, 1960: Thorpe 1998, 170; 1965, 1970, 1975, 1980: Griffith-Jones 1987, 18; 1990: Foxley 1995, 16; 1995 and 2000: Gobierno de Chile, Ministerio de Hacienda 1992, 68; 2005: OECD 2008.

TABLE A-11. Structure of exports, Mexico, percentage of the value of total exports.

Description	1992	2000	2008
1. Agricultural products (animals, grains, tea, coffee, beef)	5.29	3.10	3.30
2. Petroleum	17.58	9.65	17.35
3. Raw cotton, fibers, wood, pulp and paper	2.83	1.98	1.13
4. Food products (oils, vegetable extract, sugar, tobacco products, juices)	2.43	2.46	3.34
5. Chemical and petrochemical products	3.33	1.65	1.89
6. Mineral and mineral products (iron and steel smelting and products, copper and copper products, lead, zinc, and so on, production and products)	5.74	3.81	5.35
7. Light manufactures	15.32	17.91	14.54
Textiles/clothing	*(3.32)*	*(5.90)*	*(2.02)*
8. Capital goods, machinery, equipment, transportation	47.26	59.57	52.94
Electrical machinery, appliances, parts, electrical material**	*(24.77)*	*(28.53)*	*(25.80)*
Automobiles, tractors	*(12.26)*	*(16.92)*	*(14.64)*
TOTAL MANUFACTURES (excludes 1–6)	62.58	77.48	67.48
TOTAL MANUFACTURES and PROCESSED PRODUCTS (includes 3–7)	76.91	87.20	82.01
Not classified	.22	.05	.03

*Food products, minerals and mineral products, chemical and petrochemical products, raw cotton and fibers, wood, pulp and paper.

**Includes materials, parts, accessories, and final products (for example, cables, connectors, transformers, electrical motors, parts for electrical appliances, electrical appliances).

Source: Data from Banco Interamericano de Desarrollo. Instituto para la Integración de América Latina y el Caribe. DATAINTAL. Retrieved on May 3, 2010, from www.iadb.org/dataintal/totalpais.aspx?Tipo=P.

TABLE A-12. Structure of exports, South Korea, percentage of the value of total exports.

Description	1990	2000	2007
Animal, vegetable oils, products, beverages	3.32	1.53	.90
Crude material, mineral fuels	2.60	6.50	7.76
Chemicals	3.86	8.00	10.11
Basic manufactures	22.08	17.64	14.01
Iron and steel products	(8.25)	(6.60)	(8.50)
Machines, transport equipment		58.21	58.34
Machinery, precision equipment	39.29	(6.96)	(9.73)
Ships, boats, warships	(5.37)	(4.78)	(7.23)
Telecommunications, sound recording, reproducing apparatus, and equipment	(4.32)	(13.58)	(13.64)
	(5.98)		
Miscellaneous manufactured goods	28.57	7.22	8.68
Unclassified goods	.28	.91	.21

Source: Data from Asian Development Bank 2008.

TABLE A-13. Structure of exports, Chile, percentage of the value of total exports.

Description	1996	2000	2008
Mining	46.19	45.36	60.34
Copper	(40.60)	(41.20)	(51.97)
Agrolivestock/forestry/fishing	10.76	9.57	6.23
Fruit	(8.47)	(7.74)	(5.63)
Industry	43.05	45.06	33.43
Food and beverages/tobacco (salmon, fishmeal, juices, wine)	(20.73)	(18.25)	(13.38)
Forestry products (sawed wood, chips, pulp and paper)*	(11.73)	(13.25)	(8.49)
Chemical products	(3.92)	(6.88)	(6.05)
Basic and manufactured metals, machinery, equipment, and transport material	(4.88)	(4.83)	(4.95)
Other	(1.78)	(1.40)	(.53)

Source: Data from Gobierno de Chile.

*Wood furniture was included in the category "timber and wood furniture," a category that accounted for only 3.30 percent of total exports in 2008.

FIGURE A-1.   Critical conjunctures, path-dependent and reactionary sequences, and social outcomes: South Korea, Chile, and Mexico.

South Korea Critical Conjuncture 1930–1953	Chile Critical Conjuncture 1929–1941	Mexico Critical Conjuncture 1890–1925
High level of peasant mobilization	• Great Depression	• Peasant and worker mobilization
WWII ends; U.S. military occupation; division of Korea	• Popular Front, 1938: working class and middle class gain access to power	• The Mexican Revolution
Korean War, 1950–1953	• Import substitution industrialization	• Growth of U.S. economy
Land redistribution, 1948–1952	• Reform/social improvement in the countryside is blocked	• Emergence of new agrarian export class
1961: Gen. Park comes to power		• Land redistribution and other redistributive measures stall; growing political unrest
1961–1970:		

South Korea

1961–1970:
• Support for rural dwellers
• Employment-generating industrialization
• Independent bureaucracy

↓

Path-Dependent Sequence
• Success of industrial growth model, dramatic decline in poverty
• Generates public support for state-led development
• Rise in inequality in 1970s; government takes measures to mitigate it

1980s:
• By 1980: emergence of large urban middle class with social justice concerns; organizes trade unions
• Sympathetic to rural welfare; significant transfers to poor rural kin
• Impact of debt crisis is quickly overcome through state action stimulating exports

Chile

↓

Reactive Sequence
(1941–1973)

1941: Exit of Socialist Party from Popular Front; turn to revolutionary Marxism
• 1946: Communists are expelled from Popular Front
• Trade unions repressed; peasant unions outlawed
• Increasing mobilization and political polarization, 1960s–1973
• Propertied class plots to overthrow the government in alliance with middle class
• 1973 military coup

↓

Second Critical Conjuncture: 1973–1984
• Decline of copper prices followed by international debt crisis
• Radical neoliberal economic restructuring; model modified after 1983
• Poverty and inequality increase

Mexico

↓

Second Critical Conjuncture, 1930–1940

Great Depression: increased worker and peasant mobilization

Extensive land redistribution under Cárdenas, 1934–1940

Living standards improve

↓

Reactive Sequence 1938–1976
• Intense opposition from propertied classes, mobilization of middle class against the regime
• Cárdenas is replaced with a more conservative leadership
• The PRI becomes a mechanism of political control
• Growth with inequality; high level of rural poverty; land redistribution reversed
• Workers and peasants mobilize

(continued)

- State bureaucrats, *chaebols,* and public resist pressures for market reform
- Social programs begin to expand in response to public concerns

1987–1992:
Political transition

- Middle-class and worker mobilization for both democracy and social justice, combined with sharp criticism of *chaebols*
- Pressure from civil society for expansion of social welfare protection begins to bear fruit
- State, however, is weakening, in face of *chaebols*

1997 Financial crisis
and after

- Immediate impact: sharp rise in poverty and inequality
- But rapid economic recovery; poverty and inequality decline and remain comparatively low
- Although weakened, state continues to play an important role in economic recovery
- Power of *chaebols* increases
- Pressures from *chaebols* for labor flexibility
- Goverment orchestrates labor flexibility in exchange for expanded social welfare protection
- Irregular labor force increases

- Highly flexible labor code (1979)
- Mobilization against the regime

1986–1989
Pacted Political Transition

- With adjustment of economic model, export-led growth produces a decline in poverty

Civilian Rule, 1990–2010
1990–2000 Path Dependency

- Institutional path-dependent features from military period stall social improvements
- Powerful private sector, quiescent civil society and weak labor movement
- Poverty continues to decline largely due to economic growth
- But inequality remains high

2000–2010: Rise in Popular Mobilization

- Election of socialist presidents
- Civil society mobilization increases: 2006
- Produces legislation addressing equity in education and pensions
- High degree of labor flexibility remains for rural workers
- Inequality begins to decline

- 1970–1975, land redistribution and social improvements
- Intense opposition from propertied interests (capital flight)
- Attempt at redistribution ends

Third Critical Conjuncture, 1980–1994

- Debt crisis and decline in petroleum prices hits economy
- Opposition of private sector to regime
- Import substitution model discredited
- Poverty increases, then falls
- Inequality remains high

1995–2010

- Peso crisis 1995; rise in poverty
- Mobilization for electoral democracy accelerates
- Social issues on the back burner
- Old PRI authoritarian structures fall
- 2000: PRI presidential candidate is defeated
- Middle class shifts support to the opposition PAN party
- From 2006 on: Center right government supports labor flexibility, subsidies to support the middle class
- Poverty increase in 2006
- Inequality remains high

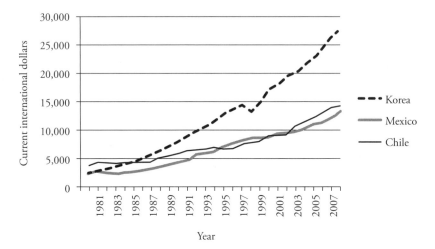

FIGURE A-2. Gross national income (GNI) per capita (current international dollars) PPP, 1980–2008. PPP, or purchasing power parity, is a method of measuring the relative purchasing power of different countries' currencies over the same types of goods and services, despite differential rates of inflation. PPP allows us to make more accurate comparisons of standards of living across countries because goods and services may cost more in one country than in another. Source: Data from World Bank Indicators.

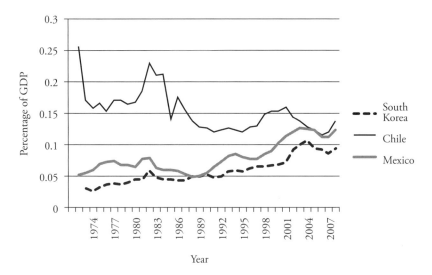

FIGURE A-3. Social expenditures as a percentage of GDP, 1973–2008. Sources: Data from IMF, *Government Finance Statistics Yearbooks,* 1977, 1985, 1991, 2001, 2005, 2007, 2008 except Mexico 2000–2006 and Korea 2004–2008 from OECD 2010 and Mexico 2008 from CEPAL 2010.

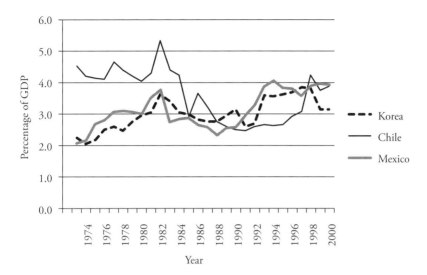

FIGURE A-4. Education expenditures as a percentage of GDP, 1973–2000. Source: Data calculated from: IMF, *Government Finance Statistics Yearbooks,* 1977, 1985, 1991, 2001, 2005, 2007, 2008.

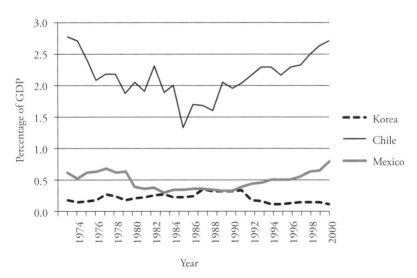

FIGURE A-5. Health expenditures as a percentage of GDP, 1973–2000. Source: Data from: IMF, *Government Finance Statistics Yearbooks,* 1977, 1985, 1991, 2001, 2005, 2007, 2008.

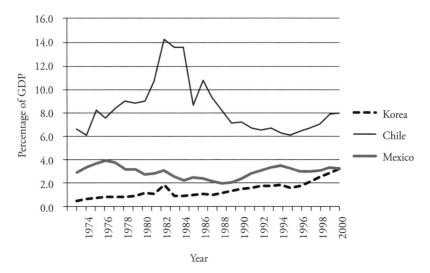

FIGURE A-6. Social security and welfare expenditures as a percentage of GDP, 1973–2000. Source: Data calculated from: IMF, *Government Finance Statistics Yearbooks,* 1977, 1985, 1991, 2001, 2005, 2007, 2008.

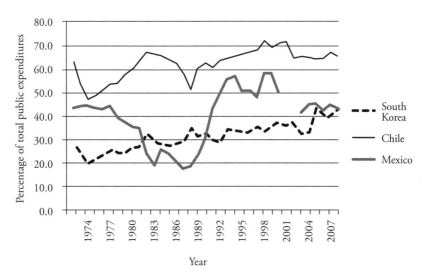

FIGURE A-7. Social spending as a percentage of total public expenditures, 1973–2008. Source: Data from IMF, *Government Finance Statistics Yearbooks,* 1977, 1985, 1991, 2001, 2005, 2007, 2008; except Mexico, 2003–2008: Secretaría de Hacienda y Crédito Público, "Estructura del ingreso y financiamiento del sector público presupuestario. Retrieved on September 10, 2010, from www.apartados.hacienda.gob.mx/estadisticas_oportunas/esp/index.html.

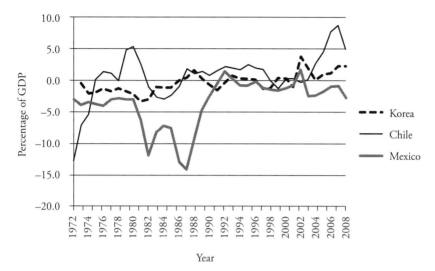

FIGURE A-8. Public deficit or surplus as a percentage of GDP, 1973–2008. Source: Data from 1973–2000: IMF, *International Statistical Yearbooks,* 1998 and 2008; from 2001–2009: World Bank Indicators.

Notes

Chapter 1

1. This recent increase in inequality levels marks a change in comparison with what was observed during the thirty years following World War II when, with the exception of Latin America and parts of sub-Saharan Africa, a widespread move toward greater egalitarianism occurred in the majority of societies, both developed and developing (Cornia et al. 2004, 26).

2. Figures on South Korean inequality have come under considerable criticism for, among other things, their failure to take into account asset concentration (Joung-woo 2006, 204; Kwon 1993, 136–140). Similar criticisms have also been made of the Latin American figures on inequality (Guerrero, López-Calva, and Walton 2006, 2). Hence, the argument that South Korea has maintained comparatively lower levels of inequality appears valid. Definitions of poverty and are also disputed, particularly in the case of Mexico. See the note at the bottom of Table A-1 regarding the sources and comparability of figures used in this study.

3. The term *newly industrializing countries* or NICs arose originally in the 1970s to refer to the four East Asian cases already referred to, in addition to two Latin American countries (Mexico and Brazil) in the process of increasing manufactured exports.

4. Chile's average annual per capital growth rate between 1950 and the mid-1960s was only 1.6 percent (see Table A-5).

5. The only other comparable case is Taiwan, with similar achievements in per capita income, equality, and export performance. The city-states of Hong Kong and Singapore are not comparable due to the absence of the land reform issue and their early status as trading centers and later as international financial hubs.

6. In contrast, civil society is weaker and more quiescent in Taiwan (S. Kim 2000; Koo 1993b).

7. In addition, Korea, like Mexico and Chile and unlike Taiwan, struggled with a fragmental health system that it was able to unify in the face of stiff resistance from social forces (Wong 2004, 88). This topic is discussed in Chapter 7.

8. Of course, frustrated power contenders may also manipulate a social force's interests.

9. This did not occur in South Korea. The reasons are explored in Chapter 5.

10. Exceptions are the edited volume by Boyd, Galjart, and Ngo (2006) and Davis's comparative study (2004). While the former does not give systematic attention to the explanation of distinct poverty and inequality outcomes across specific cases, the latter is not concerned with the ability of Asian NICs to maintain low levels of poverty and inequality long after they have industrialized and the rural population has declined.

11. Haggard, Kang, and Moon (1997), however, contest this viewpoint because the Japanese colonial rule was not as enduring as assumed.

12. It took Latin America some fifty years of almost incessant civil wars to consolidate its nation-states, and this period was followed by cycles of electoral democracy and military rule in the twentieth century.

13. International factors, which also played an important role, are discussed later in the chapter.

14. See Chapter 7.

15. Admittedly, this is somewhat of an oversimplification because import substitution policies were also employed in East Asia.

16. Examples include Guatemala, 1954; the Dominican Republic, 1965; and, through the 1970s, U.S. military support for right-wing Central American governments seeking the defeat of insurgent groups demanding land redistribution.

17. Theoretically, redistribution is possible without economic growth, but it is usually politically extremely difficult. Kerala, India, is a case of radical redistribution in a context of slow growth, but the particular circumstances that made this possible are relatively rare in the global south. See Sandbrook et al., 2007.

18. Most of this work, however, deals with Western liberal democracies (Hadenius 1992; Lipset and Lakin 2004, 38; Londregan and Poole 1996; Przeworski and Limongi Neto 1997).

19. A response might be that this occurs because these are low-quality democracies, in the sense of weak labor organizations and weak civil societies.

20. A full discussion of the political transitions of each of the cases occurs in the country chapters, Chapters 2, 3, and 4.

21. Distinct political settlements produced different welfare states with varying redistributive consequences. Esping-Andersen (1990) identifies three distinct welfare state regimes: the liberal (the United States), the conservative corporatist (Germany, Italy), and the social democratic (Sweden).

22. The most widely known example of the use of *coyuntura* is Cardoso and Faletto (1979). An example of use of the concept of critical juncture in comparative historical sociology is Ertman 1997.

23. In this work, *middle class* denotes that portion of the urban population employed in job categories described as "white collar." These include: professionals, administrators, office workers, technicians, owners of small businesses, and the self-employed. Generally, this group of the population has a living standard and a lifestyle that sets it apart from the working and agricultural classes.

Chapter 2

1. Inequality increased in the 1970s, but the figure declined thereafter. As discussed later in the chapter, most observers attribute the increase of inequality in the 1970s to the policy turn to heavy and chemical industries.

2. In 1950, 79.4 percent of the labor force was engaged in agriculture (see Table A-7).

3. The extent of the participation of former landowners in the industrial expansion that began in the 1960s is a topic of considerable debate. There does appear to be some continuity, particularly among those landowners who had invested in small Korean firms during the period of Japanese rule. However, Woo points out that of the top fifty *chaebols,* only three had founders who accumulated wealth during the period of Japanese colonial rule (1991, 66–69).

4. The example of the radical North Korean land reform that had begun in 1946 also had an important impact in encouraging the South Korean peasantry to demand land redistribution.

5. The concept of private property had been in existence in the precolonial period and was reinforced during Japanese colonial rule (Kim and Roemer 1979, 1).

6. The first postliberation election occurred in 1948.

7. The Korean government did not offer much in the way of compensation to land-lords. The government paid landlords with bonds that rapidly deteriorated to only about 10 percent of their face value (Mason et al. 1980, 420). This fact caused landlords to turn their land over to tenants in private deals.

8. Legislation placing a three-*chongbo* (one *chongbo* is about 2.2 acres) limit on farm size was effective in preventing an immediate return to inequality in land ownership (Mason et al. 1980, 329). By 1974, tenancy had increased to 31.4 percent of farmers and to 43.7 percent by 1980 (Boyer and Ahn 1991, 46)

9. The Gini coefficient is a number measuring inequality that ranges from zero (for complete equality) to 1.0 if one person has all the land or income.

10. In addition, educational opportunities were broadly similar with children using the same texts and writing the same national examinations across the country (Song 2003, 56).

11. A couple of socialist parties did arise in the 1960s. Led by intellectuals, they did not establish roots in the masses. The intense ideology of anticommunism set the narrow parameters within which acceptable political activity could occur.

12. This explanation diverges from Davis (2004), who attributes state capacity to the regime's social basis in the middle, yeoman class.

13. This scenario runs counter to expectations given the conventional wisdom regard-ing the central role of trade unions and leftist political parties in redistributive outcomes in the industrialized countries.

14. According to Mason et al., when the impact of revenue and expenditure is com-bined, the net effect is to make the budget a modest influence for reducing inequality in both the urban and rural areas (1980, 439).

15. While the southeast prospered during the 1960s and 1970s, the southwest and central provinces experienced both a dramatic fall in population and economic stagna-tion. Investment went largely to the southeast and Seoul region (Yea 2002, 38).

16. Indeed, the sympathy of the regime for rural issues has caused at least one observer to describe the 1961 coup as "a revolt of the countryside" (B. Kim 2000, 74).

17. The nature of the regime's support base has been an issue of considerable contention. Probably the most common interpretation sees the regime as "a political alliance of civilian bureaucrats, technocrats, and industrialists centered on the military elite" (Choi 1993, 26).

18. The extent to which presidential elections were a good gauge of public sentiment varied. Large-scale fraud characterized the 1960 election, while the 1963 election was relatively fair (Lee 2001, 148). There is some dispute about the extent of fraud in the 1967 presidential election (Cole and Lyman 1971, 238; Lee 2001, 148), while there is a consensus that there was a high degree of fraud in the 1971 election (Lee 2001, 149). With the authoritarian Yushin constitution, electoral fraud declined as it became less necessary.

19. However, the impact of elections was only a contributing factor in accounting for concern for rural social welfare. As discussed later in this chapter, prorural policies continued even after the regime's turn to a much tougher form of authoritarianism.

20. Indeed, 72 percent of the military men who participated in the coup and in the subsequent government were born in rural areas (Mason et al. 1980, 461). The fact that the military provided free educational opportunities for new recruits had made it particularly attractive to the poor, particularly the rural poor (Kim 2001, 174).

21. While in 1965 urban and rural incomes were about equal, by 1970 rural incomes had declined to 67 percent of urban incomes (Song 2003, 197).

22. However, the government continued to maintain low prices in urban areas through an outright government subsidy (Mason et al., 423).

23. *Minjung,* meaning the "people" or the "masses," rose up as an alliance of the popular sectors and the middle class in opposition to the authoritarian regime. It also advocated a radical restructuring of the economy to achieve redistributive justice (Koo 1993a, 143). This is discussed further in the following pages.

24. Critics, however, argue that the tax system has been particularly remiss in taxing the windfall income due to property ownership (Kwon 1993, 224).

25. The U.S. threat to withdraw aid was an additional pressure propelling Korean industrial policy forward. The threat forced Korea to develop an effective export profile in order to earn foreign exchange (Haggard 1990, 61; Woo 1991, 77).

26. In the second half of the 1960s, 60 percent of investments in manufacturing went to only three industries: petrochemicals, steel, and machinery. Initially, the process of allocating large investments discretionally fostered many incompetent firms. Hence, in 1969–1971, over 100 incompetent firms were either liquidated or acquired by other firms (Jwa 2002, 21, 24).

27. By the early 1990s, South Korea had become the world's second largest exporter of ships after Japan (Woo 1991, 135).

28. One important difference from the Latin American cases, however, is that only employers and employees contributed. The state did not contribute until 1988.

29. Arita's data is drawn from a 1990 "Survey on Inequality and Equity" conducted by the Korean Social Science Research Council. The analysis is limited to males only. The working class includes sales and service workers, skilled and unskilled workers. The middle class is divided into the "old" and "new" middle class, although both groups expanded rapidly during the period of industrialization. The new middle class includes specialists, technicians, employed administrators, and office workers, while the old middle class includes employers and the self-employed (excluding farming, forestry, fishing) and company owners employing five or more people (2003, 204). Both old and new middle classes had incomes substantially above the working and agrarian classes but well below the capitalist class.

30. This comparative dimension of the Korean versus the Latin American experiences is explored further in Chapter 5.

Chapter 3

1. Diego Portales was never president of Chile. He was unofficial dictator from 1830 through 1831, following the civil war, and served as minister of the interior between 1835 and 1837 when he was assassinated.

2. The alternative would have been to invest in capital improvements. Agriculturalists did not do so because of the extreme uncertainty of the grain trade (Bauer 1975, 162).

3. The *inquilino* system itself responded to the belief that laborers were not sufficiently motivated by wages to make themselves available for the crucial harvest time (Bauer 1975, 142).

4. Zeitlin sees the defeat of 1851 as a vital turning point in Chilean history, marking the defeat of an alternative development through a bourgeois revolution (1984).

5. The expansion of the service sector was also a function of the predisposition of both Chilean elites and the emerging middle and professional classes to favor public expenditure on urban services (roads, public works, and education) over investment in services for mining and rural communities (Mamalakis 1976, 49).

6. Originally, the Chilean elite had sought to dilute what it regarded as the "ignorant and idle rabble" that constituted the country's population through encouraging European immigration (Collier 2003, 116). However, this immigration failed to materialize.

7. The most notable case of state repression was the state massacre of some 1,000 nitrate workers and family members in Iquique during a protest demanding higher wages and better working conditions (Hall and Spalding 1989, 188).

8. In 1922, the Socialist Workers Party became the Communist Party of Chile with its trade union arm as the FOCH (Morris 1966, 115).

9. Confronted with widespread political unrest, President Ibañez resigned in 1931. His rule was followed by a succession of military coups over the next seventeen months until the last military government presided over new elections and the return of civilian government.

10. Alguirre Cerda, Popular Front president from 1938–1941, was a large landowner.

11. The congressional political right would grant approval for the establishment of the new state industrial development bank, CORFO (Chilean Production Development

Corporation), only if the Popular Front agreed to suspend legislation allowing rural union-ization (Fáundez 1988, 44). The government outlawed peasant unions in law until 1947 and in practice (given official support for their repression) until 1967 (Drake 1978, 36).

12. White-collar workers in the public sector are particularly important (Guardia B. 1979, 509).

13. Between 1940 and 1950, the salaries of white-collar workers increased 46 percent, while the wages of workers increased only 7 percent (Fáundez 1988, 56).

14. President Ibañez's 1955 measures involving the restriction of public expenditure, wages, and credit generated riots, and by 1957 the program was abandoned. Another effort at stabilization attempted by President Jorge Alessandri (1958–1964) was also aban-doned in the face of rising criticism from both business and labor. He followed with an expansionary program involving increased wages for workers and expanded credit. Infla-tion ensued (Sigmund 1977, 26).

15. President Alessandri (1920–1924 and 1932–1938), for example, reduced congress's initiative on economic matters, while President Eduardo Frei (1964–1970) created an Economic Committee of Ministers to increase presidential oversight over economic pol-icy (Montecinos 1998, 7).

16. However, an important fraction of the Christian Democratic Party also called for the eradication of capitalism (Sigmund 1977, 24 26).

17. By 1970, three holding companies controlled about 70 percent of Chilean capital in business corporations (Roxborough, O'Brien, and Roddick 1977, 56), and 7 percent of landowners owned 65 percent of the land and 78 percent of the arable irrigated land (Sigmund 1977, 29).

18. Spontaneous rural and urban land takeovers (not organized by any party) in-creased from the late 1960s onward (Angell 1988, 57; Martner 1988, 154). With the ac-celeration of land invasions, the government disregarded its own agrarian reform law by authorizing (after the fact) the seizure of properties under the legal minimum size (Hira 1998, 52).

19. Meanwhile, Congress, where Allende lacked a majority, repeatedly blocked his efforts to increase taxation to pay for the increases in wages and social programs.

20. The military apparently liked the Chicago boys because they too appeared to be independent of social groups (Valdés 1995 163).

21. The Chicago boys were named for their education in economics at the Univer-sity of Chicago, an experience that occurred as a consequence of an exchange program established between the Catholic University and the University of Chicago in the 1950s.

22. The military was exempt.

23. This is explained in more detail in Chapter 7.

24. Driabe and Riesco suggest that there was an important political motivation be-hind these measures: the facts that rural teachers had supported radical agrarian reform and that universities had been centers of agitation for social change (2009, 21).

25. Nevertheless, the infant mortality rate continued to improve during the period, probably due to highly targeted support for the extremely poor and an infant feeding program (Olivarria-Gambi 1980, 109; UNDP 2004, 168).

Chapter 4

1. With the center of the Aztec empire located where modern Mexico City stands today and with the Mayan civilization extending into much of southern Mexico, Mexico was a center of pre-Columbian high culture.

2. Due to Mexico's policy of assimilation, the indigenous population declined to between 28 percent and 37 percent of the total population by the middle of the twentieth century (Lambert 1967, 42).

3. The Spanish crown had granted land to Indian village brotherhoods known as *confradías*. Over time, these lands came to be regarded as village (communal) property (Hart 1997, 30).

4. There were two periods during the years that Porfirio Díaz dominated Mexican politics when he was not actually president: in 1876, when he left an interim president in charge; and another, between 1880 and 1884, when his political ally, Manuel González, was president.

5. This was not true of some of the northern landowners, however, as we will see in the following pages.

6. An estimated 50 percent of communal landholdings were lost because of railway expansion (Haber 1989, 29).

7. Many of the firms established between 1890 and 1910 became the backbone of the post-1940 industrialization process (Haber 1989, 3).

8. Capital goods, at 10 percent of imports in 1877, had increased to 30 percent by 1910–1911 (King 1970, 3).

9. Indeed, Mexican revolutionary nationalism has its origins in the brutal repression of fierce worker resistance to the privileges granted foreign investors and foreign workers (Basurto 1984, 103; Parkes 1962, 3).

10. Meanwhile, the revolutionary leaders who had arisen from the lower classes (Emiliano Zapata and Pancho Villa) were defeated in the conflicts between the various revolutionary armies that occurred in the aftermath of the Revolution.

11. Calles established the precursor to the Institutional Revolutionary Party (PRI), the National Revolutionary Party (PNR), in 1929.

12. The year 1920 saw the ascendancy of the so-called northern dynasty with the overthrow of Carranza by Obregón. Both Obregón and Calles were lower-middle-class mestizos who became large landowners in the north (Hansen 1980, 119).

13. Steps taken to benefit the peasant population included the building of more than 1000 rural schools between 1920 and 1924, more than had been built in the previous fifty years (Parkes 1962, 338).

14. In 1933, President Calles had proposed an agrarian reform program involving the creation of small properties, which the peasantry would purchase. His successor, President Rodríguez, could not get the cabinet to agree to the program (Cline 1961, 216).

15. In 1934 and 1937, the government revised the constitution to acknowledge and support the *ejido* (Cline 1962, 135).

16. In 1990, during a debate with Mexican writer, Octavio Paz, the Peruvian writer Mario Vargas Llosa described Mexico's political system as a "perfect dictatorship."

17. These political arrangements did not eliminate unrest, as illustrated by the upsurge of independent unionism in the petroleum, miners, and railway unions in the 1950s. The state did not hesitate to use repression if other methods failed.

18. The middle class, defined as employees in nonmanual occupations, excluding low-level office and retail clerks, increased from 4.5 percent of the population in 1940 to 9.4 percent by 1960. If all white-collar workers are included, however menial their employment, these figures rise to 15.9 percent and 21.0 percent, respectively. The former set of figures is more congruent with the definition of middle class presented in Chapter 1, as by 1940 the comparatively low level of pay of menial white-collar workers would not have afforded a lifestyle distinguishable from workers of their income level (Gilbert 2007, 28, 29).

19. Two institutions provide social security: IMSS (Mexican Institute for Social Security) for private sector workers and ISSSTE (Institute of Security and Social Services for State Workers).

20. There were social supports "by other means," such as subsidies on basic foodstuffs, and these went some way in mitigating general hardship. However, these benefited mainly urban dwellers.

21. However, between 1941 and 1945, production in the *ejido* sector was the same or slightly better than that of large commercial producers (Hewitt de Alcántara 1976, 210).

22. Increasing foreign debt now became the means to keep public investment going and to ensure that public and private industry had access to needed imported inputs.

23. NAFINSA provided between one-third and one-fifth of the total financing going to industry (Bennett and Sharpe 1982, 185).

24. Although in 1945 NAFINSA held stock in some thirty-five companies, as of 1961 it was creditor, investor, and guarantor of some 533 enterprises of all kinds (Blair 1964, 196).

25. The term was coined to refer to a decline in the manufacturing sector because of the increase in natural resource exploitation, something that happened in the Netherlands after the discovery of a large natural gas field.

26. Meanwhile, the banks were left to function, for the most part, with their existing management. The government compensated bankers generously, sometimes for more than the actual worth of their banks (Teichman 1988, 140).

Chapter 5

1. On the path-dependent impact of hierarchies established by Spanish colonial rule, see Mahoney 2003. Mahoney's argument that those Latin American countries with dense indigenous populations (and intense racial stratification) during the colonial period would experience a greater degree of social underdevelopment (lower levels of literacy and health) than those with a smaller indigenous population coincides with the Mexican and Chilean experiences (82).

2. These developments may have reinforced the cultural predisposition for equity present in Confucian philosophy, in contrast to Latin American Positivism, which in its extreme form (the case of Mexico) took on the racist features of social Darwinism. See Chapter 4 on Mexico.

3. Recall the examples of Presidents Cárdenas and Echeverría in Mexico and the Frei and Allende administrations' land redistribution efforts in Chile.

4. In Chile, redistribution of 50 percent of the land benefited only 20 percent of rural households, while in Mexico redistribution of 43 percent of the land benefited about the same proportion of rural households (Borras and McKinley 2006, 2).

5. The elimination of the ideological political left in Korea with the division between North and South Korea was an important ingredient, making possible the avoidance of land redistribution programs that rejected the notion of private property.

6. Industrialization was initiated by the Japanese, but recall that this industrialization occurred largely in the northern part of the colony. Hence, when the division between North and South Korea occurred, South Korea was left largely without an industrial base.

7. The ideological heterogeneity of the military during this early period is illustrated by the 1932 military intervention, led by General Marmaduque Grove, which produced the short-lived (twelve-day) Socialist Republic.

8. Early Mexican labor organizations such as the General Confederation of Workers and Peasants of Mexico had integrated both peasants and workers in the same organization.

9. The exception, of course, was the student movement of the late 1960s. By the early 1970s, the influx of students, radicalized by the 1968 government repression of the student protest movement, into poor rural areas contributed to the rise in independent unionism (Hansen 1980, 229). However, the students' organizational efforts among the rural poor were not as pervasive or as sustained as the Korean middle-class efforts to organize the working class.

10. In the state of Morelos, for example, between 1942 and 1962 peasants, faced with broken government promises and state repression, took up arms on three occasions in their struggle for better crop prices, credit, and land reform (Padilla 2007). In the 1960s in Guerrero, one of the poorest states in Mexico, where peasants had given strong support to Zapata during the Mexican Revolution, peasants backed a guerrilla band led by Lucio Cabañas; it took seven years, 24,000 army troops, and the initiation of a "dirty war" to finally diminish the guerrilla threat in Guerrero.

11. Social security spending is described as "unequalizing" because, in late industrializing countries, including Korea, it benefits the most organized and leaves out the majority of workers, both formal and informal. There were also sharp inequalities within Korea's social security regime, but because social security protection was limited the unequalizing impact was more restrained.

12. The ability of Chile to reduce poverty substantially after the late 1980s and its more recent success at some inequality reduction will be dealt with in later chapters. However, this later success had much to do with earlier developments.

13. One could argue, however, that while lower poverty and inequality (compared with Mexico) were the short-term outcome of dynamic mineral-led growth in Chile, the longer-term consequences were considerably more problematic. The elite intransigence and ideological polarization this type of development gave rise to were instrumental in the 1973 coup, after which social gains were reversed.

14. However, it is important to bear in mind that while these advantages produced a better poverty outcome than was the case for Mexico, inequality remained fairly high.

15. During the period of the "parliamentary republic" (1891–1925), which featured a weak executive, the mining and landed oligarchy exercised control through their control of parliament.

16. Recall that when opposition center-left parties began to experience electoral success with the election of the Popular Front, the landed oligarchy, because of its continued overrepresentation in congress, was able to broker a deal that left its power in rural areas in tact. See Chapter 3.

17. As we will see in the following chapter, CORFO was instrumental in shaping the emergence of a new economic growth model based on the exportation of nontraditional agricultural exports.

18. Recall that Mexican entrepreneurs were more predisposed to use capital-intensive methods that reduced employment. As we saw in Chapter 4, this was a problem, with a long historical legacy dating back to Mexico's initial industrialization phase under Porfirio Díaz. However, additional factors likely encouraged the continued use of such methods. These factors include the following: proximity to the United States and the important role of U.S. investment; government rebates and tax holidays, granted for the importation of capital goods; pressure from labor for increased wages, which encouraged capitalists to replace labor with capital; and the policy of pegging the peso, which made it cheaper for domestic producers to use imported capital intensive methods (Aspe and Beristain 1984, 121; Aspra 1977, 117). It would have required a strong and highly capable state to chart a different type of industrial path given these circumstances and pressures.

19. Had there been larger middle- and working-class groups in Korea, particularly ones without concern for rural welfare, General Park would have found it much more difficult to maintain his pro-rural-poor policies.

Chapter 6

1. In the Chilean case, civil society pressure would not begin to have an important impact until after 2000. See Chapter 7.

2. Most of the poverty reduction after 1987 (between 73 and 80 percent), including the reduction that occurred under civilian rule before 2000, was a consequence of the job creation arising from export-led economic growth (Beyer 1995, 21; Meller 2000; World Bank 2002, 8).

3. Similarly, CEPAL found that only a minority of Chileans (34 percent in 1997 and 30 percent in 2002) believed that the distribution of income was very unjust (2010, 79).

4. The Concertación was elected in 1990. Four Concertación governments ruled between 1990 and 2010: Patricio Alywin (1990–1994), Eduardo Frei (1994–2000), Ricardo Lagos (2000–2006), and Michelle Bachelet (2006–2010). This chapter focuses on the Alywin and Frei administrations.

5. The trade union movement never regained the strength it enjoyed prior to the military coup. In 1990, the national unionization rate was low at 12.5 percent (Haagh 2002, 99).

6. Time spent in exile in Eastern Europe, where the problems of centrally planned economies became abundantly clear; graduate study in the United States; advanced training in the social sciences; and shared experience as researchers in the think tank CIEPLAN (Corporation for Economic Research on Latin America) all predisposed opposition civilian leaders to a shared acceptance of the new economic model (Silva 1991).

7. One important difference from the Chilean case was that there was no increase in commodity prices to spur economic recovery following the debt crisis.

8. The most notorious example occurred in 1993 when the country's top business leaders were each invited to pledge $25 million (U.S.) to the PRI's 1994 election campaign; public outcry resulted in a reduction of contributions to a third of a million each (Teichman 1996, 256).

9. It gave communal farmers the legal right to hold title to land and therefore the right to sell or rent the land or to form joint ventures with private agribusinesses.

10. In 1989, President Salinas introduced the National Solidarity Program or PRO-NASOL, which provided matching funding for locally generated projects by poor communities.

11. On the overwhelming evidence of electoral fraud perpetrated against the leftist National Democratic Front, see Gómez Tagle, 1989.

12. Prior to the market reform era, with the exception of the *maquila* program (incentives to encourage investment in export processing zones) and a few sectoral development programs (auto parts, pharmaceuticals), there had been few sectoral policies to promote exports. The new trade regime (NAFTA) did not include any new incentives.

13. This caused increased hardship among the poor urban dwellers (the majority), who lacked social security protection.

14. These other reforms in the social security institutions occurred later. See Chapter 7.

15. Depreciation of the Japanese yen was important because South Korea is so heavily dependent on imported Japanese inputs and technology.

16. Another very important difference was the fact that much of Korea's debt was acquired in support of its HCI economic strategy, with the loans going into productive investment rather than for general budget support, as occurred in Mexico. The Korean investments would eventually bear fruit in the area of export performance.

17. Although the Chun regime came to power by military coup, it relied even more heavily than had the Park regime on civilian technicians and bureaucrats (Jun 2001, 131).

18. This event, involving fierce repression in a stronghold of government opposition, has been described as *the* defining episode in the development of civil society and worker consciousness (Gray 2008, 55).

19. By the 1990s, divisions within the middle class began to emerge with less educated and older members of the middle class becoming less sympathetic to labor demands (Sang-jin 2002, 267).

20. Another important middle-class-led organization was the Citizens Coalition for Economic Justice (CCEJ), established in 1989 by some 500 professionals (doctors, lawyers, professors, writers, and journalists). It was primarily concerned with wealth formation and income distribution. By 1993, it had a membership of 7,000 (Koo 2007, 119).

21. Named the National Council of Korean Trade Unions, NCTU, in 1990, this organization was established as the KCTU in 1995.

22. Parliamentary elections would not occur until 1991.

23. Financial unification did not occur until 2000. This is discussed in Chapter 7.

24. Taxes from copper account for approximately 15 percent of Chile's tax revenue and petroleum about 35 percent of Mexico's tax revenue.

25. *Labor flexibilization* refers to changes in the norms and laws governing labor relations that give employers the ability to more easily hire and fire workers. In practice this ability has usually meant, among other things, the greater use of temporary and part-time labor and the increasing use of subcontracting. Reasons that have been advanced in support of labor flexibilization include the belief that it allows enterprises to adjust quickly to the market, to lower costs, and to increase labor productivity, thereby increasing competitiveness. Probably the most widely touted reason for its adoption was the belief that labor flexibilization would stimulate the expansion of employment. Popular during the early 1990s, the purported positive benefits of labor flexibilization have come under increasing criticism. As noted, the labor reforms under Pinochet produced a highly flexible labor regime. Although Mexico's labor law provided substantial labor protection, labor flexibility was not an issue during these years due to the fact of considerable de facto labor flexibility. I return to this issue in more detail in the following chapter.

26. The government's response to the 1997 financial collapse is more fully explored in the next chapter.

27. However, the government's (financial) contribution to this program was small (Kim and Mo 1999, 88).

28. In large firms, corporate welfare came to amount to one-third of the monthly wage (Song and Hong 2005, 186).

29. This is discussed in more detail in the next chapter.

30. See Chapter 3 on this point.

Chapter 7

1. While the impact of taxes and transfers on inequality in Chile is considerably less than for European countries, a recent ECLAC study found that in 2008 taxes and transfers did reduce inequality (as measured by the Gini coefficient) by 4.2 percent, the second-highest percentage reduction among six Latin American countries (ECLAC 2010, 233). A 2009 study, covering the period 2000–2006, found that increases in per capita health care and educational investments, targeted to the poor areas, contributed to the reduction of poverty, especially extreme poverty (Glick and Menon 2009, 277).

2. The data on these three countries do not give much support to Haggard and Kaufman's argument (2008, 260) that the rise in social protection and social spending after 2000 in the Asian NICs countries is explained by their healthier fiscal situation compared with the comparatively weaker fiscal situation of Latin American countries. Korea's increase in social expenditure began in 2001 when its deficit became larger than Mexico's and Chile's, and Chile, with the healthiest fiscal situation of all three countries after 2003, saw a decline (up to 2006) in social spending. After 2005, both Mexico's defi-

cit and social spending increased (Figures A-3 and Figure A-8). The most important difference in welfare regimes lay not in their level of spending but in their distinct principles, as discussed later in the chapter.

3. The CCEJ also continued to be important (Lim and Jang 2006, 449).

4. Opposition to a unified system occurred due to the fear that the self-employed would underreport their incomes to minimize their contributions while employees had their contributions deducted by the employer (Gray 2008, 135).

5. Others, however, see the new social policies as reflecting the development of a real commitment to social citizenship (Kuhnle, 2004).

6. Lomeli (2008, 10) claims that, by the beginning of the 1990s, Koreans were paying about 50 percent of their medical expenses, amounting to about 5 percent of their incomes on health (Gough 2004, 176). However, there are compensatory and ceiling provisions designed to prevent bankruptcy caused by co-payments (Lomeli 2008, 29).

7. Irregular low-paying jobs are increasingly being filled by foreign workers, most of whom work illegally and lack any form of social protection (Kim and Park 2006, 445).

8. "Informal" employment in Chile (and Mexico) is not exactly comparable to "irregular" employment in Korea. The most important difference is that irregular employment excludes self-employed workers, while informal employment includes them.

9. Some of the gains included an increase in the fines on businesses for unjustified dismissals and increased compensation to workers, the requirement that employers specify reasons for layoffs, and the right of workers fired due to union activities to be rehired (*La Tercera,* August 31, 2001).

10. FONASA users were means tested and charged a co-payment according to their income (Taylor 2003, 36). Although the Concertación had consistently increased spending in public health, the extent of the deterioration in infrastructure during the period of military rule meant that inadequacies in public health care continued to be substantial. Additional pressure on the public system occurred because the private system did not cover all ailments nor provide care for the elderly.

11. The psychological and social support provided by an army of social workers, seeking to bring existing social services to those living in extreme poverty, became a much more important aspect of the program than the small cash benefit.

12. Targeting (of poor areas, youth, and indigenous people) was also a feature of the Alywin and Frei administrations.

13. Furthermore, with the rise of copper prices on the international market, she also had the fiscal resources for new initiatives.

14. The state provided the difference between low private pensions and the minimum state-guaranteed amount, which was still very low. In addition to lack of consistent formal employment, other factors producing low pensions included low salaries, the high cost of administration, and the ups and downs of the market.

15. The figures for Mexico were forty-seventh for reading and fifty-first for math.

16. Calderón won by a fraction of a percentage point in 2006. Gilbert argues that the election turned on the middle-class vote, which moved disproportionately to the PAN in 2006 (2007, 83, 103).

17. The most notable example includes Francisco Gil Díaz, his finance minister, who moved in and out of the private sector.

18. These demands occurred despite the fact that there is considerable de facto labor flexibility in Mexico.

19. This is defined as spending for health that is higher than 30 percent of disposable income of the household (OECD 2005, 67).

20. The government subsidizes family contributions of the bottom two deciles of the population only. Hence, the take-up rate by those in the third decile and higher is likely to be very low (OECD 2005, 117). This will also contribute to the inadequacy of funding.

21. During the administration of President Fox, the head of the Teachers' Union, Elba Gordillo, and her political party, Alianza Nueva, played the role of power broker in a Congress where no single party had control (*Mexico and NAFTA Report* July 2007, 2).

References

Agosín, Manuel R. 1999. "Comercio y crecimiento en Chile." *Revista de Cepal* 68: 79–100.

Agosín, Manuel R., and Ernesto Pastén H. 2003. "Corporate Governance in Chile." Central Bank of Chile Working Papers, No. 209.

Aguilar, Alonso, and Fernando Carmona. 1973. *México: Riqueza y miseria.* Mexico City: Editorial Nuestro Tiempo S.A.

Aguilera Reyes, Máximo. 1994. "La economía chilena en el período 1974–1993." Documentos Docentes. Santiago: Universidad Central de Chile, Facultad de Ciencias Económicas y Administrativas.

Albala-Bertrand, José Miguel. 1999. "Industrial Interdependence Change in Chile, 1960–1990: A Comparison with Taiwan and South Korea." *International Review of Applied Economics* 13(2): 161–191.

Amparo Casar, María, and Wilson Peres. 1988. *El Estado Empresario en México. ¿Agotamiento o renovación?* Mexico City: Siglo Veintiuno Editores.

Amsden. Alice.1989. *Asia's Next Giant: South Korea and Late Industrialization.* New York: Oxford University Press.

———. 1994. "The Spectre of Anglo Saxonization is Haunting South Korea." In *Korea's Political Economy: An Institutional Perspective,* edited by Lee-Jay Cho and Yoon-Hyun Kim, 87–136. Boulder, CO: Westview.

An, Jaewook, Sang Kun Bae, and Ronald A. Ratti. 2002. "Government vs. Private Control, Political Loans, and the Privatization of Korean Banks." *Social Science Research Network.* Available at http://ssrn.com/abstract=308364.

Angell, Alan. 1988. *De Alessandri a Pinochet: En busca de la Utopía.* Santiago: Editorial Andrés Bello.

Arellano, José Pablo. 1985. *Políticas sociales y desarrollo: Chile 1924–1984.* Santiago: Corporación de Investigaciones Económicas para Latinoamérica.

Arita, Shin. 2003. "The Growth of the Korean Middle Class and Its Social Consciousness." *The Developing Economies* 41(2): 201–220.

Asian Development Bank. 2008. *Key Indicators for Asia and the Pacific, 2008, Country Tables, Korea.* Mandaluyong City, Philippines: Asian Development Bank. Retrieved on May 3, 2010, from www.adb.org/Statistics/Ki.asp .

———. 2010. *Key Indicators for Asia and the Pacific, 2010.* Mandaluyong City, Philippines: Asian Development Bank.

Aspe, Pedro, and Javier Beristain. 1984. "The Evolution of Income Distribution Policies in the Post Revolutionary Period in Mexico." In *The Political Economy of Income Distribution in Mexico,* edited by Pedro Aspe and Paul E. Sigmund, 15–25. New York: Homes and Meier Publishers.

Aspra, Antonio L. 1977. "Import Substitution in Mexico: Past and Present." *World Development* 5 (1–2): 111–122.

Atkinson, A. B., and John Mills. 1991. "Social Security in Developed Countries: Are There Lessons for Developing Countries?" In *Social Security in Developing Countries,* edited by Ehtisham Ahmad, Jean Dréze, and Amartya Sen, 81–111. Oxford, UK: Clarendon Press.

Atunes, Ricardo. 2000. "The World of Work, the Restructuring of Production, and the Challenges to Trade Unionism and Social Struggle in Brazil." *Latin American Perspectives* 27(6): 9–26.

Ayala Espino, José. 1988. *Estado y desarrollo: La formación de la economía mixta mexicana (1920–1982).* Mexico City: Fondo de Cultura Económica.

Bąkiewicz, Anna. 2008. "Small and Medium Enterprises in South Korea: In the Shadow of Big Brothers." *Asia and Pacific Studies* 5: 45–70.

Ban, Sung Hwan, Pal Yong Moon, and Dwight H. Perkins. 1980. *Rural Development.* Cambridge, MA: Harvard University Press.

Banco de México. 1995. *The Mexican Economy 1994.* Mexico City: Banco de México.

Banco Interamericano de Desarrollo. Instituto para la Integración de América Latina y el Caribe. DATAINTAL. Retrieved on May 3, 2010, from www.iadb.org/dataintal/totalpais.aspx?Tipo=P.

Barrientos, Armando. 2004. "Latin America: Towards a Liberal-informal Welfare Regime." In *Insecurity and Welfare Regimes in Asia, Africa and Latin America,* edited by Ian Gough and Geof Wood, 121–168. Cambridge, UK: Cambridge University Press.

Basurto, Jorge. 1984. *La clase obrera en la historia de México: de avilocamachismo (1940–1952),* Tomo 11. Mexico City: UNAM.

Bauer, Arnold J. 1975. *Chilean Rural Society from the Spanish Conquest to 1930.* Cambridge, UK: Cambridge University Press.

Bennett, Douglas, and Kenneth Sharpe. 1982. "The State as Banker and Entrepreneur: The Last Resort Nature of the Mexican State's Intervention, 1917–1970." In *Brazil and Mexico: Patterns in Late Development,* edited by Sylvia Ann Hewlett and Richard S. Weinert, 168–205. Philadelphia: Institute for the Study of Human Issues.

Betcherman, Gordon. 2002. "An Overview of Labor Markets Worldwide: Key Trends and Major Policy Issues." Social Protection Discussion Paper, World Bank, Social Protection Unit. Washington, DC: World Bank.

Berg, Janine. 2004. *Miracle for Whom? Chilean Workers under Free Trade.* New York: Routledge.

Berger, Stefan. 2002. "Democracy and Social Democracy." *European History Quarterly* 32(1): 13–37.

Beyer, Harald. 1995. "Logros en pobreza: Frustración en la igualdad." *Estudios Públicos* 60: 16–31.

Birdsall, Nancy, and Juan L. Londoño. 1997. "Asset Inequality Matters: An Assessment of the World Bank's Approach to Poverty Reduction." *American Economic Review* 87(2): 32–37.

Blackmore, Harold. 1974. *British Nitrates and Chilean Politics, 1886–1896: Balmaceda and North.* London: University of London and the Athlone Press.

Blair, Calvin. 1964. "Nacional Financiera: Entrepreneurship in a Mixed Economy." In *Public Policy and Private Enterprise in Mexico,* edited by Raymond Vernon, 193–238. Cambridge, MA: Harvard University Press.

Blanton, Robert, T. David Mason, and Brian Athow. 2001. "Colonial Style and Post-Colonial Conflict in Africa." *Journal of Peace Research* 38 (4): 473–491.

Borras, Saturnino M. Jr., and Terry McKinley. 2006. "The Unresolved Land Reform Debate: Beyond State-Led or Market-Led Models." *Policy Research Brief.* United Nations Development Program. 2 November.

Borzutsky, Silvia. 2002. *Vital Connections: Politics, Social Security and Inequality in Chile.* Notre Dame, IN: University of Notre Dame Press.

———. 2006. "Cooperation or Confrontation between the State and the Market: Social Security and Health Policies." In *The Chilean Road to Democracy and the Market,* edited by Silvia Borzutsky and Lois Hecht Oppenheim, 142–166. Gainsville: University of Florida Press.

Boyd, Richard. 2006. "Modes of Rent-Seeking and Economic Outcomes: A Comparison of Japan and Mexico." In *Political Conflict and Development in East Asia and Latin America,* edited by Richard B. Boyd, Richard, F. Galjart and Tak-Wing Ngo, 148–212. New York: Routledge.

Boyd, Richard B., F. Galjart, and Tak-Wing Ngo, eds. 2006. *Political Conflict and Development in East Asia and Latin America.* New York: Routledge.

Boyer, William W., and Byong Man Ahn. 1991. *Rural Development in South Korea: A Sociopolitical Analysis.* Newark: University of Delaware Press.

Boylan, Delia M. 1996. "Taxation and Transition: The Politics of the 1990 Chilean Tax Reform." *Latin American Research Review* 31(1): 7–31.

Bronstein, Arturo. 2009. *International and Comparative Labour Law.* Geneva: Palgrave Macmillan and International Labour Office.

Brown, Jonathan C. 2000. *Latin America: A Social History of the Colonial Period.* Fort Worth, TX: Harcourt.

Buzo, Adrian. 2002. *The Making of Modern Korea.* Routledge: London and New York.

Camp, Roderic. 1989. *Entrepreneurs and Politics in Twentieth Century Mexico.* New York: Oxford University Press.

Cardoso, Fernando H. 1972. *Ideologías de la burguesía industrial en sociedades dependientes (Argentina y Brasil)*. Buenos Aires: Siglo Veintiuno.

Cardoso, Fernando H., and Enzo Faletto. 1979. *Dependency and Development in Latin America*. Berkeley: University of California Press.

Castells, Manuel. 1974. *La lucha de clases en Chile*. Buenos Aires: Siglo Veintiuno.

Centeno, Miguel Angel. 1999. *Democracy within Reason*, 2nd ed. University Park: The Pennslyvania State University Press.

Chase-Dunn, Christopher. 1987. "The Korean Trajectory in the World System." In *Dependency Issues in Korean Development*, edited by Kyong-Dong Kim, 207–304. Seoul: Seoul National University Press.

Cho, Yoon Lo. 1997. "Government Intervention, Rent Distribution and Economic Development in Korea." In *The Role of Government in East Asian Development*, edited by Masahiro Okuno-Fujiwara, 208–232. Oxford, UK: Clarendon Press.

Choi, Jang Jip. 1993. "Political Change in South Korea." In *State and Society in Contemporary Korea*, edited by Hagen Koo, 13–15. Ithaca, NY: Cornell University Press.

Choi, Soo Ho. 2000. "Land Is Thicker Than Blood. Revisiting 'Kinship Paternalism' in a Peasant Village in South Korea." *Journal of Anthropological Research* 56(3): 349–363.

Choi, Young Back. 1996. "The Americanization of Economics in Korea." In *The Post-1945 Internationalization of Economics*, edited by A. W. Coats, 97–211. Durham, NC: Duke University Press.

Chun, Moo-Kwon. 2008. "Institution Complementarities and Change: The Relationship between Production and Welfare Regimes in Korea." Paper presented at the EASP (East Asian Social Policy) 5th International Conference, National Taiwan University, Tapei, Taiwan, November 3–4. Retrieved on August 23, 2009, from www.welfareasia .org/5thconference/session-2/.

Clark, Marjorie Ruth. 1973. *Organized Labor in Mexico*. New York: Russell and Russell.

Cleaves, Peter S. *Bureaucratic Politics and Administration in Chile*. 1974. Berkeley: University of California Press.

Cline, Howard. 1961. *The United States and Mexico*. Cambridge, MA: Harvard University Press.

———. 1962. *Mexico. Revolution to Evolution, 1940–1960*. London: Oxford University Press.

Cockcroft, James D. 1983. *Mexico: Class Formation, Capital Accumulation and the State*. New York: Monthly Review.

Cole, David C., and Princeton N. Lyman. 1971. *Korean Development: The Interplay of Politics and Economics*. Cambridge, MA: Harvard University Press.

Collier, Simon. 2003. *Chile: The Making of a Republic, 1830–1865. Politics and Ideas*. Cambridge, UK: Cambridge University Press.

Collins, Susan M. 1994. "Savings, Investment and External Balance in South Korea." In *Macroeconomic Policy and Adjustment in Korea 1970–1990*, edited by Stephan Haggard, Richard N. Cooper, Susan M. Collins, Choongsoo Kim, and Sung-Tae Ro, 231–259. Cambridge, MA: Harvard Institute for International Development and Korea Development Institute.

CEPAL (Comisión Económica para América Latina y el Caribe). 2010. *Panorama Social de América Latina, 2009.* Santiago: CEPAL.

Constable, Pamela, and Arturo Valenzuela. *A Nation of Enemies.* 1991. New York: W. W. Norton and Co.

Cooper, Richard N. 1994. "Fiscal Policy in Korea." In *Macroeconomic Policy and Adjustment in Korea 1970–1990,* edited by Stephan Haggard, Richard N. Cooper, Susan M. Collins, Choongsoo Kim, and Sung-Tae Ro, 111–144. Cambridge, MA: Harvard Institute for International Development and Korea Development Institute.

Corbacho, Ana, and Gerd Schwartz. 2002. "Mexico: Experiences with Pro-Poor Expenditure Policies." IMF Working Paper. Washington, DC: IMF, Fiscal Affairs Department.

Cornia, Giovanni Andrea, Tony Addison, and Sampsa Kiiski. 2004. "Income Distribution Changes and Their Impact in the Post Second World War Period." In *Inequality, Growth and Poverty in an Era of Liberalization and Globalization,* edited by Giovanni Andrea Cornia, 26–56. Oxford, UK: Oxford University Press.

Cortés, Fernando. 2000. *La distribución del ingreso en México en épocas de estabilización y reforma económica.* Mexico City: Miguel Angel Porrúa.

Cortés Conde, Roberto. 2006. "Fiscal and Monetary Regimes." In *The Cambridge Economic History of Latin America: The Long Twentieth Century,* edited by John H. Coatsworth, Victor Bulmer Thomas, and Roberto Cortés Conde, 209–248. Cambridge, UK: Cambridge University Press.

Couch, Colin, and Henry Farrell. 2004. "Breaking the Path of Institutional Development? Alternatives to the New Determinism." *Rationality and Society* 16 (1): 5–43.

Cumberland, Charles C. 1968. *Mexico: The Struggle for Modernity.* New York: Oxford University Press.

Cumings, Bruce. 1987. "The Origins and Development of the Northeast Asian Political Economy: Industrial Sectors, Product Cycles and Political Consequences." In *The Political Economy of the New Asian Industrialism,* edited by Frederick C. Deyo, 44-83. Ithaca, NY: Cornell University Press.

Daly, Jorge, and Thibault Muzart. 2007. "Business Environment. SME Exports: The Case of Chile." Technical Brief No. 2. Washington, DC: U.S. Agency for International Development.

Davis, Diane E. 2004. *Discipline and Development: Middle Classes and Prosperity in East Asia and Latin America.* Cambridge, UK: Cambridge University Press.

De Ferranti, D., G. E. Perry, F. H. G. Ferreira, and Michael Walton. 2004. *Inequality in Latin America: Breaking with History?* Washington D.C.: World Bank.

De Gortari, Hira, and Alicia Ziccardi. 1996. "Instituciones y clientelas de la politica social: Un ebozo histórico 1867–1994." In *Las políticas sociales de México en los noventa,* edited by R. Casas, 201–227. Mexico City: Instituto de Investigaciones Sociales de la Universidad Nacional Autónoma de México, la Facultad Latinoamericana de Ciencias Sociales y Plaza y Valdés.

Deininger, Klaus, and Lyn Squire.1998. "New Ways of Looking at Old Issues: Inequality and Growth." *Journal of Development* Economics 57(2): 257–285.

Deyo, Fredrick C. 1987. "Coalitions, Institutions and Linkage Sequencing—Toward a Strategic Capacity Model of East Asian Development." In *The Political Economy of New Asian Industrialism,* edited by Fredrick C. Deyo, 227–247. Ithaca, NY: Cornell University Press.

Díaz, Alvaro. 1997. "Chile: Neoliberal Policy, Socioeconomic Reorganization, and Urban Labor Markets." In *Global Restructuring, Employment, and Social Inequality in Urban Latin America,* edited by Richard Tardanico and Rafael Menjívar. Miami: University of Miami Press.

Dion, Michelle. 2006. "Globalization, Democratization and Social Security Reform in Mexico." Paper presented at the 2006 Southern Political Science Association Meeting. Atlanta, GA, January 5–7.

Dong-A-Ilbo. 2006. "National Pension Plan Has 'Blind Spots.'" *Global Action on Aging.* Retrieved on July 29, 2009, from www.globalaging.org/pension/world/2006/blindspot.htm.

Drake, Paul W. 1978. *Socialism and Populism in Chile, 1932–52.* Urbana: University of Illinois Press.

Driabe, Sônia M., and Manuel Riesco. 2009. *El estado de bienestar social en América Latina: Una nueva estrategia de desarrollo.* Documento de Trabajo No. 31. Madrid: Fundación Carolina CeACI. Retrieved on January 10, 2010, from www.funcacióncarolina.es.

ECLAC (Economic Commission for Latin America and the Caribbean). 2007. *Social Panorama of Latin America.* New York: ECLAC.

———. 2010. *Time for Equality: Closing Gaps, Opening Trails.* New York: ECLAC.

Edwards, Sebastian, and Cox Edwards, Alejandra. 1987. *Monetarism and Liberalization: The Chilean Experiment.* Cambridge, MA: Ballinger Publishing Co.

Ertman, Thomas. 1997. *Birth of the Leviathan: Building States and Regimes in Early Modern Europe.* Cambridge, UK, and New York: Cambridge University Press.

Esping-Andersen, Gøsta. 1990. *The Three Worlds of Welfare Capitalism.* Princeton, NJ: Princeton University Press.

Esquivel, Gerardo. 2009. "The Dynamics of Income Inequality in Mexico since NAFTA." Research for Public Policy, Inclusive Development, ID-02-2009, RBLAC-UNDP, New York.

Esteva, Gustavo. 1983. *The Struggle for Rural Mexico.* South Hadley, MA: Bergin and Garvey Publishers.

Estrategia. 1994. *El Gran Salto de Chile. La historia económica y empresarial.* Santiago: Publicaciones Editorial Gestión.

Estrategia. (Santiago) April 10, 2002.

Evans, Peter. 1987. "Class, State and Dependence in East Asia: Lessons for Latin Americanists." In *The Political Economy of the New Asian Industrialism,* edited by Frederick C. Deyo, 203–226. Ithaca, NY: Cornell University Press.

———. 1995. *Embedded Autonomy: States and Industrial Transformation.* Princeton, NJ: Princeton University Press.

Fábrega, Jorge. 2010. "Education: Three Years after Chile's Penquin Revolution." *Americas Quarterly.* Retrieved on February 3, 2010, from www.americasquarterly.org/node/982.

Fajnzylber, Pablo, Daniel Lederman, and Norman Loayza. 1998. *Determinants of Crime Rates in Latin America and the World: An Empirical Assessment.* Washington, DC: The World Bank.

Fáundez, Julio. 1988. *Marxism and Democracy in Chile: From 1932 to the Fall of Allende.* New Haven, CT: Yale University Press.

Ffrench-Davis, Ricardo. 2002. "El Impacto de las exportaciones sobre el crecimiento en Chile." *Revista de Cepal* 76: 143–160.

Fitzgerald, E. V. K. 1978. "The State and Capital Accumulation in Mexico." *Journal of Latin American Studies* 10(2): 263–282.

Foxley, Alejandro. 1987. "The Neoconservative Economic Experiment in Chile." In *Military Rule in Chile: Dictatorship and Opposition,* edited by J. Samuel Valenzuela and Arturo Valenzuela, 13–43. Baltimore, MD: The Johns Hopkins University Press.

———. 1995. "Los objetivos económicos y sociales en la transición a la democracia." In *Políticas económicas y sociales en el Chile democrático,* edited by Crisóstomo Pizarro, Dagmar Raczynski, and Joaquín Vial. Santiago, 11–29. Santiago: CIEPLAN and UNICEF.

Foxley, Alejandro, Eduardo Aninat, and J. P. Arellano. 1979. *Redistributive Effects of Government Programs: The Chilean Case.* Oxford, UK: Pergamon Press.

Frenk, Julio, Miguel Angel González-Block, and Rafael Lozano. 2000. "Seis tesis equivocadas sobre las políticas de salud en el combate a la pobreza." In *Familia, género y pobreza,* coordinated by María de la Paz López and Vania Salles, 339–365. Mexico City: Miguel Angel Porrúa.

Frías, Patricio, and Jaime Ruiz-Tagle. 1992. *Situación y dinámica del sindicalismo chileno en el contexto económico y sociopolítico.* Santiago: Programa de Económica del Trabajo.

Furtado, Celso. 1976. *Economic Development of Latin America,* second edition. Cambridge, UK: Cambridge University Press.

Garrido, Celso. 1998. "El liderazgo de las grandes empresas industrials mexicanas." In *Grandes empresas y grupos industriales latinoamericanos,* coordinated by Wilson Peres, 397–472. Mexico City: Siglo Veintiuno Editores.

Gereffi, Gary, and Peter Evans. 1981. "Transnational Corporations, Dependent Development and State Policy in the Semi-Periphery: A Comparison of Brazil and Mexico." *Latin American Research Review* 21(3): 31–64.

Gideon, Jasmine. 2007. "A Gendered Analysis of Labour Market Informalization and Access to Health in Chile." *Global Social Policy* 7(1): 75–94.

Gilbert, Denis. 2007. *Mexico's Middle Class in the Neoliberal Era.* Tucson: University of Arizona Press.

Gilbert, Neil. 2004. "Productive Welfare and the Market Economy: Korea's Enabling State." In *Modernizing the Korean Welfare State: Toward the Productive Welfare Model,* edited by Ramesh Mishra, Stein Kuhnle, Neil Gilbert, and Kyungbae Chung, 11–26. New Brunswick, NJ: Transaction Publishers.

Glick, David, and Nidhiya Menon. 2009. "Public Programs Pare Poverty: Evidence from Chile." *Bulletin of Economic Research* 61 (3): 249–282.

Gobierno de Chile. Ministerio de Hacienda, Chile. Base de Datos Estadísticas. Retrieved on May 2, 2010, from http://si2.bcentral.cl/Basededatoseconomicos/951_417.asp?m =BP_102&f=A&i=E .

Godoy Urzúa, Hernán. 1971. *Estructura social de chile. Estudio selección de textos y bibliografía.* Santiago: Editorial Universitaria S.A.

Goldberg, Mike, and Eric Palladini. 2008. "Chile: A Strategy to Promote Small Innovative Small and Medium Enterprises." Policy Research Working Paper 4518. Poverty Reduction and Economic Management Department. Latin American Finance and Private Sector Unit. Washington, DC: The World Bank.

Gollás, Manuel, and Adelberto García Rocha. 1976. "El Desarrollo económico reciente de México." In *Contemporary Mexico,* edited by James W. Wilkie, Michael C. Meyer, and Edna Monzón de Wilkie, 405–440. Berkeley: University of California Press.

Gómez Tagle, Silvia. 1989. "La demanda democrática del 6 de Julio." Paper presented at the 15th International Congress of the Latin American Studies Association, September 21–23, Miami.

González Gómez, Mauricio A. 1998. "Crisis and Economic Change in Mexico." In *Mexico under Zedillo,* edited by Susan Kaufman Purcell and Luis Rubio, 37–65. Boulder, CO: Lynne Rienner.

Gough, Ian. 2004. "Welfare Regimes in Development Contexts: A Global and Regional Analysis." In *Insecurity and Welfare Regimes in Asia, Africa and Latin America,* edited by Ian Gough and Geof Wood, 15–48. Cambridge, UK: Cambridge University Press.

Grant, Geraldine. 1983. "The State and the Formation of a Middle Class: A Chilean Example." *Latin American Perspective* 10(1–2): 151–170.

Gray, Kevin. 2008. *Korean Workers and Neoliberal Globalization.* New York: Routledge.

Grayson, George. 1984. *The United States and Mexico: Patterns of Influence.* New York: Praeger.

Greenburg, Harry. 1970. *Bureaucracy and Development: A Mexican Case Study.* Lexington, MA: D. C. Heath and Company.

Gribomont, C., and M. Rimez. 1977. "La política económica del gobierno de Luís Echeverría (1971–1976): Un primer ensayo de interpretación." *El Trimestre Económico* 44(4): 771–833.

Griffith-Jones, Stephany. 1987. *Chile to 1991: The End of an Era?* Special Report No. 1073. London: The Economic Intelligence Unit.

Guardia B., Alexis. 1979. "Clases sociales y subdesarrollo capitalista en Chile." *Revista Mexicana de Sociología* 41(2): 495–541.

Guerrero, Isabel, Luis Felipe López-Calva, and Michael Walton. 2006. "The Inequality Trap and Its Links to Low Growth in Mexico." Working Paper Number 298. Stanford, CA: Stanford Center for International Development.

Haagh, Louise. 2002. *Citizenship, Labor Markets and Democratization.* New York: Palgrave.

Haber, Stephen H. 1989. *Industry and Underdevelopment: The Industrialization of Mexico, 1890–1940.* Stanford, CA: Stanford University Press.

Hadenius, Axel. 1992. *Democracy and Development.* Cambridge, UK: Cambridge University Press.

Haggard, Stephan. 1990. *Pathways from the Periphery: The Politics of Growth in the Newly Industrializing Countries.* Ithaca, NY, and London: Cornell University Press.

Haggard, Stephan, and Susan M. Collins. 1994. "The Political Economy of Adjustment in the 1990s." In *Macroeconomic Policy and Adjustment in Korea 1970–1990,* edited by Stephan Haggard, Richard N. Cooper, Susan M. Collins, Choongsoo Kim, and Sung-Tae Ro, 75–107. Cambridge, MA: Harvard Institute for International Development and Korea Development Institute.

Haggard, Stephan, David Kang, and Chung-In Moon. 1997. "Japanese Colonialism and Korean Development: A Critique." *World Development* 25(6): 867–881.

Haggard, Stephan, and Robert R. Kaufman. 2008. *Development, Democracy and Welfare States: Latin America, East Asia and Eastern Europe.* Princeton, NJ: Princeton University Press.

Hall, Michael M., and Hobart A. Spalding Jr. 1989. "Urban Labor Movements." In *Latin America Economy and Society, 1870–1930,* edited by Leslie Bethell, 183–223. Cambridge, UK: Cambridge University Press.

Hall, Peter A., and Rosemary Taylor. 1996. "Political Science and the Three Institutionalisms." *Political Studies* 44(5): 936–957.

Hamilton, Nora. 1982. "The State and the National Bourgeoisie in Post Revolutionary Mexico, 1920–1949." *Latin American Perspectives* 9(4): 31–50.

Hamilton, Nora, and Sunhyuk Kim. 2004. "Democratization, Liberalization and Labor Politics: Mexico and Korea." *Comparative Sociology* 3(1): 67–91.

Han, Seung-Mi. 2004. "The New Community Movement: Park Chung Hee and the Making of State Populism in Korea." *Pacific Affairs* 77 (1): 69–93.

The Hankyoreh (Seoul). 2009, May 22. Retrieved on September 12, 2010, from http://english.hani.co.kr/arti/english_edition/e_business/356266.html.

Hansen, Roger D. 1980. *The Politics of Mexican Development.* Baltimore, MD: The Johns Hopkins University Press.

Harrison, Lawrence E. 1998. *The Pan American Dream.* Boulder, CO: Westview.

Hart, John Mason. 1997. *Revolutionary Mexico: The Coming and Process of the Mexican Revolution,* tenth anniversary edition. Los Angeles: University of California Press.

Harvey, Neil. 1998. *The Chiapas Rebellion: The Struggle for Land and Democracy.* Durham, NC: Duke University Press.

Heredia, Blanca. 1996. *Contested State: The Politics of Trade Liberalization in Mexico.* PhD thesis. Columbia University.

Hernández, Silvia. 1973. "El desarrollo capitalista del campo chileno." In *Chile: Reforma agraria y gobierno popular,* edited by Solon Barraclough, Almino Alfonso, Silvia Hernández, Hugo Zemelman, Sergio Gómez, and José Bengoa, 132–141. Buenos Aires: Ediciones Periferia S.R.L.

Heston, Alan W., Bettina Aten, and Robert Summers. 2001. *Penn World Tables, 6.2.* Philadelphia: Center for International Comparisons, University of Pennsylvania.

Hewitt de Alcántara, Cynthia. 1976. *Modernizing Mexican Agricultura: Socio-economic Implications of Technological Change, 1940–1976.* Geneva: U.N. Institute for Social Development.

Hira, Anil. 1998. *Ideas and Economic Policy in Latin America: Regional, National and Organizational Case Studies.* Westport, CT: Praeger.

Holliday, Ian. 2000. "Productivist Welfare Capitalism: Social Policy in East Asia." *Political Studies* 48(4): 706–723.

———. 2005. "East Asian Social Policy in the Wake of the Financial Crisis: Farewell to Production." *Policy and Politics* 33(1): 142–162.

Hong, Kyong Joon. 2002. "An Analysis of the Anti-Poverty Effectiveness of Public and Private Income Transfers since the Enactment of the National Basic Livelihood Act." *Korean Journal of Social Welfare* 50: 61–84. (In Korean).

Huber, Evelyne. 2005. "Globalization and Social Policy: Developments in Latin America." In *Globalization and the Future of the Welfare State,* edited by Miguel Glatzer and Dietrich Rueschemeyer, 75–105. Pittsburgh, PA: University of Pittsburgh Press.

Huber, Evelyne, and John D. Stephens. 1998. "Internationalization and the Social Democratic Model: Crisis and Future Prospects." *Comparative Political Studies* 31(3): 353–397.

———. 2001. *Development and Crisis of the Welfare State: Parties and Policies in Global Markets.* Chicago: University of Chicago Press.

Hudson, Rex A. 1994. *Chile: A Country Guide.* Washington, DC: GPO for the Library of Congress. Retrieved on May 5, 2009, from http://countrystudies.us/chile/.

Human Rights Watch. 2005. "Mexico: Fox's Labor Reform Proposal Would Deal Serious Blow to Workers' Rights. Letter to Mexico's Chamber of Deputies." Retrieved on July 15, 2008, from hrw.org/english/docs/2005/02/09/mexico10156 txt.htm.

Ick-jin, Seo. 2006. "Industrialization in South Korea: Accumulation and Regulation." In *Developmental Dictatorship and the Park Chung-Hee Era,* edited by Lee Byeong-cheon, 51–79. Paramus, NJ: Homa and Sekey Books.

Index Mundi, Chile, "Chile GDP, Real Growth Rate." Retrieved on April 22, 2010, from www.indexmundi.com/chile/gdp_real_growth_rate.html.

Infante, G. Richard, and Osvaldo Sunkel. 2009. "Chile: Towards Inclusive Development." *Cepal Review* 97: 133–152.

ISLA (Information Services on Latin America). Oakland, CA: Various dates.

Inter-American Development Bank Database. *Latin American and Caribbean Watch Data Mexico.* Retrieved on April 22, 2010, from www.iadb.org/research/Latinmacrowatch/CountryTable.cfm.

IMF (International Monetary Fund). *Government Finance Statistics Yearbooks.* Various years.

Jacobs, Norman. 1985. *The Korean Road to Modernization and Development.* Urbana and Chicago: University of Illinois Press.

Jomo, K. J. 2006. "Growth with Equity in East Asia." Working Paper Number 33. New York: Department of Economic Development and Social Affairs, United Nations, 1–52.

Joung-woo, Lee. 2006. "Development Dictatorships: Disparity between the 'Haves' and the 'Have-Nots.'" In *Development Dictatorship and the Chung-Hee Era: The Shaping of Modernity in the Republic of Korea,* edited by Lee Byeong-cheon, 185–201. Paramus, NJ: Homa and Sekey Books.

Jun, Jinsok. 2001. "South Korea. Consolidating Democratic Civilian Control." In *Coercion and Governance: The Declining Political Role of the Military in Asia,* edited by Muthiah Alagappa, 121–142. Stanford CA: Stanford University Press.

Jwa, Sung-Hee. 2002. *The Evolution of Large Corporations in Korea: A New Institutional Economics Perspective of the Chaebol.* Northampton, MA: Edward Elgar Publishing.

Kalinowski, Thomas. 2008. "Korea's Recovery since the 1997/98 Financial Crisis: The Last Stage of the Development State." *New Political Economy* 13 (4): 447–462.

Kay, Cristobal. 2006. "East Asia's Success and Latin America's Failure: Agrarian Reform, Industrial Policy and State Capacity." In *Political Conflict and Development in East Asia and Latin America,* edited by Richard B. Boyd, F. Galjart, and Tak-Wing Ngo, 21–52. New York: Routledge.

Kim, Andrew Eungi, and Innwon Park. 2006. "Changing Trends of Work in South Korea." *Asian Survey* 46(3): 437–456.

Kim, Byung-kook. 2000. "Party Politics in South Korea's Democracy: The Crisis of Success." In *Consolidating Democracy in South Korea,* edited by Larry Diamond and Byung-kook Kim, 53–85. Boulder, CO: Lynne Rienner.

Kim, Choongsoo. 1990. "Labor Market Developments in Macroeconomic Perspective." In *Korean Economic Development,* edited by Jene K. Kwon, 302–321. Westport, CT: Greenwood Press.

———. 1994. "Wage Policy and Labor Market Development." In *Macroeconomic Policy and Adjustment in Korea, 1970–1990.* edited by Stephan Haggard, Richard N. Cooper, Susan Collins, Choongsoo Kim, and Sung-Tae Ro, 185–230. Cambridge, MA: Harvard University Press.

Kim, Jun ll, and Jongrun Mo. 1999. "Democratization and Macroeconomic policy." In *Democracy and the Korean Economy,* edited by Jongryn Mo and Chung-in Moon, 73–86. Stanford, CA: Stanford University Press.

Kim, Ki Duk, and Son, Byong Don. 1995. "The Transition in Income Distribution of Working Class families from 1982–1992." In *Salwe Bokji Yonku* 6: 91–118. (In Korean).

Kim, Kwang Sik, and Michael Roemer. 1979. *Growth and Structural Transformation, Studies in the Modernization of the Republic of Korea, 1945–1975.* Cambridge, MA: Council on East Asian Studies, Harvard University.

Kim, Kwang Woong. 1990. "The Role of Bureaucracy in the Politics of Economic Development." *Korean Journal of Public Administration* 28(1): 92–112. (In Korean).

Kim, Kyo Sung. 2002. "The Effect of Income Transfer on the Poverty Rate." *Korean Journal of Social Welfare.* 48: 119–149 (In Korean).

Kim, Pil Ho. 2010. "The East Asian Welfare State Debate and Surrogate Social Policy: An Exploratory Study on Japan and South Korea." *Socio-economic Review* 8(3): 411–435.

Kim, Pyung Joo. 1990. "Korea's Financial Evolution, 1961–1986." In *Korean Economic Development,* edited by Jene K. Kwon, 185–205. New York: Greenwood Press.

Kim, Sunhyuk. 2000. "Democratization and Environmentalism: South Korea and Taiwan." *Journal of Asian and African Studies* 35(3): 287–302.

Kim, Woon-Tai. 2001. "Korean Politics: Setting and Political Culture." In *Understanding Korean Politics: An Introduction,* edited by Soong Hoom Kil and Chung-in Moon, 9–32. Albany: State University of New York Press.

Kim, Yeon-Myung. 2006. "Towards a Comprehensive Welfare State in South Korea: Institutional Features, New Socio-economic Political Pressures, and the Possibility of the Welfare State." Asia Centre Working Paper 14. London School of Economics and Political Science. Retrieved on January 12, 2011, from www.lse.ac.uk/collections/asiaResearchCentre.

King, Timothy. 1970. *Mexico: Industrialization and Trade Policies since 1940.* London: Oxford University Press.

Kleinberg, Remonda Bensabat. 1999. *Strategic Alliances and Other Deals: State Business Relations and Economic Reform in Mexico.* Durham, NC: Carolina Academic Press.

Kohli, Atul. 1994. "Where Do High Growth Political Economies Come From? The Japanese Lineage of Korean 'Development State.'" *World Development* 22 (9): 1269–1293.

———. 2004. *State Directed Development: Political Power and Industrialization in the Global Periphery.* Cambridge, UK: Cambridge University Press.

Kong, Tat Yan. 2000. *The Politics of Economic Reform in South Korea: A Fragile Miracle.* London and New York: Routledge.

Koo, Hagen. 1993a. "The State, Minjung and the Working Class in South Korea." In *State and Society in Contemporary Korea,* edited by Hagen Koo, 131–162. Ithaca, NY: Cornell University Press.

———. 1993b. "Strong State and Contentious Society." In *State and Society in Contemporary Korea,* edited by Hagen Koo, 231–249. Ithaca, NY: Cornell University Press.

———. 2006. "The Irony of Labor Strength and Income Inequality: A Comparison of Brazil and South Korea." In *Political Conflict and Development in East Asia and Latin America,* edited by Richard Boyd, Benno Galjart, and Tak-Wing Ngo, 53–73. New York: Routledge.

———. 2007. " Engendering Civil Society: The Role of the Labor Movement." In *Korean Society. Civil Society, Democracy and the State,* edited by Charles K. Armstrong, 109–131. London: Routledge.

———. 2008 "The Changing Faces of Inequality in South Korea in the Age of Globalization." *Korean Studies.* 31(1): 1–18.

The Korean Times. 2009. "Non-regular Workers." June 8. Retrieved on December 15, 2009, from www.koreatimes.co.kr/www/opinion/2009/202_46458.html.

Kuhnle, Stein. 2004. "Productive Welfare in Korea: Moving Towards a European Welfare State Type." In *Modernizing the Korean Welfare State: Toward the Productive Welfare Model,* edited by Ramesh Mishra, Stein Kuhnle, Neil Gilbert, and Kyungbae Chung, 47–64. New Brunswick, NJ: Transaction Publishers.

Kurtz, Marcus J. 2001. "State Developmentalism with a Development State: The Public Foundations of the 'Free Market' Miracle in Chile." *Latin American Politics and Society* 43(2): 1–25.

———. 2004. *Free Market Democracy and the Chilean and Mexican Countryside.* Cambridge, UK: Cambridge University Press.

Kuznets, S. 1955. "Economic Growth and Income Inequality." *American Economic Review* 45(1): 1–28.

Kwon, Seung-Ho, and Michael O'Donnell. 2001. *The Chaebol and Labor in Korea: The Development of a Management Strategy in Hyundai.* London and New York: Routledge.

Kwon, Soonwon. 1993. *Social Policy in Korea: Challenges and Responses.* Seoul: Korean Development Institute.

———. 1999. *The Welfare State in Korea: The Politics of Legitimization.* New York: St. Martin's Press.

La bastida Martín, Julio. 1980. "Los grupos dominantes frente a las alternativas de cambio." In *El perifil de México en 1980,* 7th ed, 100–164. Mexico City: Siglo Veintiuno.

Laclau, Ernesto. 1977. *Politics and Ideology in Marxist Theory: Capitalism, Fascism, Populism.* London: Verso Editions.

Lambert, Jacques. 1967. *Latin America. Social Structures and Political Institutions.* Berkeley: University of California Press.

Larraín, Felipe. 1991. "Public Sector Behaviour in a Highly Indebted Country: The Contrasting Chilean Experience." In *The Public Sector and the Latin American Crisis,* edited by Felipe Larraín and Marcelo Selowsky, 89–136. San Francisco: ICS Press.

Larrañaga, Osvaldo. 2008. "Inequality, Poverty and Social Policy: Recent Trends in Chile." OECD Social, Employment and Migration Working Papers, No. 85.

Latin America Weekly Report. (London). 2002. January.

Laurell, Asa Cristina. 2003. "The Transformation of Social Policy in Mexico." In *Confronting Development: Mexico's Economic and Social Policy Challenges,* edited by Kevin Middlebrook and Eduardo Zepeda, 320–349. Stanford, CA: Stanford University Press.

Lee, Hye Kung. 2005. "Civil Society and Welfare Reforms in Post-Crisis Korea." Paper presented at the Canada-Korea Social Policy Symposium II, Toronto, January 27–28. Retrieved on May 9, 2008, from www.utoronto.ca/ai/canada-korea/papers/Lee.CanadaCSOfa.doc.

Lee, Jung Bock. 2001. "The Political Process in Korea." In *Understanding Korean Politics: An Introduction,* edited by Soong Hoom Kil and Chung-in Moon, 141–173. Albany: State University of New York Press.

Lee, Namhee. 2007. *The Making of Minjung: Democracy and the Politics of Representation in South Korea.* Ithaca, NY: Cornell University Press.

Lee, Sook Jong. 2008. "The Politics of *Chaebol* Reform in Korea." *Journal of Contemporary Asia* 38(3): 439–452.

Lee, Yeon-ho. 1997. *State, Society and Big Business in South Korea.* London: Routledge.

Lefort, Fernando, and Eduardo Walker. 2000. "Ownership and Capital Structure of Chilean Conglomerates: Facts and Hypotheses for Governance." *Revista Abante.* 3(1): 3–27.

Lim, Hyun-Chin, and Jin-Ho Jang. 2006. "Neoliberalism in Post Crisis Korea: Social Conditions and Outcomes." *Journal of Contemporary Asia* 36 (4): 442–463.

Lipset, Seymour Martin. 1967. "Values, Education and Entrepreneurship." In *Elites in Latin America,* edited by Seymour M. Lipset and Aldo Solari, 3–60. New York: Oxford University Press.

Lipset, Seymour Martin, and Jason M. Lakin. 2004. *The Democratic Century.* Norman: University of Oklahoma Press.

Loaeza, Solidad. 1983. "El papel político de las clases medias en el México contemporáneo." *Revista Mexicana de Sociología.* 45(2): 407–439.

Lomeli, Enrique Valencia. 2008. "Korean and Mexican Welfare Regimes: A Historical Comparison. "ESAP 5th conference. Taiwan University, Tapei, Taiwan, November 3–4. Retrieved on August 23, 2009, from www.welfareasia.org/5thconference/session-4/stream-6-1/.

Londregan, John Benedict, and Keith T. Poole. 1996. "Does High Income Promote Democracy?" *World Politics* 49(1): 1–30.

López, J. Humberto. 2004. "Pro Poor Growth: A Review of What We Know (and What We Don't Know)." Washington, DC: World Bank. Available at www.eldis.org/assets/Docs/18547.html.

López Monjardin, Adriana. 1996. "A contracorriente: Expresiones de la resistencia a las reformas de la legislación agraria." In *Neoliberalismo y organización social en el campo*, edited by Hubert Cartón Grammont, 441–479. México City: UNAM, Institución de Investigaciones Sociales.

López Obrador, Andrés Manuel. 1999. *Fobaproa: Expediente abierto, reseña y archivo.* Mexico City: Editorial Grijalbo S.A.

Loveman, Brian. 1976. *Struggle in the Countryside: Politics and Rural Labor in Chile.* Bloomington: Indiana University Press.

———. 1988. *The Legacy of Hispanic Capitalism,* 2nd ed. Oxford, UK: Oxford University Press.

Ludovic, Comeau. 2003. "The Political Economy of Growth in Latin America and East Asia: Some Empirical Evidence." *Contemporary Economic Policy* 21(4): 476–489.

Lustig, Nora. 1998. *Mexico: The Remaking of an Economy,* 2nd ed. Washington, DC: The Brookings Institute.

Mahoney, James. 2000. "Path Dependence in Historical Sociology." *Theory and Society* 29(4): 507–548.

———. 2003. "Long-Run Development and the Legacy of Colonialism in Spanish America." *American Journal of Sociology* 109(1): 50–106.

Mahoney, James, and Dietrich Rueschemeyer. 2003. "Comparative Historical Analysis: Achievements and Agendas." In *Comparative Historical Analysis in the Social Sciences*, edited by James Mahoney and Dietrich Rueschemeyer, 3–40. Cambridge, UK: Cambridge University Press.

Mai, Jai S. 2006. "Export Promotion and Economic Development: The Case of Korea." *Journal of World Trade* 40(1): 153–166.

Mamalakis, Markos J. 1976. *The Growth and Structure of the Chilean Economy: From Independence to Allende.* New Haven, CT: Yale University Press.

Mamalakis, Markos J., and Clark Winton Reynolds. 1965. *Essays on the Chilean Economy.* Homewood, IL: Richard D. Irwin.

Marshall, Ray, and Adams, Arvil Van. 1994. "Labor Market Flexibility and Job Security Measures in a Global Economy: New Challenges Ahead." *Estudios de Economía* 21(9): 149–176.

Martínez, Gabriel, and Guillermo Fárber. 1994. *Desregulación económica (1989–1993).* Mexico City: Fundo de Cultura Económica.

Martínez, Javier, and Alvaro Díaz. 1996. *Chile: The Great Transformation.* Washington, DC: The Brookings Institution.

Martínez Nava, Juan M.1984. *Conflicto estado empresarios.* Mexico City: Editorial Nueva Imagen.

Martner, Gonzalo. 1988. *El gobierno del presidente Salvador Allende, 1970–1973: Una evaluación.* Santiago: Ediciones Literatura Americana Reunida.

Mason, Edward S., Mahn Je Kim, Dwight H. Perkins, Kwang Sur Kim, and David C. Cole. 1980. *The Economic and Social Modernization of the Republic of Korea.* Cambridge, MA: Harvard University Press.

Maxfield, Sylvia. 1990. *Governing Capital. International Finance and Mexican Politics.* Ithaca, NY: Cornell University Press.

McGuire, James. 2010. *Wealth, Health and Democracy in East Asia and Latin America.* Cambridge, UK: Cambridge University Press.

Meller, Patricio. 2000. "Pobreza y distribución del ingreso en Chile (Década del 90)." Working Paper No. 69. Santiago: Departamento de Ingeniería Industrial, Universidad de Chile.

Mesa-Lago, Carmela. 1978. *Social Security in Latin America.* Pittsburgh: University of Pittsburgh Press.

Meyer, Lorenzo. 1973. "Desarrollo político y dependencia externa: México en el siglo XXI." In *Críticas constructivas del Sistema Político Mexicano,* edited by William P. Glade and Stanley R. Ross. Austin: University of Texas Press.

Meyer, Michael C., and William L. Sherman. 1979. *The Course of Mexican History.* New York: Oxford University Press.

Mexico and NAFTA Report. London. Various dates.

Middlebrook, Kevin J. 1995. *The Paradox of Revolution. Labor, the State and Authoritarianism in Mexico.* Baltimore, MD: The Johns Hopkins University Press.

Midgley, J. 1987. "Need and Deprivation in Developing Societies." In *Comparative Social Policy and the Third World,* edited by Steward Macpherson and James Midgley, 15–51. New York: St. Martin's Press.

Migdal, Joel S. 1988. *Strong Societies and Weak States: State-Society Relations and State Capabilities in the Third World.* Princeton, NJ: Princeton University Press.

———. 1994. "The State in Society: An Approach to Struggles for Domination." In *State, Power and Social Forces. Domination and Transformation in the Third World,* edited by Joel S. Migdal, Atul Kohli and Vivienne Shue, 7–34. Cambridge, UK: Cambridge University Press.

Miller, Robert Ryal. 1985. *Mexico: A History.* Norman: University of Oklahoma Press.

Minns, John. 2001. "Of Miracles and Models: The Rise and Decline of the Development State in South Korea." *Third World Quarterly* 22(6): 1025–1043.

Mishra, Ramesh. 2004. "Productive Welfare: Its Significance and Implications." In *Modernizing the Korean Welfare State: Toward the Productive Welfare Model,* edited by

Ramesh Mishra, Stein Kuhnle, Neil Gilbert, and Kyungbae Chung, 307–317. New Brunswick, NJ: Transaction Publishers.

Mo, Jongryn, and Chung-in Moon. 1999. "Epilogue: Democracy and the Origins of the 1997 Korean Economic Crisis." In *Democracy and the Korean Economy*, edited by Jongryn Mo and Chung-in Moon, 171–198. Stanford, CA: Stanford University Press.

Montecinos, Veronica. 1998. *Economists, Politics and the State: Chile, 1958–1994*. Amsterdam: CEDLA, 1998

Moon, Chung-in. 1999. "Democratization and Globalization as Ideological and Political Foundations of Economic Policy." In *Democracy and the Korean Economy*, edited by Jongryn Mo and Chung-in Moon, 1–33. Stanford, CA: Stanford University Press.

Moon, Chung-in, and Sunghack Lin. 2001. "The Politics of Economic Rise and Decline in South Korea." In *Understanding Korean Politics: An Introduction*, edited by Soong Hoom Kil and Chung-in Moon, 201–230. Albany: State University of New York Press.

Moon, Chung-in, and Jae-jin Yang. 2002. "Globalization, Social Inequality and Democratic Governance in South Korea." In *Democratic Governance and Social Inequality*, edited by Joseph S. Tulchin and W. Amelia Brown, 131–161. Boulder, CO: Lynne Rienner.

Moreno-Bird, Juan Carlos, Juan Ernesto Pardinas Carpizo, and Jaime Ros Bosch. 2009. "Economic Development and Social Policies in Mexico." *Economy and Society* 38(1): 154–176.

Moreno-Bird, Juan Carlos, Jesús Santamaría, and Juan Carlos Rivas Valdivia. 2005. "Industrialization and Economic Growth in Mexico after NAFTA: The Road Travelled." *Development and Change* 36(6): 1095–1119.

Morley, Samuel. A. 2001. *The Income Distribution Problem in Latin America and the Caribbean*. Santiago: Economic Commission for Latin American and the Caribbean.

Morris, James O. 1966. *Elites, Intellectuals and Consensus*. New York: W. F. Humphrey Press.

Múnoz Góma, Oscar, and Carmen Celedón. 1996. "Chile in Transition: Economic and Political Strategies." In *Economic Policy and the Transition to Democracy: The Latin American Experience*, edited by Juan Antonio Morales and Gary McMahon, 191–222. New York: St. Martin's Press.

Myers, Ramon H., and Adrienne Ching. 1964. "Agricultural Development in Taiwan under Japanese Colonial Rule." *Journal of Asian Studies* 23 (4): 555–570.

Nafziger, E. Wayne, and Juha Auvinen. 2002. "Economic Development, Inequality, War, and State Violence." *World Development* 32(2): 153–163.

Nunn, Fredrick M. 1970. "A Latin American State within a State: The Politics of the Chilean Army, 1924–1927." *The Americas* 27(1): 40–55.

O'Brien, Phil, and Jackie Roddick. 1983. *Chile: The Pinochet Decade. The Rise and Fall of the Chicago Boys*. London: Latin American Bureau.

Oh, John Kie-chiang. 1999. *Korean Politics: The Quest for Democratization and Economic Development*. Ithaca, NY: Cornell University Press.

Olivarria-Gambi, Mauricio. 2003 "Poverty Reduction in Chile: Has Economic Growth been enough?" *Journal of Human Development* 4(1): 103–123.

Oppenheim, Lois Hecht. 1993. *Politics in Chile: Democracy, Authoritarianism and the Search for Development.* Boulder, CO: Westview Press.

OECD (Organisation for Economic Co-operation and Development). 1999. *Employment Outlook, June 1999.* Paris: OECD.

———. 2005. *Reviews of Health Systems: Mexico.* OECD: Paris.

———. 2008 *Factbook 2008, Economic, environmental and Social Statistics, Public Finance, Taxes.* OECD: Paris. http://lysander.sourceoecd.org/vl=805521/cl=30/nw=1/rpsv/factbook/100401.htm.

———. 2009a. *Reviews of Labor Market and Social Policies. Chile.* Paris: OECD.

———. 2009b. *Economic Surveys: Mexico.* Paris: OECD.

———. 2009c. OECD Program for International Student Assessment (PISA). PISA 2009 Country Profiles. Available at http://stats.oecd.org/PISA2009Profiles/.

———. 2010. *Factbook 2010, Economic, Environmental and Social Statistics, Public Finance, Taxes.* Paris: OECD.

Padilla, Tanalís. 2007. From Agrarista to Guerrilleros. The Jaramillista Movement in Morelos. *Hispanic American Historical Review* 87(2): 255–292.

Padilla Aragón, Enrique. 1981. *México: Hacía el crecimiento con distribución del ingreso.* Mexico City: Siglo Veintiuno.

Pardo, María del Carmen. 2000. "El deseño administrativo de los programas de emergencia." In *Las políticas sociales de México al fin del milenio, descentralización, deseño y gestión,* coordinated by Rolando Cordera and Alicia Zicardi, 462–475. Mexico City: Miguel Angel Porrúa.

Park, Eul Yong. 1998. "The Role of Government and Technological Capability in the Development of Korean Steel Industry: The Case of POSCO." In *Asia's Development Experiences: How Internationally Competitive National Manufacturing Firms Developed in Asia,* edited by Takahushi Kazuu, 127–178. Tokyo: The Foundation for Advanced Studies in International Development.

Park, Yoon-Yeong. 2002. "A Study of the Policy-Making Process for the National Basic Livelihood Security Act." *Hanguk Sahoi bokji-hak* 49(5): 264–295. (In Korean).

Parkes, Henry Bamford. 1962. *A History of Mexico.* London: Eyre and Spotiswoode.

Peng, Ito. 2009. "The Political and Social Economy of Care: Republic of Korea." Research Report 3. Geneva: U.N. Research Report for Social Development, 1–64.

PSPD (People's Solidarity for Participatory Democracy). 2008. "The Founding Statement." Retrieved on May 18, 2008, from www.peoplepower21.org. (In Korean).

Pérez-Alemán, Poala. 2000. "Learning, Adjustment and Economic Development: Transforming Firms, the State and Associations in Chile. *World Development* 28 (1): 41–55.

Petras, James. 1970. *Politics and Social Forces in Chilean Development.* Berkeley: University of California Press.

Petras, James, and Fernando Ignacio Leiva. 1994. *Democracy and Poverty in Chile.* Boulder, CO: Westview.

Petras, James, and Morris Morley. 1975. *The United States and Chile: Imperialism and the Overthrow of the Allende Government.* New York: Monthly Review Press.

Petras, James, and Maurice Zeitlin. 1968. "Agrarian Radicalism in Chile." *The British Journal of Sociology* 19(3): 254–270.

Pierson, Christopher. 2000. "Not Just What but When: Timing and Sequences in Political Processes." *Studies in American Political Development* 14 (1): 72–92.

———. 2005. " 'Late Industrializers' and the Development of Welfare Regimes." *Acta Politica* 40 (4): 395–418

Pierson, Paul. 2004. *Politics in Time, History, Institutions and Social Analysis.* Princeton, NJ: Princeton University Press.

Polaski, Sandra. 2003. Jobs, Wages and Household Income. In *NAFTA. Promise and Reality: Lessons for the Hemisphere,* edited by John Audley, Sandra Polaski, Demetrios G. Papademetriou, and Scott Vaughan, 11–37. Washington, D.C.: Carnegie Endowment for International Peace.

Przeworksi, Adam. 1991. *Democracy and the Market: Political and Economic Reforms in Eastern Europe and Latin America.* Cambridge, UK: Cambridge University Press.

Przeworski, Adam, and Fernando Papaterra Limongi Neto. 1997. "Modernization: Theories and Facts." *World Politics* 49 (2): 155–183.

Puryear, Jeffrey M. 1994. *Thinking Politics: Intellectuals and Democracy in Chile.* Baltimore, MD: The Johns Hopkins University Press.

Quijano, José Manuel. 1982. *México: Estado y banca privada,* 2nd edition. Mexico City: Centro de Investigación y Docencia Económicas, A.D.

Reforma. (Mexico City). April 2008.

Remmer, Karen. 1984. *Party Competition in Argentina and Chile: Political Recruitment and Public Policy.* Lincoln: University of Nebraska Press.

Riesco, Manuel. 2007. *Se derrumbe, un mito. Chile reforma sus sistemas privatizados de educación y previsión.* Santiago: Centro de Estudios Nacionales de Desarrollo Alternativo (CENDA).

Roxborough, Ian, Philip O'Brien, and Jackie Roddick. 1977. *Chile: The State and Revolution.* London: The Macmillan Press.

Sam-soo, Kim. 2006. "Labour Policy and Industrial Relations in the Park Chung-hee Era." In *Developmental Dictatorship and the Park Chung-Hee Era: The Shaping of Modernity in the Republic of Korea,* edited by Lee Byeong-cheon, 153–184. Paramus, NJ: Homa and Sekey Books.

Sandbrook, Richard, Marc Edelman, Patrick Heller, and Judith Teichman. 2007. *Social Democracy in the Global Periphery: Origins, Challenges, Prospects.* Cambridge, UK: Cambridge University Press.

Sanderson, Steven E. 1981. *Agrarian Populism and the Mexican State: The Struggle for Land in Sonora.* Berkeley: University of California Press.

Sang-cheol, Lee. "Industrial Policy in the Park Chung-hee Era." In *Developmental Dictatorship and the Park Chung-Hee Era,* edited by Lee Byeong-cheon, 80–109. Paramus, NJ: Homa and Sekey Books.

Sang-jin, Han. 2002. "The Public Sphere and Democracy in Korea: A Debate on Civil Society." In Korean *Politics: Striving for Democracy and Unification,* edited by Korean National Commission for UNESCO, 255–281. Elizabeth, NJ: Hollym.

Santiago Times. (Santiago). August 30, 2007.

Scott, John. 2003. "Progresa: Contexto y relevancia. Mexico City: Centro de Investigación y Docenia Económicas (CIDE)." Unpublished.

———. 2009. "Redistributive Constraints under High Inequality: The Case of Mexico." United Nationals Development Program. Regional Bureau for Latin America and the Caribbean. Research for Public Policy Inclusive Development. ID-07-2009. New York.

Secretaría de Hacienda y Crédito Público [Mexico]. "Estructura del ingreso y financiamiento del sector público presupuestario." Retrieved on September 10, 2010, from www.apartados.hacienda.gob.mx/estadisticas_oportunas/esp/index.html.

Segura-Ubiergo, Alex. 2007. *The Political Economy of the Welfare State in Latin America. Globalization, Democracy and Development.* New York: Cambridge University Press.

Sen, Amartya. 2000. *Development as Freedom.* New York: Alfred A. Knopf.

Serrano, Mónica. 1997. "Civil Violence in Chiapas: The Origins and Causes of the Revolt." In *Mexico: Assessing Neoliberal Reform,* edited by Mónica Serrano, 75–93. London: Institute of Latin American Studies, University of London.

Seymour-Jones, Sean. 2007. "Chile: When Students Rocked Santiago." *Green Left,* July 28. Retrieved on May 5, 2008, from www.greenleft.org.au/node/38034.

Shin, Gi-Wook. 1996. *Peasant Protest and Social Change in Colonial Korea.* Seattle: University of Washington Press.

———. 1998. "Agrarian Conflict and the Origins of Korean Capitalism." *Third World Quarterly* 103(5): 1309–1351.

Shin, Kwang-Yeoung. 2008a. "The Development of Welfare Regime in South Korea." Retrieved on July 29, 2009, from http://swat.sw.ccu.edu.tw/downloads/papers/200811010108.pdf.

———. 2008b. "Globalization and Social Inequality in South Korea," 63–83. Retrieved on July 29, 2009, from www.ritsumei.jp/acd/re/k-rsc/.

Sigmund, Paul E. 1977. *The Overthrow of Allende and the Politics of Chile, 1964–1976.* Pittsburgh: University of Pittsburgh Press.

Silva, Eduardo. 1996. *The State and Capital in Chile: Business Elites, Technocrats and Market Economics.* Boulder, CO: Westview Press.

Silva, Patricio. 1991. "Technocrats and Politics in Chile: from the Chicago Boys to the CIEPLAN Monks." *Journal of Latin American Studies* 31(2): 385–410.

———. 2006. "Government-Business Relations and Economic Performance in South Korea and Chile: A Political Perspective." In *Political Conflict and Development in East Asia and Latin America,* edited by Richard B. Boyd, F. Galjart, and Tak-Wing Ngo, 74–117. New York: Routledge.

Smith, Peter H. 1979. *Labyrinths of Power.* Princeton, NJ: Princeton University Press.

Solís, Leopoldo. 1981. *La realidad económica Mexicana: Retrovisión y perspectivas.* Revised. Mexico City: Siglo XXI.

Son, Byong Don. 1999. "Poverty Reduction Effect of Income Transfers." *Korean Journal of Social Welfare* 39: 157–179. (In Korean).

Song, Byung-Nak. 2003. *The Rise of the Korean Economy.* New York: Oxford University Press.

Song, Ho Keun, and Kyung Zoon Hong. 2005. "Globalization and Social Policy in South Korea." In *Globalization and the Future of the Welfare State*, edited by Miguel Glatzer and Dietrich Rueschemeyer, 170–202. Pittsburgh, PA: University of Pittsburgh Press.

Standing, Guy. 1999. *Global Labor Flexibility: Seeking Distributive Justice*. London: Macmillan Press.

Steinmo, Sven. 2008. "Historical Institutionalism." In *Approaches and Methodologies in the Social Sciences*, edited by Donatella della Porta and Michael Keating, 118–138. Cambridge, UK: Cambridge University Press.

Subercaseaux, Bernardo. 1988. *Fin del Siglo. La época de Balmaceda: modernización y cultura en Chile*. Santiago: Editorial Aconcagua.

Székley, Gabriel. 1983. *La economía política del petróleo en México, 1976–1982*. Mexico City: El Colegio de México.

Székely, Miguel. 1998. *The Economics of Poverty, Inequality and Wealth Accumulation in Mexico*. New York: St. Martin's Press.

Tan, Hong. 2009. "Evaluating SME Support Programs in Chile Using Panel Data." Policy Research Working Paper 5082. Impact Evaluation Series. Washington, DC: World Bank, Latin American and Caribbean Region.

Tannenbaum, Frank. 1968. *Mexico: The Struggle for Peace and Bread*. New York: Alfred A. Knopf.

Taylor, Marcus. 2003. "The Reformulatin of Social Policy in Chile, 1973–2001." *Global Social Policy* 3(1): 21–44.

Teichman, Judith A. 1988. *Policymaking in Mexico: From Boom to Crisis*. Boston: Allen and Unwin.

———. 1996. *Privatization and Political Change in Mexico*. Pittsburgh, PA: University of Pittsburgh Press.

———. 2001. *The Politics of Freeing Markets in Latin America: Chile, Argentina and Mexico*. Chapel Hill: University of North Carolina Press.

———. 2002."Private Sector Power and Market Reform: Exploring the Domestic Origins of Argentina's Meltdown and Mexico's Policy Failures." *Third World Quarterly* 23(3): 491–528.

———. 2008. "Redistributive Conflict and Social Policy in Latin America." *World Development* 36(3): 446–460.

———. 2009. "Competing Visions of Democracy and Development in the Era of Neoliberalism in Mexico and Chile." *International Political Science Review* 30(1): 67–87.

Tello, Carlos. 1980. *La política económica en México, 1970–1976*. Mexico City: Siglo XXI

———. 1984. *La nacionalización de la banca*. Mexico City: Siglo XXI.

La Tercera. (Santiago). Various dates.

Thacker, S. C. 2000. *Big Business, the State and Free Trade: Constructing Coalitions in Mexico*. Cambridge, UK: Cambridge University Press.

Thelen, Kathleen. 1999. Historical Institutionalism in Comparative Politics. *Annual Review of Political Science* 61(2): 369–404.

Thorpe, Rosemary. 1998. *Progress, Poverty and Exclusion: An Economic History of Latin America in the 20th Century*. Washington, DC: Inter-American Development Bank.

Tilly, Charles. 2005. "Historical Perspectives on Inequality." In *The Blackwell Companion to Social Inequalities,* edited by Mary Romero and Eric Margolis, 15–30. Malden, MA: Blackwell Publishing.

Tironi, Ernesto B. 1988. "Parte Tercera: Una evaluación de los programas de gasto social." In *Pobreza en Chile,* edited by Eugenio Ortega R. and Ernesto Tironi B., 171–201. Santiago: Centro de Estudios del Desarrollo.

U.N. Common Database (U.N. Population Division Estimates). Retrieved in March 2008 from www.globalis,gvu.unu.edu/indicator.

UNDP (U.N. Development Program). 2004. *Human Development Report, 2004. Cultural Diversity in Today's Diverse World.* New York: UNDP.

Universidad de Chile, Facultad de Ciencias Económicas. 1963. *La economía de chile en el período 1950–1963.* Vol. 11. Santiago: Instituto de economía de la Universidad de Chile.

UN-WIDER Data Base. United Nations University, World Institute for Economics Research data base. Available at www.wider.unu.edu/research/Database/en_GB/wiid/.

Valdés, Juan Gabriel. 1995. *Pinochet's Economists: The Chicago School in Chile.* Cambridge, UK: Cambridge University Press.

Velasco, Andrés. 1994. "The State and Economic Policy: Chile 1952–1992." In *The Chilean Economy: Policy Lessons and Challenges,* edited by Barry P. Bosworth, Rudiger Dornbusch, and Raúl Labán, 379–411. Washington DC: The Brookings Institution.

Van Eyck, Kim. 2003. "Flexibilizing Employment: An Overview." Seed Working Paper no. 4. Geneva: International Labor Office.

Vergara, Pilar. 1983. "Las transformaciones del estado chileno bajo el régimen militar." In *Chile 1973–198?,* edited by Revista Mexicana de Sociología y FLACSO, 65–104. Santiago: FLACSO.

Vernon, Raymond. 1963. *The Dilemma of Mexico's Development.* Cambridge, MA: Harvard University Press.

Wade, Robert Hunter. 1990. *Governing the Market: Economic Theory and the Role of Government in East Asian Industrialization.* Princeton, NJ: Princeton University Press.

———. 2004. "Is Globalization Reducing Poverty and Inequality?" *World Development,* 32(4): 567–589.

Ward, Peter. 1986. *Welfare Politics in Mexico: Papering over the Cracks.* Boston: Allen and Unwin.

Wilkie, James W. 1967. *The Mexican Revolution: Federal Expenditures and Social Change since 1910.* Berkeley: University of California Press.

———, ed. 1999. *Statistical Abstract of Latin America.* Vol. 35. Los Angeles: UCLA Latin American Center Publications.

Wisecarver, Daniel. 1992. "El sector forestal chileno: Políticas, desarrollo del recurso y exportaciones." In *El modelo económico chileno,* edited by Daniel L. Wisecarver, 481–516. Santiago: Instituto de Economía de la Pontifica Universidad Católica de Chile y Centro Internacional para el Desarrollo Económico.

Wong, Joseph. 2004. *Healthy Democracies: Welfare Politics in Taiwan and South Korea.* Ithaca, NY, and London: Cornell University Press.

Woo, Jung-en. 1991. *Race to the Swift: State and Finance in Korean Industrialization.* New York: Columbia University Press.

Woo, Myungsook. 2004. *The Politics of Social Welfare Policy in South Korea: Growth and Citizenship.* Lanham, MD: University Press of America.

Worthington, Aida. 2003. "Estudio revela alto nivel de intolerancia hacía pobres en Chile." *La Tercera,* October 8.

World Bank. *World Bank Indicators*: Available at http://data.worldbank.org/indicator.

———. 2002. Operations Evaluation Department. *Chile: Country Assistance Evaluation.* Available at www.worldbank.org/oed.

———. 2003. *World Tables, third edition. Vol. II. Social Data.* The World Bank and The Johns Hopkins University Press: Baltimore and London.

———. 2010. *Prospects for the Economy, Country Forecasts, Chile.* Retrieved on April 22, 2010, from http://go.worldbank.org/JA8N5V7MDo.

Yea, Sallie W. 2002. "Regionalism and Political-Economic Differentiation in Korean Development: Power Maintenance and the State as Hegemonic Power Bloc." In *Korean Politics: Striving for Democracy and Unification,* edited by Korean National Commission for UNESCO, 29–61. Elizabeth, NJ: Hollym.

Yoo, Jong Goo. 1990. "Income Distribution in Korea." In *Korean Economic Development,* edited by Jene K. Kwon, 373–391. Westport, CT: Greenwood Press.

Yong-ha, Shin. 2003. *Essays in Korean Social History.* Seoul: Jisik-sanup Publishers Co. Ltd.

You, Jong-Sung. 2005. "Embedded Autonomy or Crony Capitalism? Explaining Corruption in South Korea, Relative to Taiwan and the Philippines. Focusing on the Role of Land Reform and Industrial Policy." Paper prepared for delivery at the Annual Meeting of the American Political Science Association, Washington, DC, September 1–4.

Young-chol, Cho. 2006. "The *Chaebol* Regime and the Developmental Coalition of Domination." In *Developmental Dictatorship and the Park Chung-Hee Era,* edited by Lee Byeong-cheon, 108–133. Paramus, NJ: Homa and Sekey Books.

Zeitlin, Maurice. 1984. *The Civil Wars in Chile, or, the Bourgeois Revolutions That Never Were.* Princeton, NJ: Princeton University Press.

Zeitlin, Maurice, and Richard Earl Ratcliff. 1988. *Landlords and Capitalists: The Dominant Class of Chile.* Princeton, NJ: Princeton University Press.

Index

Adams, Arvil Van, 143
Addison, Tony, 2
Agosín, Manuel R., 65, 120, 124
Aguilar, Alonso, 88, 89
Aguilera Reyes, Máximo, 58
Ahn, Byong Man, 36, 38, 201n8
Albala-Bertrand, José Miguel, 42, 68
Alemán, Miguel, 85
Alessandri, Arturo, 53, 204n15
Alessandri, Jorge, 56, 204n14
Allende, Salvador, 62, 64, 65, 66, 72,
    171, 204n19; land reform policies, 13,
    63, 105, 207n3
Alywin, Patricio, 122, 124, 208n4,
    211n12
Amparo Casar, María, 87
Amsden, Alice, 7, 26, 144
An, Jaewook, 133
Angell, Alan, 67, 204n18
Aninat, Eduardo, 63
Arellano, José Pablo, 63, 113
Argentina, 133
Arita, Shin, 47, 108, 134, 203n29
Asia: economic growth in, 1, 7, 8; educa-
    tion in, 7, 18; export-oriented policies
    in, 10–11, 13; import-substitution
    policies in, 200n15; inequality in, 18,

200n10; and Japanese colonialism,
7–8; land redistribution in, 8–9; vs.
Latin America, 2, 7–14, 18; poverty
in, 10, 18, 200n10; role of the state in,
7; social welfare in, 18–19; state in-
stitutions in, 7–8, 9–10; U.S. foreign
policy regarding, 12–13
Asian Development Bank, 187, 191
Aspe, Pedro, 208n18
Aspra, Antonio L., 87, 88, 208n18
Aten, Bertina, 186
Athow, Brian, 8
Atkinson, A. B., 18
Atunes, Ricardo, 143
Avila Camacho, Manuel, 83, 85
Avinen, Juha, 2
Ayala Espino, José, 82

Bąkiewicz, Anna, 135, 137, 145
Bachelet, Michelle, 153, 155–58, 179,
    180, 208n4
Bae, Sang Kun, 133
Balmaceda, José Manuel, 52
Ban, Sung Hwan, 30, 31, 36, 39, 187
Barrientos, Armando, 18
Basurto, Jorge, 205n9
Bauer, Arnold J., 51, 203nn2,3

foreign debt, 132–33; regarding health care, 136, 154, 195, 199n7; regarding industrialization, 7, 11, 24–25, 40, 42, 57, 68, 102–3, 106–11, 115, 116–17, 152, 158, 170–71, 173–77, 188; regarding inequality, 2, 3, 23–24, 26, 33, 70, 97–98, 107, 112, 119, 150, 169, 175–77, 178–80, 185, 186; regarding labor flexibility, 143, 152, 165, 178; regarding labor movement, 43, 44; regarding land reform, 10, 23–24, 26, 63, 103–6, 116, 169, 172, 179; regarding middle class, 71, 106–7, 112, 175–77; regarding military, 67, 110; regarding neoliberalism, 144; regarding peasantry, 50–51, 99, 100–101, 168; regarding pensions, 147, 156; regarding political conditions, 15, 16–17, 32, 48, 97, 102; regarding poverty, 2, 3, 26, 33, 36, 58, 70, 97–98, 112, 118, 150, 175–77, 178, 179–80, 184; regarding public deficit/surplus, 197; regarding social spending, 32, 111–12, 157, 194–96, 202n28, 210n2; regarding state strength, 4, 8, 10, 19, 24, 42, 57, 89, 97–98, 107, 112, 119, 141, 151, 174–75; regarding taxation, 189; regarding U.S. foreign policy, 12–13; regarding working class, 106–7, 112, 116
Ching, Adrienne, 7
Cho, Yoon Lo, 10
Choi, Jang Jip, 29, 202n17
Choi, Soo Ho, 36
Choi, Young Back, 144
Chun, Moo-Kwon, 145, 147, 148, 149
Chun Doo Hwan, 133, 134, 136–37, 209n17
Clark, Marjorie Ruth, 78
Cleaves, Peter S., 58, 64
Cline, Howard, 78, 79, 81, 205nn14,15
Cockroft, James D., 79, 81, 86, 89, 92, 188
Cole, David C., 28, 36, 39, 42, 202n18
Collier, Simon, 203n6

Collins, Susan M., 133, 134, 136
colonialism: duration of, 98–100, 170; Japanese colonialism in Korea, 7–8, 20, 23, 27–28, 29, 38, 47, 99–100, 116, 169, 170, 200n11, 201nn3,5, 207n6; relationship to critical conjunctures, 23, 98–101, 103; Spanish colonialism in Chile, 8, 24, 50, 98–99, 100, 169–70; Spanish colonialism in Mexico, 8, 24, 98–99, 101, 169–70
comparative historical analysis, 3, 19, 200n22
Confucianism, 11
Constable, Pamela, 67, 110
Cooper, Richard N., 133
copper prices, 66, 119, 120, 152, 192, 211n13
Corbacho, Ana, 128
Cornia, Giovanni Andrea, 2, 8, 199n1
Cortés, Fernando, 128
Cortés Conde, Roberto, 53, 113
Couch, Colin, 23
Cox Edwards, Alejandra, 68, 119
critical conjunctures, 19–26; of Chile, 21, 23, 24, 50, 54, 66, 72, 97, 98, 100–101, 118–19, 125, 139, 142, 151, 168, 169–70, 171, 172, 192–93; vs. *coyuntura,* 19; vs. critical junctures, 19–20, 21–22, 167, 200n22; of Mexico, 21, 23, 77, 97, 98, 118–19, 132, 142–43, 168, 169, 170–71, 172, 192–93; path dependent sequences after, 21–22, 97, 116, 122–23, 125–26, 142–43, 151, 168, 172–75, 192–93; reactive sequences after, 21, 22, 23, 24, 49–50, 55, 71, 72, 73, 77, 80, 82, 91–92, 96, 97, 99, 101, 106, 116, 167, 168, 169–70, 171, 172, 177, 179, 180, 192–93; relationship to colonial rule, 23, 98–101, 103; relationship to natural resource endowment, 23, 49, 97, 98, 115–17, 172–73, 177; of South Korea, 20, 24, 97, 98, 100, 102, 168–69, 192–93

Fitzgerald, E. V. K., 91

Fox, Vicente, 159, 160, 162–63, 212n21

Foxley, Alejandro, 63, 64, 189

Frei Montalva, Eduardo, 61–62, 65, 72; and Economic Committee of Ministers, 63-64, 204n15; land reform policies, 63, 207n3

Frei Ruiz-Tagle, Eduardo, 122, 124, 208n4, 211n12

Frenk, Julio, 91, 132

Frías, Patricio, 188

Furtado, Celso, 188

Galjart, F., 200n10

García Rocha, Adelberto, 85

Garrido, Celso, 127

Gereffi, Gary, 91

Germany, 200n21

Gideon, Jasmine, 152

Gilbert, Denis, 84, 110–11, 130, 206n18, 211n16

Gilbert, Neil, 148

Gil Díaz, Francisco, 212n17

Gini coefficient, 30, 70, 118, 185, 201n9, 210n1

Glick, David, 210n1

Godoy-Urzúa, Hernán, 113

Goldberg, Mike, 124, 152

Gollás, Manuel, 85

Gómez Tagle, Silvia, 209n11

González, Manuel, 205n4

González-Black, Miguel Angel, 91

González Gómez, Mauricio A., 129

Gordillo, Elba, 212n21

Gough, Ian, 18, 33, 44, 138, 211n6

Grant, Geraldine, 53, 55, 56, 109

Gray, Kevin, 134, 138, 139, 146, 147, 148, 149, 209n18, 211n4

Grayson, George, 92

Great Depression, 28, 79; Chile during, 21, 49, 54, 71, 171, 192

Greenburg, Harry, 89

Green Revolution, 86

Gribomont, C., 91

Griffith-Jones, Stephany, 189

Grove, Marmaduque, 207n7

Guardia B., Alexis, 55, 204n12

Guatemala, 200n16

Guerrero, Isabel, 150, 163, 164, 199n2

Haagh, Louise, 123, 208n5

Haber, Stephen H., 75, 76, 205n7

Hadenius, Axel, 200n18

Haggard, Stephan, 1, 10, 12, 15, 18, 26, 133, 134, 136, 200n11, 202n25, 210n2

Hall, Michael M., 203n7

Hall, Peter A., 3

Hamilton, Nora, 44, 45, 79

Han, Seung-Mi, 34, 36, 38

Hankyoreh, The, 185

Hansen, Roger D., 81, 85, 86, 187, 205n12, 207n9

Harrison, Lawrence E., 11

Hart, John Mason, 74, 205n3

Harvey, Neil, 127, 128

health care: in Chile, 60, 69, 125, 136, 151, 154, 162, 195, 199n7, 202n28, 204n25, 210n1, 211n10; in Mexico, 81–82, 84, 85, 91, 132, 136, 161–62, 164, 195, 199n7, 202n28, 212n20; relationship to inequality and poverty, 14; in South Korea, 33, 45, 46, 134, 136, 146, 147, 148, 149, 154, 162, 166, 178, 195, 199n7, 210n23, 211n6

Heredia, Blanca, 127

Hernández, Silvia, 62

Heston, Alan W., 186

Hewitt de Alcántara, Cynthia, 81, 85, 89, 206n21

Hira, Anil, 66, 204n18

historical institutionalism, 4

Holliday, Ian, 18, 148

Hong, Kyong Zoon, 134, 138, 145, 210n28

Hong, Kyung Joon, 150

204nn18,24, 207nn3,4; land redistribution, 8–9, 13, 20, 22, 23, 24, 28,
29–30, 48, 49, 56, 63, 64, 71, 72,
77, 79, 80, 81, 92, 100, 104–5, 112,
116, 192, 193, 200n17, 201n4, 207n4;
in Mexico, 9, 20, 21, 22, 24, 77, 79,
80, 81, 92, 94, 95, 97, 101, 104, 106,
116, 127, 170, 171, 172, 178, 179,
192, 193, 201n13, 205n14, 207nn3,4;
in South Korea, 9, 12–13, 20, 22,
23, 24, 26–32, 38, 47, 63, 97, 100,
103–5, 111, 116, 170, 172, 179, 192,
201nn4,7,8,13, 207n5; state support
for beneficiaries, 9, 30, 81, 105
Larraín, Felipe, 66
Larrañaga, Osvaldo, 151, 185
Latin America: vs. Asia, 2, 7–14, 18; Catholicism in, 11–12; economic growth
in, 7, 8, 10–11; education in, 9, 18;
import substitution policies in, 10–11,
200n15; indigenous population in, 8,
206n1; industrialization in, 9, 10–11;
inequality in, 18, 199nn1,2; labor
flexibilization in, 143; land reform
in, 8–9, 12–13, 200n17; mixed-blood
population in, 8; political conditions
in, 200n12; positivism in, 11–12,
74, 206n2; poverty in, 18; regressive
taxation in, 18; social compartmentalization in, 6–7; social structure
in, 8; social welfare protection in,
17–18; Spanish colonialism in, 7, 8,
47, 206n1; state institutions in, 4, 7, 8,
9–10; U.S. capital penetration in, 23;
U.S. foreign policy regarding, 12–13,
200n16. See also Chile; Mexico
Laurell, Asa Cristina, 128, 131, 132
Lederman, Daniel, 2
Lee, Hye Kung, 147, 148
Lee, Jung Bock, 35, 202n18
Lee, Namhee, 47
Lee, Sook Jong, 145
Lee, Yeon-ho, 11, 35

Lefort, Fernando, 124
Leiva, Fernando Ignacio, 120
liberation theology, 12
Lim, Hyun-Chin, 144, 147, 211n3
Limongi Neto, Fernando Papaterra,
200n18
Lin, Sunghack, 34, 47
Lipset, Seymour Martin, 11, 15, 200n18
Loaeza, Solidad, 79, 82
Loayza, Norman, 2
Lomeli, Enrique Valencia, 148, 149, 211n6
Londoño, Juan L., 8
Londregan, John Benedict, 200n18
López, J. Humberto, 2
López-Calva, Luis Felipe, 199n2
López Monjardin, Adriana, 127
López Obrador, Andrés Manuel, 130, 159
López Portillo, José, 93–95
Loveman, Brian, 54, 56, 59, 61, 63, 65
Lozano, Rafael, 91
Ludovic, Comeau, 10
Lustig, Nora, 87, 127, 128
Lyman, Princeton N., 28, 36, 39, 42,
202n18

Madero, Francisco, 78
Mahoney, James, 3, 19, 21, 206n1
Mai, Jai S., 39, 41, 43, 137
Mamalakis, Markos J., 52, 55, 56, 57, 58,
59, 60, 187, 188, 203n5
Marshall, Ray, 143
Martínez, Gabriel, 127
Martínez, Javier, 66
Martínez Nava, Juan M., 83, 92
Martner, Gonzalo, 63, 204n18
Mason, Edward S., 30, 31, 35, 36, 38, 40,
41, 187, 201nn7,8,14, 202nn20,22
Mason, T. David, 8
Maxfield, Sylvia, 79
McGuire, James, 15, 18
McKinley, Terry, 207n4
Meller, Patricio, 208n2
Menon, Nidhiya, 210n1

211n8; Institutional Revolutionary Party (PRI), 80–84, 91, 96, 127, 128–29, 130, 132, 140, 141, 142–43, 159, 160, 166, 167, 170, 192, 193, 205nn11,16, 209n8; Labor Congress (CT), 83; labor flexibilization in, 143, 160, 164, 165, 166, 178, 193, 212n18; labor movement in, 17, 43, 44, 76, 78, 79, 80–81, 82, 83, 84, 86, 90, 92, 93, 96, 110, 111, 128, 131, 132, 141, 159, 160-61, 162, 164, 166, 172, 180, 206n17, 207nn8,9, 208n18, 212n21; landowning class in, 74, 75–76, 77, 78, 79, 81, 85, 89, 92, 99, 101, 104, 106, 116, 170, 172, 179, 205nn5,12; mestizos in, 74, 78, 88, 98–99, 101, 110, 111, 170; Mexican Institute of Foreign Trade, 91; middle class in, 22, 24, 25, 76, 77, 78–79, 80, 82, 83–84, 86, 88–89, 95–96, 97, 104, 106, 107, 110, 111, 116, 117, 130, 141, 159, 163, 164, 166, 170, 172, 176–77, 179, 193, 206n18, 211n16; mining in, 23, 74, 75, 76, 78, 79, 80, 83, 95, 98, 101, 102, 116–17, 172, 177; Monterrey, 75–76, 82, 93; Morelos, 207n10; and NAFTA, 3, 129, 140, 160, 165, 209n12; National Democratic Front, 209n11; National Union of Education Workers (SNTE), 162; National Union of Workers (UNT), 160; National Workers Housing Fund, 91; Party of the Democratic Revolution (PRD), 131; peasantry in, 5, 9, 21, 23, 25, 77–78, 80, 81, 83, 84–86, 90, 91, 92, 95, 96, 99, 101, 104, 106, 110, 111, 113, 114, 127, 128, 170, 171, 177, 192, 205n13, 207nn8,10; pensions in, 81, 84, 131–32, 161, 164, 211n4; per capita income in, 25, 93, 118, 186, 194; peso crisis of 1995, 118, 129–31, 140, 141, 193; petroleum industry, 75, 78, 79, 80–81, 82, 83,

90, 93–95, 126, 133, 140, 164, 174, 193, 210n24; political conditions in, 4, 10, 15, 16–17, 32, 73, 74, 77–78, 79, 83, 86–87, 92, 96, 113, 114–15, 117, 128–29, 140, 141, 164, 166, 167, 168, 170–71, 172, 176, 178, 192, 193, 205nn12,16, 206n17, 209n11, 211n16; Popular Action Party (PAN), 82, 130, 141, 159, 177, 193, 211n16; poverty in, 2, 4, 8, 11, 13, 15, 17, 19, 20, 25, 33, 36, 73, 74, 77, 81, 89–90, 91, 93–94, 96, 97, 99, 105, 107, 110, 112, 118, 126, 127, 129, 130–31, 132, 140, 141, 142, 143, 158, 159, 162–63, 167, 168, 171, 173, 174, 179–80, 184, 192, 193, 199n2, 209nn10,13; privatization in, 126, 128, 131, 161; public deficit/surplus in, 86, 93, 94, 122, 127, 155, 197; railway industry, 75, 78, 80–81, 82, 205n6; relations with IMF, 92, 126; relations with United States, 75, 77, 82, 129, 160, 177, 178; Revolution of 1910–1917, 21, 73, 77–78, 95-96, 101, 102, 106, 110, 111, 113, 170, 192, 205n10, 207n10; small and medium-sized firms in, 5, 129, 134, 159, 175; social hierarchy in, 98–99, 101, 111; social justice concerns in, 131, 193; social security in, 32, 81–82, 84, 85, 91, 111, 112, 128, 131–32, 160–61, 196, 206n19, 209n13; strength of social forces in, 4, 10, 17, 19, 22, 25, 40, 73, 77–78, 79–83, 86–87, 90, 94–96, 97, 101, 104, 106, 107, 111, 113, 114–15, 116, 117, 118, 131, 132, 141, 160–61, 164, 166, 168, 179; student massacre of 1968, 90; unemployment in, 86, 131, 160–61; unemployment insurance in, 81; upper class in, 21, 22, 23, 24, 25, 50, 73, 74, 77–78, 80, 84, 95, 97, 99, 101, 104, 106, 111, 112, 118, 168, 171, 172, 173, 178, 179, 180, 192, 193; urbanization, 86;

Obregón, Álvaro, 205n12
O'Brien, Philip, 66, 67, 204n17
O'Donnell, Michael, 20
OECD, 132, 137, 143, 151, 152, 153, 155, 157, 158, 161, 162, 189, 194, 212nn19,20
Oh, John Kie-chiang, 32, 34, 35, 47
oil crisis of 1973, 92
oil prices, 94, 126, 133, 164, 193
Olivarria-Gambi, Mauricio, 204n25
Oppenheim, Lois Hecht, 68

Padilla, Tanalís, 207n10
Padilla Aragón, Enrique, 189
Palladini, Eric, 124, 152
Pardo, María del Carmen, 81, 84
Park Chung-hee, 33–46, 80, 192, 209n17; agriculture policies, 35–37, 202nn16,22, 208n19; antilabor policies, 43–45; attitudes regarding inequality, 34; attitudes regarding poverty, 34, 208n19; industrialization policies, 34, 36, 38, 174; populism of, 34–35, 38, 43, 99; social welfare programs, 45–46, 176
Park, Eul Yong, 40
Park, Innwon, 139, 145, 146, 184, 211n7
Park, Yoon-Yeong, 148
Parkes, Henry Bamford, 76, 77, 80, 81, 86, 205nn9,13
Pastén H., Ernesto, 124
path dependency: Couch and Farrell on, 23–24; after critical conjunctures, 21–22, 97, 116, 122–23, 125–26, 133, 140, 141, 142–43, 144, 151, 168, 172–75, 192–93; and critical junctures, 20, 21–22, 167; and industrialization, 172–75; and institutionalism, 4
Paz, Octavio, 205n16
Peng, Ito, 185
Peres, Wilson, 87
Pérez-Alemán, Poala, 120, 124
Perkins, Dwight H., 30
Petras, James, 13, 53, 56, 62, 66, 120

Pierson, Christopher, 18, 19, 22
Pierson, Paul, 4
Polaski, Sandra, 160, 163
Poole, Keith T., 200n18
Portales, Diego, 50, 203n1
positivism, 11–12, 74, 206n2
private property: attitudes in Chile regarding, 13, 17, 23, 49, 61, 62–63, 67, 72, 101, 102, 103, 105–6, 116, 172, 204n16; attitudes in Mexico regarding, 17, 23, 81, 95, 101, 102, 103, 106, 116, 172; attitudes in South Korea regarding, 27, 29, 106, 172, 201n5, 207n5
productivist welfare regimes, 18–19
Przeworski, Adam, 16, 200n18
Puryear, Jeffrey M., 121

Quijano, José Manuel, 95

Ratcliff, Richard Earl, 55, 56
Ratti, Ronald A., 133
Recabarren, Luis Emilio, 54
regime type: authoritarian, 14, 15–16, 17; democratic, 15–17; relationship to inequality, 14–15, 16; relationship to poverty, 14–15, 16; relationship to social forces, 15–16
Remmer, Karen, 114
rent seeking, 2, 10
Reynolds, Clark Winton, 57, 58
Rhee, Syngman, 38–39
Riesco, Manuel, 156, 157, 204n24
Rimez, M., 91
Roddick, Jackie, 66, 67, 204n17
Rodríguez, Abelardo, 205n14
Roemer, Michael, 29, 40, 201n5
Roh Tae-woo, 135–37
Roxborough, Ian, 204n17
Rueschemeyer, Dietrich, 3
Ruiz-Tagle, Jaime, 188

Salinas de Gotari, Carlos, 126, 127, 129, 130, 209n10
Sam-soo, Kim, 44